CW00551791

A TRAIN TO PALESTINE

Dedicated to the memory of Nelly Rosenbaum and the 1.5 million Jewish children murdered in the Holocaust.

A Train to Palestine

The Tehran Children, Anders' Army
and their Escape from Stalin's Siberia,
1939-1943

Randy Grigsby

VALLENTINE MITCHELL
LONDON • CHICAGO, IL

First published in 2020 by *Vallentine Mitchell*

Catalyst House,
720 Centennial Court,
Centennial Park, Elstree WD6 3SY, UK

814 N. Franklin Street,
Chicago, Illinois,
IL 60610 USA

www.vmbooks.com

Copyright © Randy Grigsby 2020

British Library Cataloguing in Publication Data:
An entry can be found on request

ISBN 978 1 912676 27 9 (Paper)
ISBN 978 1 912676 28 6 (Ebook)

Library of Congress Cataloging in Publication Data:
An entry can be found on request

All rights reserved. No part of this publication may be reproduced in any form or by any means, electronic, mechanical, photocopying, reading or otherwise, without the prior permission of Vallentine Mitchell & Co. Ltd.

Printed by CMP (UK) Ltd, Poole, Dorset

Contents

Author's Note

This book has always been about Joe Rosenbaum's experiences from 1938 to 1943. However, as research, outlining and the writing of the story progressed from the initial stages, it became evident that, by placing Joe as a character within a vast, historical canvas, that of the German invasion of Poland in September 1939, and then through those war years that followed, presented a problem. I was writing, after all, about an 8-year-old boy who was much too young to remember many details, and was terribly ill throughout most of the journey.

To fill in those events, I searched for sources from which to draw experiences and accounts of events in Poland and Siberia in the late 1930s. I discovered two informative books published in the 1990s on the experiences of other Tehran Children, books which proved to be invaluable in texture and detail. *Escape from Siberia: A Jewish Child's Odyssey of Survival* by Dr Dorit Bader Whiteman relates the experiences of Elliot 'Lonek' Jaroslawicz. Her book also provided information about Hadassah, the Jewish Women's Organization, and negotiations in Washington D.C. during the autumn of 1942 to obtain release of the Tehran Children to Palestine. Devora Omer's book *The Teheran Operation: The Rescue of Jewish Children from the Nazis* narrates the story of David Laor, director of the Tehran Children's Refugee Station, on the journey offering insight into the Jewish Agency arriving in Tehran. Omer was one of Israel's foremost writers. A third book, filled with vivid aspects of the journey is *Children of Zion* by Henryk Grynberg, providing personal input from the children during their struggles. If one desires to know more about the Holocaust, and specifically about the 1.5 million Jewish children murdered in those years, I would suggest an incredible record of those times: *Children with A Star: Jewish Youth in Nazi Europe,* and *Flight from the Reich: Refugee Jews, 1933-1946* (co-written by Robert Jan Van Pelt) by Deborah Dwork, historian, and Rose Professor of Holocaust History and director of the Strassler Family Center of Holocaust and Genocide Studies at Clark University.

To understand the brutal experiences of the Polish army-in-exile in Siberia, read the personal words of General Wladyslaw Anders in his autobiography *An Army in Exile*. Once I uncovered Anders, I knew I had my second main character, and his experiences, to draw from. I would also suggest several other books on the Polish army experiences in Siberia, Iran, and later the North Africa and Italian campaign as they fought alongside the American and British armies: Norman Davies, *Trail of Hope: The Anders Army, An Odyssey Across Three Continents,* and Halik Kochanski, *The Eagle Unbowed: Poland and the Poles in the Second World War.*

In the genre of memoirs and history of Polish refugees in Siberia during the war, one should consider several impressive, recent works that are also listed in the bibliography. Shimon Redlich, a professor at Ben-Gurion University in Israel and a graduate of Harvard University, survived the Holocaust after being saved by a Ukrainian family. His trilogy, spanning from 1939 to 1954 when he began his new life in Israel, is a noteworthy series on the history of the Jews in Eastern Europe. A professor at The Cooper Union for the Advancement of Science and Art, Atina Grossman's book *Shelter from the Holocaust: Rethinking Jewish Survival in the Soviet Union,* published in 2017, details the lives of about 1.5 million East European Jews, mostly from Poland, who survived the Second World War in the unoccupied regions of the Soviet Union. As for documentaries, Polish-born American producer Slawomir Grunberg's full-length film *Saved by Deportation: An Unknown Odyssey of Polish Jews,* captures the dramatic story of Polish Jews who escaped the Holocaust through exile to the Soviet Union.

In February 2013 Joe Rosenbaum's grandson, Simon, began a series of interviews with Joe, which became a college thesis on his grandfather's experiences during the war. Entitled *My Saba* (my grandfather), Simon's interviews and recounting of those times through his grandfather's words was an important resource during the writing of this book. The story that Joe told his grandson ends, however, as Joe and Rina marry, shortly after that move to America. Except for Chapters 30 and 31, the life of Joe Rosenbaum was admirably portrayed in Simon's paper. What a gift for a writer, one I treasured during the research and writing of Joe's story…for what better way to learn of a man, only a child during the journey, than through a grandson's words and heart and love?

Acknowledgments

The writing of a book, as I learned during the last five years, is not a journey of one, but a voyage of many. There are numerous people, more than can be mentioned here, throughout those times who never allowed me to give up on this story, offering encouragement and prayers, suggestions and, yes, criticism, when it was most needed. In the space allowed, I would like to extend appreciation to a few. In a church in Shreveport, Louisiana, there is Pastor Tim Carscadden and his wife, Susan, who both possess an over-powering heart for Israel. He taught me that love is where the seed for this book was planted. Also, there is Associate Pastors Jimmy and Karen Hudgens, with whom I first shared the idea for Joe's story. During that beginning, when the idea for a book about the Tehran Children was but a thought, I made contact with Ruti Marshansky (whose name I was given during a visit to Yad Vashem in Jerusalem). In those moments when I pondered the odds of even finding a Tehran Child alive and willing to tell their story, she led me to Joe Rosenbaum. So to Pastor Tim, his wife Susan, Jimmy and Karen, and Ruti, there is a debt of gratitude that can never be repaid.

I would like to offer thanks to Simon Rosenbaum, Joe's grandson, for writing his college thesis, *My Saba*, about his grandfather. Those pages were an invaluable guide from which to begin and outline the book, and I state without exaggeration, that if not for Simon's guidance, there may well have never been *A Train to Palestine*. To Joe and Rina Rosenbaum, whom my wife and I have come to love so much over the years, I will never forget the long hours of interviews, the flood of tears and wonderful echoes of laughter that your friendship has brought us. To Joe, thank you for the courage to tell this poignant story. To Rina, thank you for sharing your husband and family with us. The first to read the early pages was Caitlin Sattler, a precious young business woman, who was perhaps much too busy starting her career to humor my idea, but still she took the time to read those first pages that would become the initial chapters. Another dear friend, Peggy Stovesand, completed editing the second draft. I still remember her quiet voice as she suggested a change here, more emphasis there. As the manuscript developed into a third draft, Mary Speranza in Baton Rouge, suggested that a friend of hers, Judy Klobucar, a retired schoolteacher who taught Holocaust Studies in high school, would be a good editor for this book. Mary, of course, was right. Judy went through the manuscript focused with a surgeon's precision, constantly reminding me to 'stay close to the story,' a suggestion that resulted in the elimination of 15,000 words from the final draft. The last reader was my sister, Jan Chanler who, like myself, inherited from our mother a strong, binding love for books. Those final suggestions, and the love that only a sister can offer, were invaluable. To the editors at Vallentine Mitchell in London, Toby Harris and Lisa Hyde, please know that in the everyday routine of bringing books to market, you also help dreams come true.

And to my wife, Joyce. I can never repay the support and encouragement that she provided during those years. All those times she unselfishly allowed me to retreat into a small, cluttered office, even on Saturdays when inspiration struck, and a movie or dinner had to be cancelled. She never doubted for a moment, during that time, that this book held a higher purpose. Most of all, I remember that hers was the gentle hand that reached and touched me in bed when the nightmares began, emerging from some unknown, dark passageway. Researching and reading those books that vividly described how over 1.5 million Jewish children were murdered during the days when the world slipped into madness became, at times, too much. Her touch brought me back to the safety of the present and that 'other purpose' of which she always talked about. I love you.

List of Images

12. Eliahu Dobkin of the Jewish Agency (left) and Henrietta Szold, founder of the Hadassah Women's Zionist Organization (second from left) await the arrival of the Tehran Children in Athlit, Palestine, 18 February 1943. Copyright Unites States Holocaust Memorial Museum, courtesy of Israel Government Press Office.

13. Younger members of the Tehran children's transport are led away from the train after their arrival at the station in Athlit. United States Holocaust Memorial Museum, courtesy of David Laor.

14. Eva Litman is pictured, greeting General Wladyslaw Anders with flowers. United States Holocaust Memorial Museum, courtesy of Halina Peabody.

15. Nelly and Mina's 'Stone of Memory' in Cologne, 23 Alexander Strasse, 2007. Courtesy of Rina Rosenbaum.

16. Rosenbaum family portrait, today. Courtesy of Rina Rosenbaum.

Prologue

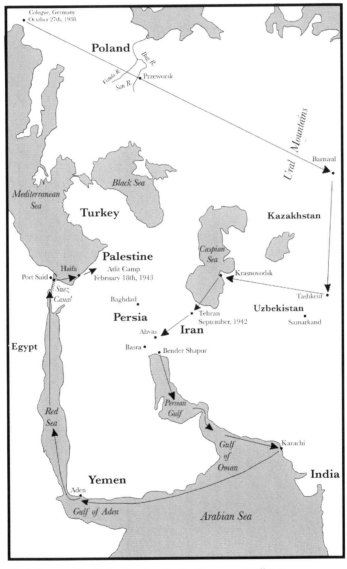

1. Map of Joe's Journey; Lunisolar Creative Productions.com. Will Baten.

...the train on its way up from Egypt was stopped at every station by crowds bearing gifts and flowers and sweets for the children. The arrival of the train at Athlit was tumultuous. Out of every window waved hands holding the little white flags with the blue Star of David that they had been given. From the mob on the platform the names of families and Polish towns were shouted in the hope that some long-lost child might be found...

...and when the children detrained she [Henrietta Szold] saw that they would present her with problems beyond any she had yet encountered. They were pathetic beyond description – they looked indeed like 'the wretched refuse' whom Emma Lazarus welcomed in the poem engraved on the Statue of Liberty. Many of them were still dressed like ragamuffins, in remnants of clothing picked up God-knows-where in the world – broken pith helmets, cut-down adults' trousers and dresses. And, worse yet, many of them, driven for years from pillar to post in a hostile world, uncared for and unschooled, were not merely sick – and many had to be carried from the train – they were wild, frightened creatures who went to bed with their clothes on, clutching the bread they had been unable to devour.

Woman of Valor, Irving Fineman[1]

PART ONE

October 1938 – March 1940

1

Germany was Home

[What] fascinated me…how an advanced and cultured society at the heart of Europe, with one of the most liberal constitutions imaginable, could undergo such a rapid and immense collapse of civilization that within a few years it unleashed the most terrible war in history with, at its heart, the most appalling genocide ever – yet – perpetrated.

British historian, Ian Kershaw[2]

There is a time-worn, faded photograph, a family keepsake placed away for many years in a drawer in a Tel Aviv home, which was then passed down by relatives through the generations; a vivid reminder of those awful, dark days as the world slipped into madness. The image captured is one taken

2. Joe, Inez and Nelly in the backyard at 23 Alexander Strasse, summer 1937. Courtesy of Rina Rosenbaum.

during the summer of 1937 in the backyard of the Rosenbaum apartment at 23 Alexander Strasse in Cologne, Germany; one of happiness, with swelling contentment on the face of seven-year-old Josef Rosenbaum smiling at the camera as he poses beneath the shade of a birch tree. He has the dark, wide eyes of his mother, reflecting the same warm kindness and child-like humour. Hovering over Josef is his sister Inez, older by five years, long arms at her side, the awkwardness of youth, but there is also a gentle smile, hints of a young lady, already. Between them is the youngest, Nelly, just two years old, so short that she must stand on her tiptoes so that she can be seen at the bottom of the photograph. The evening sun washes their amused faces. It is a good time to be a child. Life is carefree, it is summer and there is no school.

But this photograph, like so many others taken in Europe during the 1930s, portrays the fallacies of those fragile times, especially if one is a Jew living in Germany. For these pictures depicted those carefree present times, the laughter and warmth of childhood, and not the unfamiliar future that was quickly approaching, set in motion just three years before.

On 30 January 1933, Adolf Hitler had been appointed Chancellor of Germany, an act that had surprised and shocked even his most astute political opponents with the swiftness in which it had happened. From that day forward, the impending threat to the over nine million European Jews erupted with brutal swiftness. Now possessing the power that he had wished for, Hitler had, within six months, systematically introduced wholesale discrimination against the Jews, creating a wave of concern and fear throughout the Jewish community. The Nuremberg Laws, prohibiting marriage and extra-marital sex between Jews and non-Jews, passed on 15 September 1935. The Reich Citizenship Law stripped Jews of their German citizenship, and encouraged Germans to discontinue shopping at Jewish stores. Jews could no longer work in the medical or education fields, and they were forced to take lower paying jobs.

For Hitler, it was the beginning of a powerful and wonderful dream. For European Jews their future will dissolve into an endless nightmare.

These events went unnoticed by the Rosenbaum children. The only occasion that would connect Josef with the Führer was when Simon Rosenbaum took his son to watch Hitler parade down a Cologne boulevard on 29 March 1936. On that chilled winter afternoon, caught up in a sea of admirers, staring out over unbroken row after row of blood-red and black Nazi flags, Josef leaned forward anxiously perched atop his father's broad shoulders. Then, a black polished Mercedes-Benz slipped past, the Führer standing in the front seat, glaring sternly over the throng, his arm stretched out in perfect salute. Nazi banners, mounted on the sedan fenders, crackled in the breeze, as the chilled air pulsated with echoing, rhythmic roars – 'Seig Heil. Seig Heil. Seig Heil!'

Reflecting back on that day, Josef remembers that even he was caught up in the moment: 'As the automobile passed, with everyone yelling out "Heil Hitler", riding high on my father's shoulders, and leaning forward to catch a glimpse of the famous leader, I did also. I yelled out, "Heil Hitler". What could be so wrong with that? Why, everyone was yelling it…everyone was caught up in the moment.'[3]

But certainly Josef and his sisters had noticed their parents gathered in low-voiced conversations at the kitchen table; after all, talk hidden from the children had never happened before in the Rosenbaum home. And there was the fact that the Jewish children had been forced to attend new schools, but then again, children adjust quickly. For Josef and his sisters during that summer of 1937 the sun shone warmly on their faces, the grass was, at long last after winter, green and lush, and the days no longer filled with classrooms and studying. For Josef each day was an adventure, while Inez leisurely read a book resting on her lap on the back stoop. At that moment, in these children, there still beat hearts with a false assurance that their world would never change.

Within two years, their father Simon Rosenbaum travelled to America seeking employment, fully expecting his family to follow soon. To make daily family matters easier to manage for his wife Mina, Inez, by now fourteen, goes to live with an uncle in Belgium. The fate of Josef, his mother and younger sister Nelly, would within seven months be swept up in Hitler's decree that all German Jews be expelled from their homeland. The deportation began Josef's cruel odyssey as he and his family headed eastward into Poland.

Over four long and difficult years later, Palestine would be his journey's end.

***

Six hundred-ninety-three miles east in Warsaw, Poland, there is another photograph that will be proudly passed from generation to generation after the war. It is also taken in the summer of 1937, in fact on the first day of August, in the town of Baranowicze. A sparsely-built soldier, mostly bald, with a thin moustache, stiffly stands at attention in front of a row of men holding colourful banners. Polish General Wladyslaw Anders is about to take over command of the Nowogródzka Calvary Brigade stationed in eastern Poland. Within twenty-four months, Anders would find his command directly in the path of the German army flooding across the border.

From that summer day forward, the fate of a young German-Jewish boy, and that of a dedicated Polish general, will be forever linked.

Such is the destiny of those swept up in the swirling maelstrom of war.

***

Joe Rosenbaum was born into this turbulent, disquieting world on 25 March 1931. Cologne, a centre of industry and trade in western Germany, was also by the 1930s home to over 15,000 Jews, and like many European municipalities, was two cities, the old and the new, separated by ancient buildings and narrow streets of an earlier time. Cologne was also recognized as a major cultural centre for the Rhineland, home to more than 30 museums and hundreds of galleries, displaying articles from ancient Roman archaeological discoveries, fashionable art and sculpture.

Joe's mother, Mina, was born there in 1898 within a large family of seven brothers and sisters. His father Simon Rosenbaum had arrived in Germany during the First World War when he was fifteen, because his family, who had lived in Poland when the nation was controlled by the Austro-Hungarian Empire, feared that their son would be forced to join the Russian Army. A year later, when he was sixteen, Simon fell in love with Mina, a short, funny girl who was a year older. Simon came from a religious family, and so their family in Germany was also religious, 'but not as devout as the family in Poland'.[4]

In 1925, Simon and Mina were married. 'My parents were first cousins, my mother's mother and my father's mother were sisters, and this was very common among Jewish people in those days. Other families, too. According to Jewish law it's kosher. It's okay.'[5]

Because Simon came from such a religious family, he wore *peyot*, long locks of hair on each side of his face, and one of Joe's favourite stories was when his mother snuck into his father's bedroom one night and cut off one of the *peyot* with scissors. They quarrelled as to why she had cut it off like that, and Simon argued that he would have to wear a big handkerchief around his face as if he had a toothache. He had to do just that until Mina took pity on him, sneaked in several nights later, and cut off the second *peyot*.

Joe's older sister, Inez, was born a year after Simon and Mina married, and to support his growing family Simon drove a truck and worked for his older brother, Moshe, who owned a junkyard. Simon knew only Yiddish, a German dialect, a mixture of Hebrew and Slavic spoken by Jews in Central and Eastern Europe before the Holocaust, and he also spoke a little Polish, all of which hampered his attempts to get a better job. He began to learn German and to read. Five months after his daughter was born, Simon moved his family into a comfortable second-floor apartment located at 23 Alexander Strasse.

It was on this narrow, bustling street that life unfolded for Joe with cherished memories when he was four. 'We lived in a small apartment, I can [still] draw it up in my mind,' Joe remembers:

> We lived on the second floor. Up the stairs, and our apartment was on the left, another apartment on the right. Down the hallway was a bathroom and washroom that we shared. When you walked in our apartment door, you came right into the kitchen, and then into a large living room with a large bed. And that's where our parents slept. I remember on Saturday mornings, we children would run and jump in the bed with father and mother, and we'd have a big party, laughing and joking. But what was important to me is that we had a very close family, and I don't remember my parents ever arguing or yelling…this was a very good point for me to remember.[6]

A balcony overlooked the streets, his personal viewpoint on the world from where young Joe looked down on the busy streets filled with people and automobiles. At the corner sat several wagons where vendors sold vegetables and fruit. A small wagon nearest the curb, bananas hanging from hooks, and a sign '*Est mecht Fuichte.*'

Off in the distance stood the Roman Catholic Cathedral. Taking over 600 years to complete from the 1200s to 1880, the structure served as a landmark into the suburb of Deutz. As a small boy, Joe marvelled at this towering silhouette over 500 feet tall with easily recognizable twin spires. He remembers that when his father took him there, his father seemed even more amazed than he was with the building. In the later years of the war, Allied bombers would destroy most of the city, but amid the terrible destruction the legendary cathedral would suffer only minimal damage. For Joe, this historic building would much later in his life symbolize strength and the will to survive. But for now, life on Alexander Strasse was one of happiness and contentment.

That is what Joe remembered from his youth. But for any Jewish child from a middle-class family living in Germany during the 1930s, possibly there was more to recollect. There was mother standing in front of the oven in the narrow kitchen, a ruffled white apron around her waist. On the wall behind hung an assortment of cups, and spoons, and a ladle, all things that held a sort of magic for a small boy. On a table in the corner sat a single piece of brass Jewish art, a *menorah*, washed in the golden softness of a lamplight. Across the living room above the fireplace, white-chocolate porcelain figurines, neatly arranged, danced along the mantle. An angel, perhaps. A dog. A horse. Next to these were several jars filled with coins for when mother sent the children to the market located on the next block to fetch a last item needed for dinner. A clock was on the far corner of the mantle, with very good woodwork and expensive, a wedding gift from an aunt who now lived in Palestine. And at the other edge a kerosene lamp, for those occasions when the electricity source went out. The kitchen table was covered with glasses and plates, and several books rested at the edge. Whenever an aunt or an uncle visited, the adults would sit around the table that remained cluttered with glasses and plates. They discussed Hitler and what he was doing to their country. Most voices argued that this clownish man was simply a passing fad, soon to disappear behind a passion of common sense as soon as more level-headed leaders came to power.

It was, after all, a common apartment where Joe's family lived, like that owned by so many Jews. They lived and worked and enjoyed life – that is, until 1936.

Joe remembered that his father was tall and handsome, always smiling. Mother was short and chubby, with a great sense of humour, never passing up the opportunity to pull a joke on someone, enjoying life even as she worked in the demanding position of office secretary. Once, at a busy traffic intersection, she walked up behind a policeman standing on a wooden box directing traffic. As he pointed first left, and then right – Mina mocked him. The crowd laughed until the policeman glanced behind him and saw what Mina was doing.

Then came the day when Mina was expecting a baby. Being a wise mother, she saw that young Yossi, Josef's nickname, didn't understand what was happening. His father had simply told him that a stork would bring the baby. But Mina knew her inquisitive son needed to be more involved. 'So, my mother said to put a piece of sugar cube on the window, and if in the morning the cube was gone, it means you were a good boy yesterday, and that the stork is going to bring, sooner or later, the baby. So, I was afraid that if I didn't eat the sugar, we wouldn't get a baby.'[7]

Several weeks passed, and one morning Joe woke up early to voices in the kitchen. 'What happened?' He asked as he crawled out of bed.

'Mama went to the hospital to get the baby,' Inez told him.[8]

'Why?' Joe asked. 'The stork was supposed to bring the baby to the window.'

Inez and Simon comforted Joe telling him that everything was fine, but that his mother needed to go to the hospital. Joe didn't understand everything that was going on, and he didn't see his mother for four and five days, so he worried.

When they finally brought home the new baby sister, Nelly, Joe immediately loved her. Unfortunately, she would suffer throughout her short life with a physical defect, a split lip broken in the upper part of the mouth that had been sewed up at the hospital, but not in a professional way. Nelly couldn't eat normally, so feeding her was a problem, and she had to eat lying on her side with the bottle.

Mina, a person who took charge of a situation, said they should travel to America, where Nelly could have proper surgery performed on her mouth. Mina planned to contact her cousins and ask them to sponsor her family and bring them to America. Unknown to Inez and Joe, leaving Germany was a topic Simon and Mina had discussed frequently within the recent weeks sitting at the small kitchen table, late at night once the children were in bed. Certain that Germany was no longer a safe place for a Jew to live, Simon planned to get his family out as soon as possible. Even Mina's brother, Anschel, was already living in Palestine.

The news from America wasn't encouraging, once her cousins informed Mina that sponsoring a family of five wasn't possible. But they suggested that it would be more likely for her to bring her family to America if Simon travelled to America first and obtained work. Mina was very much against this; breaking up a family was simply unacceptable. She insisted that either the family could all go to America together, or they would remain in Germany.

However, in the following weeks, living conditions worsened for German Jews and Simon lost his job when the Nuremburg Laws, restricting Jews living in Germany, were enacted. Mina, fearing that conditions were only going to worsen, conceived a plan to take the family to Palestine. But she soon learned that Palestine was such a small desert country with only 100,000 Jews and a limited number of good hospitals. Besides, she found out the British government allowed only a small number of Jews to immigrate to Palestine.

Within several months Hitler enacted more restrictions. Jews were forced to wear the Star of David on their clothing while walking the city streets. If the unfolding events weren't hurtful enough, it pained Mina to witness how Hitler's law affected her children's lives.

By 1936, Jewish children, segregated from mainstream school classes, were concentrated in special classes taught by Jewish retirees because Jewish teachers were dismissed from positions in government schools. Following the *Kristallnacht* pogroms in November 1938, Jewish pupils were shut out completely from all German schools. Impoverished and drained of resources, the Jewish community now faced ruin.

While Jewish children were constrained as to which schools they could attend, and removed from sharing in certain school events, German children

3. Joe in first grade at Cologne elementary school, just before deportation. Courtesy of Rina Rosenbaum.

attending Cologne schools were required to deliver an invocation dedicated to Hitler:

> *'Fuhrer, my Führer, bequeathed to me by the Lord,*
> *Protect and preserve me as long as I live!*
> *Thou hast rescued Germany from deepest distress,*
> *I thank thee today for my daily bread.*
> *Abide thou long with me, forsake me not,*
> *Fuhrer, my Fuhrer, my faith and my light!*
> *Heil, my Fuhrer!'*[9]

Learning of these oaths taught to the German youth prompted the British Ambassador to report back to London, 'The German schoolboy is being methodically educated, mentally and physically, to defend this country – but I fear that, if this or a later German government ever requires it of him –he will be found to be equally well-fitted and ready to march on foreign soil.'[10]

* * *

At the beginning of 1938, Mina reconsidered her plans and finally wrote to her cousins in America, informing them that Simon would indeed travel

4. Last family photograph, April 1938, with Josef, Mina, Inez, Simon and Nelly. Courtesy of Rina Rosenbaum.

alone to America and obtain work. After *Pesach*, Passover, in April 1938, Simon departed Germany by train and then boarded a ship to America, leaving Mina to raise three children. To manage daily matters more easily, Mina sent twelve-year-old Inez to Antwerp, Belgium, to live with her brother Yoachim, who had a son and three daughters all about the same age as Inez. Joe's heart ached when he was told his father was going away, but the young boy was reassured by his mother that, 'they would be apart only a few months'.[11]

Simon, on that fateful day when he departed Cologne, had no idea that only seven months later his family would be uprooted from their home, and sent on a passage of hardship and death.

For the next four years, Simon Rosenbaum's family simply vanished from the earth.

***

For a boy of seven, even after his father had departed for America, life in Cologne wasn't that different for Joe. He missed his father and older sister terribly of course, but his mother reassured Yossi every day that the proper papers from his father would soon arrive. Then they would send for Inez, and they would all travel to America and be a family again. During the following months, the three of them continued living their lives and they were never alone because there was family nearby to support them. Two of Mina's sisters and her mother lived close by, and there was Moshe, who came by daily to check on them.

In the fall of 1938, on 27 October, Hitler ordered the expulsion of the 17,000 Jews living in Germany. Their removal eastward towards the Polish border, proved to be swift and brutal. A senior British diplomat in London, upon reading the reports from the British Embassy in Berlin, wrote: 'The Germans were out to eliminate the Jews at any cost to the latter, and nothing we can do or say will stop them.'[12]

On a Thursday morning, four months after his father left for America, Joe was abruptly taken out of the Jewish school and instructed to go home immediately. When he arrived at the apartment on Alexander Strasse, halfway up the stairs, Joe froze.

A policeman dressed in a starched grey-green uniform stood at the apartment door as Joe slipped past him and ran inside. His mother was furious, arguing with the policeman that her son was born in Germany, and that all her children were born in Germany, and with her husband not present, she should stay.

The policeman stepped menacingly toward her, jabbing his finger in her face, telling her, 'That you and your family must take any possessions you need and arrive at the train station by evening. Or else.'[13]

The deportation of the Jews proved to be just the beginning of a new wave of humiliation. A month later, *Kristallnacht*, 'the Night of Broken Glass', erupted on the streets, announced by Nazi officials as a public reaction to the assassination of a German embassy official. During the violence, so named because of the large amounts of shattered glass covering the streets, over 30,000 Jews, between the ages of sixteen to sixty, were arrested; a hundred persons were beaten to death, over a thousand synagogues were destroyed and damaged, and 7,500 Jewish businesses were looted. Jewish hospitals, schools and cemeteries were randomly vandalized, and all six synagogues in Cologne were destroyed.

After the policeman left the apartment, Mina hurriedly went about gathering items that she thought they'd need, which proved to be a difficult task. *How long of a journey would her family be taking?* She wondered how many days or months they should expect to be away from home, but one thing she knew for certain was that that they had to leave, and there wasn't much time.

After collecting the small amount of money hidden away in the apartment, along with the possessions she had gathered, Mina packed a single suitcase. Joe would have to carry Nelly.

When they walked outside into the hallway Mina turned back, taking a moment to lock the door. Then, patiently, with a long moment of thoughtful hesitation, she placed the key in her pocket. That simple act of his mother locking the apartment assured Joe that they would soon return home. And, with that reassurance, he hoisted Nelly into his arms, headed down the stairs, walked out into the street at his mother's side, and followed her towards the train station.

It would be over seventy years later before Joe again stood in front of their apartment at 23 Alexander Strasse.

***

Zindel Grynszpan was also among the thousands of Jews expelled that day. Born in the town of Radomsko, he had lived in Hanover since 1911. He described the tragedy unfolding that late October day:

> When we reached the border, we were searched to see if anybody had any money, and anybody who had more than ten marks, the balance was taken from him…the SS were giving us, as it were, protective custody, and we walked two kilometers on foot to the Polish border…the SS men were whipping us, those who lingered they hit, and blood was flowing on the road. They tore away their little baggage from them, they treated us in a most barbaric fashion – this was the first time that I'd ever seen the wild barbarism of the Germans.[14]

As they walked through the town after sunset, Grynszpan found the night streets black with people shouting out of the shadows, 'The Jews out to Palestine'.[15]

The train station was crowded and frantic. The sour smell of the unwashed, trapped and frightened deportees soaked the air as wave after wave flooded into the building. A British woman sent to help those who had been expelled later recalled: 'I found thousands crowded together in pigsties. The old, the sick, and children herded together in the most inhuman conditions. Conditions were so bad,' she added, 'that some actually tried to escape back to Germany and were shot'.[16]

Joe, his mother, and Nelly arrived at the station as German soldiers hurriedly directed them down the crowded loading station and towards a

5. View of Zbaszyn, the site of a refugee camp for Jews of Polish nationality who were expelled from Germany. United States Holocaust Memorial Museum, courtesy of Michael Irving Ashe.

passenger train. Instructed to get on the train car directly in front of them, they stepped inside. The car was uncomfortably hot, as so many people were crammed into such a small space, Joe thought, that there wasn't room to even lie down. 'This was a regular train, a passenger train, and we went to the Polish border. It was very crowded, but it didn't take too long. I remember we left at noon, and arrived at night; it was dark.'[17]

They had reached Zbaszyn, located between Poland and Germany, the border traversing the city through the middle, once a part of the German Empire in 1871, and then part of the Second Polish Republic. In 1938, the city's population stood at 5,400, which included 360 Germans and only 52 Jews. But by October 1938, the town's Jewish population had swollen to a number simply too large to estimate.

Thirty-nine-year-old Emanuel Ringelblum was also, at that time, in Zbaszyn. A Polish historian, he recollected testimony from many deportees, and later used this evidence against the Nazis during war crime trials conducted after the war. Grynszpan, who had arrived earlier in the night, recalled: 'The Jews were put in stables still dirty with horse dung. At last a lorry with bread arrived from Poznan, but at first there was not enough bread to go around.'[18] He decided to send a postcard to his son Hirsch, in Paris, describing his family's travails. The young man, enraged by what he read, went to the German embassy in Paris and on 6 November shot the first German official who received him. *Kristallnacht*, 'the Night of Broken Glass,' would soon follow.

Mina, with her two children, found herself stranded at the train station, unable to escape the unbearable heat and without any means of support. They lived for three days in a small corner of the station in horribly cramped conditions with little food and water. The harshness of that experience remains fresh in Joe's mind: 'Let's go home, Mama. Let's get out of here,' he had pleaded.[19] Mina took her son aside and tried to explain, 'But we have to stay here, Yossi. I have to take care of my sick sister.' The calm way in which his mother explained it to him satisfied the boy for the moment.

Those deportees possessing papers proving that they were Polish citizens were able to move on, but Joe's mother had no such papers, so it wasn't possible for them to cross over the Polish border. Sending a telegram to her husband in America and another message to her brother in Belgium, Mina asked that they wire money for them to live. Then she waited for any response. By now, there were two families together – Mina and her two children, sister Yechen, and her two children, 17-year-old Paola, and Shlomo, a cousin who was a year older than Joe. Years later, Joe will learn that his father had sent papers for his family to follow him to America, as Mina had requested. However, the papers arrived too late at the Alexander Strasse address in Cologne. By then, Simon's family was in Zbaszyn at the Polish border.

Finally, three days later, Joe's mother received money wired from her brother in Belgium. These funds allowed her to leave the train station with her two children and the other family members, as they stumbled through a flurry of worsening, desperate conditions in the border town. People milled about with nothing to eat, no money and hardly any shelter available, although the Germans still allowed the Poles who possessed proper papers to cross the border into Poland. But Mina decided that they should stay and rent a room in the village.

***

In early February 1939, Mina and the others finally crossed over the border into Poland where they travelled to Joe's grandfather's house in Przeworsk. Before departing, Mina sent Simon a last photograph of his family. Despite the demanding ordeal over the last five months of being forced from home and to live in deplorable conditions, they still appeared healthy and were smiling.

***

Unbeknownst to the thousands of refugees crowded into this small border village, at a state dinner in the Kremlin the foreign minister of Nazi Germany, Joachim von Ribbentrop, had signed a non-aggression agreement with Soviet Union Foreign Minister, Vyacheslav Molotov. Germany and Russia were now allies, sworn not to attack each other. Two years later, on 22 June 1941, Hitler would violate the treaty and invade his ally. For the moment, however, there existed an impending problem between the two military powers – exactly what would they do with the Jews in Poland? Within days, thousands of Jewish refugees would be forced across the border and transported by train to inhumane camps located in the immense Siberian forest where death awaited them from disease, slave labour and agonizing hunger.

By late 1939, European Jews were caught up in a web of furious evil. At the innocent age of eight, Joe Rosenbaum simply found it hard to comprehend the tragedy unfolding around him. For a boy that age, Joe admitted, it seemed an adventure without the tiniest hint, at the moment, of danger. Joe simply learned to trust his mother as they escaped farther from Germany, unable to recognize the enormity of the maelstrom enveloping Poland, unfolding not only in Joe's life, but also on the world stage.

As the war front shifted, first eastward, and then back westward towards Germany in the later years of the war, mass graves and tortured bodies were discovered in the thousands in wells, village streets and forests. During the period 1939 to 1941, while the Russians occupied a smaller part of Poland than the Germans, they murdered far more people than the Nazis. When Germany attacked Russia in June 1941, 1.25 million Poles were forced into labour camps or prisons located in remote settlements scattered over the

Soviet Union. During the brutal reigns of Hitler and Stalin, over fourteen million people were murdered between 1930 and 1947 in Poland, Ukraine, the Baltic region and Belarus. Three million starved to death in what the Ukrainians refer to as the *Holodomor*, an orchestrated artificial famine brought about by sealed borders and grain confiscated from the rural areas and shipped to the cities.[20]

Eastern Europe, that region into where Joe and his family along with thousands of Jewish refugees were forced to travel, became known in history as the 'Bloodlands'.[21]

2

Eastward

The headline of 1 September morning edition of the *Los Angeles Times* informed its readers that the Second World War had begun: 'German Army Invades Poland. Battle Rages Along Border.'[22] German forces, consisting of thousands of tanks, armoured cars and troop-carrying vehicles flooded across the border, prompting a young Wehrmacht infantryman to pencil in his diary: 'Such a wonderful feeling, now, to be a German....'[23]

Along the Paris' Champs-Élysées, Saturday boulevardiers took what they suspected to be their last leisurely strolls and aperitifs, while several blocks away at the Élysée Palace, France's ministers were drafting a declaration of war on Germany.

Meanwhile, at a Berlin café table in the German capital, a young Luftwaffe officer with an open newspaper laid out before him on a small table read of the war's first weekend. William L. Shirer, American journalist, war correspondent and historian, was stationed in Berlin at the time of the invasion. On what he described as a gray, sultry morning in the German city, he reflected on those fateful hours in his book, *The Rise and Fall of the Third Reich*:

> The people in the streets (of Berlin), I noticed, were apathetic despite the immensity of the news, which had greeted them from their radios and from the extra editions of the morning newspapers. (The Army reports were first broadcast over the German radio at 5:40 a.m.)... perhaps, it occurred to me, the German people were simply dazed at waking upon this first morning of September to find themselves in a war which they had been sure the Führer somehow would avoid. They could not quite believe it, now that it had come.[24]

While German citizens went about their daily routines that fateful morning, occasionally glancing above for signs of rain from low clouds covering Berlin, 357 miles away Polish citizens stared into the skies over Warsaw, nervously searching for German warplanes reported to be sweeping over the border since dawn.

In the London streets shoppers and businessmen read the Friday morning edition of *The Star*: 'Poland Invaded, Several Towns Bombed – Hitler Launches a Full-Scale Attack.'[25] For several days afterwards, until the reality of war sank into the senses of the population, life appeared to go on as normal, except for what the people considered precautionary actions. In London sandbags lined walls and stairways, anti-aircraft barrage balloons appeared over the city, and woman and children began evacuating to the countryside.

Shortly before 6pm on 1 September, the appointed time for the British Parliament to convene, Winston Churchill was driven up to London where he would later meet with Neville Chamberlain and accept an invitation from the Prime Minister to join the War Cabinet. Churchill had first learned of the attack at 8:30 that morning when Count Edward Raczynski, the Polish ambassador, telephoned Churchill informing him of the attack on his homeland.

After several messages went unanswered to the German government insisting they withdraw their army from Poland, Churchill sent a note to Chamberlain: 'I remain here at your disposal.'[26]

President Franklin Roosevelt was awakened at 2.50am to receive a telephone call from William C. Bullitt, his ambassador in Paris, informing him that Poland had been invaded. 'Several German divisions are deep in Polish Territory,' Bullitt said, 'and fighting is heavy…there were reports of bombers over the city [Warsaw].'[27]

Roosevelt listened silently until Bullitt finished relating the details.

After thanking his ambassador, the President ended the phone call and then issued orders that all Army commands and the fleet of Navy ships be advised immediately. Remaining in bed, Roosevelt reached to the side table, picked up a pencil and notepad, and began documenting how, and the precise time, he was notified of Hitler's actions.

The note ended: 'In bed 3:05 a.m., Sept. 1 – FDR '39'.[28]

***

Such a strange sight, Joe thought.[29]

A boy, not that much older than himself, was standing in the town square beating on a drum. It was just after noon in Przeworsk, Poland (Pshevorsk in Yiddish), a city that, within days, would find itself directly in the path of the invading German army spreading out eastward. It was where Mina Rosenbaum brought her family after being granted permission by officials to leave Zbaszyn on the Polish border. 'We went to my father's parents,' Joe remembers:

And the first time I saw them, I was shocked because I remembered the story my mother would tell me of Hansel and Gretel, and I saw two old people coming out of that little hut with a roof covered with hay. That old man with a long white beard was my grandfather, Ja'akov-David, but he was called Jankel-Duvid. His wife was the sister of my mother's mother, the aunt to my mother. She was Sarah-Esther. When I saw them in the little hut, and we came inside, [and] it was already late at night, pitch dark. My mother saw them for the first time. They were her in-laws, and also her uncle and aunt...but she had never seen them before.[30]

It was several days later when Joe and his cousins went to the centre of town: 'In the square was a big market, and a church, it was market day, and this boy, maybe fourteen, was beating on a drum.'[31] A large crowd had gathered to watch the boy, standing erect on the steps of the town hall – a towering, gray façade building topped with an impressive black clocktower from where flags hung. With his eyes straight forward, the boy rapped on the drum hanging at his waist. His ankles shone trout-white from beneath canvas trousers too short to cover his long thin legs, as he hesitated for a moment while adjusting the strap over his shoulder. Then he began again, rhythmically smacking on the drum military style – 'brrdum, brrdum, brrdum', and shouted out Polish phrases. Because Joe was a German Jew, he didn't understand a word the boy spoke, so he leaned closer to one of his cousins who had taught him some Polish and a little Yiddish since coming to Poland. 'What is he saying?' Joe asked.

The cousin leaned closer and whispered, 'The war has come.'

What war? Joe wondered, because for him the statement made very little sense. And the boy beating a drum and yelling words. What could he really know? 'What war is the boy yelling about?' Joe asked his cousin.

'Hitler and the Germans have attacked Poland,' his cousin said, his face wrinkling with concern. Joe didn't understand because he had found Przeworsk to be such a simple, pleasant place, much different than busy, crowded Cologne. No radio, no telephone, and no German soldiers or police. 'We were isolated there', Joe said, and he felt safe.[32]

Przeworsk was a town located in southeastern Poland. A settlement since the tenth century, Jews had always played a part in the town's rich heritage, especially as the city went through a long period of economic success. In 1921, over 1,400 citizens of the 3,000 living there were Jews. Nine years later, a great fire in 1930 destroyed a large portion of the town, leaving many of the Jews homeless until they found poor houses on a narrow and dirty street named Zydowska Street. This was the same street where Joe and other boys soon played soldiers, replicating the war erupting around them.

For Joe, he admits, leaving Cologne and arriving in rural Poland, was 'for me…like I had landed five hundred years ago…to sleep on the barn hay at my grandfather's house was exciting, like an adventure, except for the lice, of course. They were everywhere, constantly biting and bothering everyone so badly that one could hardly sleep.'[33] So, except for the dreadful lice, Przeworsk turned out to be a great place for such an inquisitive boy as Joe, a perfect place to explore, with horses, the Gothic abbeys, the towering town hall, a large wonderful palace and even a monastery. On the north side of the square was a two-storey brick building that served as an evening school for Jewish girls, and in the afternoons, lines of pretty, flushed-faced teenagers wearing thick sweaters would run out into the street laughing and pulling at each other's hair. Just outside the town was the sugar factory built on low, flat ground, a series of long white-painted buildings constructed behind a sparse tree line and a round smokestack that was always billowing dark smoke.

Every day brought strange and wonderful sights. Each morning the sun came up over open pastures with cows, horses, and mules, shining on wide fields and crops of rye, and wheat and sugar beets. Sunflowers grew along long, wooden fences. There were forests thick with birch, pine and oak trees for Joe and the other boys to play. Joe had been used to seeing the men in Cologne wearing suits, but the Polish men were dressed in white shirts worn over loose, baggy trousers and waistcoats, with high dull leather boots. The women wore long skirts and white blouses, with bright-coloured kerchiefs wrapped over their heads.

There was *Pierogi*, a dumpling, to eat. Every day, Joe and his cousins ran through the open market where the women sold vegetables and fruit, row after row of tables burdened with butter churns along the downtown streets. The roads leading out of town were lined with eight-sided small roadside stands, wooden buildings with a cross on top and a large open window, where the vendor sold flowers to the Christian women on their way to church.

Joe had cousins to play with here. There was a lot he didn't know about, or understand, such as the war starting, but he knew one thing for certain – if German soldiers were anything like the police officer who had made them leave their apartment, Joe didn't want them to ever come to Przeworsk. But the Germans soon arrived.

Przeworsk would be captured by the Wehrmacht on 9 September 1939, and remain under German occupation until 27 July 1944.

After a time, the boy with the drum grew weary, and as he grasped the drumsticks, his hands dropped to his side, and he simply walked away through the crowd. Joe and his cousins watched as the people walked quietly away also, from the market, down the streets, disappearing past the large church and common-coloured buildings. Then Joe and his cousins ran as fast as they could to his grandfather's house. Joe knew grandfather could explain to them what was going on. He would know what this war would mean for them.

Joe's grandfather was by then an old man with his long, white beard and narrow spectacles that rested at the end of his bulbous nose. His skin was like worn leather, which made him look funny enough, and when he was amused, the children could hear his deep laughter echoing throughout the small house.

Joe loved to listen to his grandfather's stories. On this late afternoon, as the children sat around him on the the floor in front of a cramped stone fireplace, Grandfather told them exciting stories of the last war when the Germans used gas against its enemies. He told them that the German planes would be here in a few days and how he was very afraid it would be a gas war again. When the old man told the children about being afraid, Grandmother frowned and shook her head. Still, Joe couldn't fully understand what was happening or what Grandfather was telling them. Maybe his older cousins understood. Over the next several days, Joe noticed that his grandparents, aunts and uncles took large sheets of wet cloth and blocked the windows so that the air inside would remain clean.

As Joe's grandfather had said it would, the bombing of towns and villages throughout Poland arrived with brutal swiftness as the Polish army fell back, attempting to regroup. One soldier described those early days:

> Throughout the battle, the enemy planes circled overhead...But they were not dropping bombs yet, for fear of hitting their own men. The deafening sound of the planes, the sight of the swastikas on their wings, even the pilots, whose faces could clearly be seen as they flew low, filled us with alarm. They looked like monsters in their flying helmets and goggles.[34]

The first German plane appeared over Przeworsk two days later. The Polish children referred to them as 'black crosses'. Joe ran out with the others and stared up at the sky as the lone aircraft circled over the city like a large, lazy bird. Grandfather explained that there was nothing for them to worry about, at least for the moment, because it was a German spy plane flying over to find out what was going on, attempting to locate what remained of the Polish army. Joe recalls that the boys thought it was humorous when, 'the Polish soldiers came out into the street, with long rifles like from the time of

Napoleon…pointed the rifles at the sky…boom, boom…they shot at the plane, but never hit anything.'[35] As the plane flew away westward, Grandfather told them that this plane had no bombs or machine guns, but that the next planes that appeared overhead would carry such weapons. For this reason, Grandfather instructed the children that they should stay close to the house.

As Joe and his cousins continued to play war on Zydowska Street, conditions worsened along the battlefront. The Polish army desperately attempted to fall back and regroup; such efforts were made worse by the thousands of refugees clogging the roadways. This was the situation General Wladyslaw Anders, commander of the Nowogrodzka Calvary Brigade, found as he futilely attempted to reposition his troops outside the city of Lublin.

> Crowds of refugees, their belongings piled on all manner of vehicles, and driving their cattle ahead of them, blocked the roads as they tried to escape to the eastern provinces. All roads were blocked by refugees with their belongings and by the [chaotic clutter] of military vehicles. The crowds had no idea in which direction to move, and from time to time were bombed and machine-gunned by the enemy. On our way south, we were frequently forced to move across country and to cross rivers over which the bridges had been blown up by partisan German settlers. German shell-fire from the east and from beyond the Vistula [River], although not very accurate, threw the refugee crowds into disorder…the whole advance was extremely fatiguing .[36]

During the second week of September, General Anders passed through Warsaw weeping at the sight unfolding before him in the capital. 'Many houses in Praga, the suburb of the right bank of the Vistula, lay in ruins as the result of German bombing. In the streets were barricades improvised from overthrown tram-cars…there was utter confusion in the city…'[37]

By late afternoon, long lines of weary refugees reached Przeworsk, streaming through mostly on foot, but also riding on horses and wagons. Following was an endless parade of retreating soldiers as the bitter smell of petrol and sweating cavalry horses choked the air. Joe and his cousins watched the strange sight of retreating soldiers, mud-caked sedans, tanks and trucks grinding through the streets, stirring huge dust clouds. By nightfall, the town fell eerily quiet as the refugees and soldiers continued eastward. Always to the east.

Two days later, the German planes appeared again over the town, and as Grandfather had warned, they dropped bombs. After the planes flew away and the bombing stopped, Joe, his grandfather and cousins followed the crowd to the factory. 'They bombed the railroad station and the sugar factory and so we had all the sugar we wanted. So, the whole town went to the factory after they bombed and took sugar, sacks of sugar, whatever we could *schlep*, we took it home. It was free.'[38] Then the baker stopped baking bread, so the women baked their bread at home. Joe's grandmother baked cake. She baked so much cake that Joe thought of it as a big holiday. But eventually he tired of eating cake and searched the kitchen for plain bread.

The next day, the German warplanes bombed the city again, and there were so many explosions that Joe and his cousins couldn't count all the blasts. With the war drawing closer, Joe's grandfather decided to move the family to Kaintshuk, eleven kilometres away. Joe was familiar with Kaintshuk, a town about the same size of Przeworsk, because once a week he accompanied his grandfather to a marketplace stall in the centre of town where they sold clay pots.

Late the next morning, Joe and his family walked out of Przeworsk beneath a dark, whirling sky, the air thickly humid and miserable because September days could be eleven hours long in Poland. The road to Kaintshuk was jammed with civilians and Polish soldiers with horses and cannons fleeing the German army, and it was along this road for the first time in his young life that Joe witnessed people being killed as German soldiers moved along in the woods on both sides of the road, shooting the Polish soldiers.

That first night in Kaintshuk turned out to be a nightmare, nothing like Joe's grandfather thought it would be. For most of the night, Joe lay on a blanket listening to the passing sounds of war:

> I remember sleeping there at night, and the first night we slept there, we heard a big noise. Heavy armament was coming through. First the Polish army was running away, and the Germans were chasing them from behind. They came with tanks, with motorcycles and would make a horrendous noise.[39]

Because the war had found them here also, Grandfather gathered the family together one morning and told them, 'What are we doing here? We should go back to Przeworsk, and back to our house, our place. I don't believe that we have to run anymore.'

The next morning, they travelled the eleven kilometres back to Przeworsk. The sky was clear that day, but the air remained stifling. Careful not to travel on the road as often, they circled through pastures and woods, always on the lookout for German soldiers. Once they reached the town, his grandfather was relieved to find out that there were neither Polish nor

German soldiers remaining. The war had not followed them. Peace wouldn't last long.

After the Polish army fell back, German soldiers poured into Polish towns and villages. Eliott 'Lonek' Jaroslawicz anxiously watched that morning as the soldiers arrived in his town:

> There was a big soccer place and here came the Germans. They came with their motorcycles and trucks and bayonets. They put up their rifles, standing up three of them together, like triangles with bayonets on top. They used to take off their shirts and get washed up, though it was September and the weather was getting cold. And they used to eat and drink beer.[40]

***

The Germans finally arrived in Przeworsk. Most of them continued marching eastward, but a small group of the German soldiers stayed in the town. They settled in the marketplace, where only days before the boy had beaten his drum and announced the war was coming. To Joe, that seemed like years ago because he and his cousins were so tired from walking to Kaintshuk and back.

On the third day, the soldiers gathered all the Jews together in the marketplace. A stern-faced German officer dressed in a starched, gray uniform stood before them announcing what they could and couldn't do. Incidents erupted over the next several weeks as soldiers beat up Jews, taunting them with hateful words and cutting their beards. Joe only heard about these terrible episodes because his mother was afraid of the Germans, and she kept her son inside. 'They took the Jews', Joe remembers hearing the grown-ups saying, 'made them clean the floor. This is what put panic in the situation, and fear, a lot of fear.'[41] Then gradually, something strange happened – life went back to normal. The baker began baking bread again, and Joe's mother let them play outside.

However, within several days and without warning, the Germans again gathered all the Jews into the marketplace. Joe watched in horror as the soldiers badly beat up a group of the younger men, and cut off the older men's beards. Then the Germans violated the cemetery and carried the gravestones to the centre of town to pave the streets with. The next day the soldiers set fire to the synagogue and the *beis medrash,* the house of learning. When the Jews tried to put out the fire, the soldiers forced them back. The Holy Books perished, and the afternoon air was filled with crying and weeping from the crowd who had gathered across the street.

One morning, the German officer with the serious face once again stood in front of them and announced, 'You have to leave within 24 hours! If you're here at this time tomorrow, we will shoot you.' Joe and his family hurried back to the house and gathered the possessions they wanted to take with them. Grandfather tried to calm everyone and announced, 'We have to go to the Russian side. I'm certain that we'll be safe there.'[42]

***

As the violence and tragedy swirled around Joe and his family, there was no way such a young boy could know just how fortunate his family had been, because Przeworsk was located to the east, close to the border between the Russians and the Germans. The Germans simply wanted the Jews out. In the towns and villages closer to the Polish-German border, from where Hitler's attack came, the situation was much different, and the consequences terrifyingly worse.

Stories spread of looting, brutality and the murdering of Jews as the Germans swept through Poland. The Germans took Lancet, a city in southeastern Poland with a flourishing Jewish community. Later in the war, on 2 August 1942, German SS soldiers led over 2,750 Jews into the nearby Falkinia Forest, lined them up in front of a mass grave, and murdered them by machine gun fire.

In 1939, the opening days of the war itself brought much bloodshed. Three days before *Rosh Hashanah*, the Jewish new year, the Germans captured Lezajsk. Events that unfolded there were much the same story as repeated all over Poland – the beatings, the tearing out of beards along with tatters of flesh, the stealing of the Jews' possessions, the ransacking of their homes. The soldiers took away many people, and they were never seen or heard from again. They looted valuables, and then set fire to the *beis medrash* and the synagogues. At the river outside the town of Pultusk, both Jews and Poles were lined up along the bank. Then the Germans shot them, and they fell into the water. The Germans entered Tomaszow Lubelski during *Rosh Hashanah*. The very first day they killed Rabbi Nachum, Rafal Bernsztajn and a boy called Lipe. Mieliec was captured the next day, and the soldiers went directly to the *Mikva*, the ritual bathhouse. They shot 64 Jews that day. Then they set fire to the synagogue, the *beis medrash*, and the house where Rabbi Hurwicz lived with an orphan boy. The rabbi escaped out of the window, but as the boy climbed the fence he was shot in the back.[43]

These brutal scenes were repeated in villages and towns throughout Poland. Jews were the target – men, women and children – it didn't matter to the German soldiers. Jews were ordered from their homes, assembled in the town squares and randomly shot to set an example, a warning of what was to come. The Germans moved in and murdered, the Russians looted, as non-Jewish Poles assisted in rounding up Jews, who only days before had been their neighbours from whom they had purchased milk, cheese and vegetables.

Civilization quickly disappeared behind a disquieting cloak of mass graves, firing squads and brutal attacks. The invaders were imposing their will on the captured populations, and there was no one to stop them. In the midst of this horror, the conquered Jews would soon learn to live by faith, scarce amounts of food and water and inadequate shelter or medicines.

They also soon learned to live on the smallest of hope, only to survive, at least, for one more day.

***

During that first week of September, General Halder, Hitler's Chief of Staff, reviewed just how successfully the attack into Poland had progressed over the last several days with General von Brauchitsch, Commander in Chief of the German Army. After the discussions concluded, Halder penned in his diary, that 'the enemy is practically beaten'.[44]

***

The inevitable war, however, was hardly a surprise to Warsaw residents. During the last days of August 1939, any optimism that Hitler would somehow change his posture melted away due to blackouts, the opening of gas shelters and civilians being trained to use gas masks. During the nights, behind the darkened windows of cafés and bars, patrons danced, drank and sang patriotic songs, as a brief escape from the reality facing their city. In the late-night hours, they would walk home or take taxis, gas masks slung over their shoulders, along streets that were eerily different now, darkened and abandoned, foretelling the oncoming danger.

Wladyslaw Szpilman, a 27-year-old Polish pianist and classical composer who performed classical and jazz music for Polskie Radio (Polish Radio), remembered the morning the war came to Warsaw. He was living with his parents, my sisters and a brother on Sliska Street, working for Polskie Radio as a pianist. Their flat was on the third floor, and on that last day of August, Szpilman was late getting home and went straight to bed.

> The noise of explosions woke me. It was light already. I looked at the time: six o'clock. Obviously military exercises were in progress, we had

become accustomed to them over the last couple of days…[So] I decided to read until breakfast time. It must have been at least eight when my bedroom door opened. Mother stood there, dressed as if she was off into town any minute. She was paler than usual, and could not conceal a certain disapproval when she saw me still in bed reading. She opened her mouth, but at the very first word her voice failed her and she had to clear her throat. Then she said, in nervous, hurried tones, 'Get up! The war…the war's begun.'[45]

Because Szpilman wasn't a soldier and didn't own a firearm, two weeks later as the German infantry fought their way into Warsaw, the pianist used as his platform Polskie Radio with his piano as his weapon, performing a bold act of defiance against the invaders.

Late in the afternoon on that same day: an automobile pulled into Zamosc [247 kilometres from Warsaw and only 67 kilometres from the Ukraine border], loaded with refugees escaping Warsaw. The black-caftanned, white-bearded Jewish owner of a wine bar served them scrambled eggs and asked for news of the invasion. He shook his head as they told him of mass bombings from a sky filled with Luftwaffe planes, of the Germany army sweeping across the Vistula River, seemingly unstoppable, and long lines of exhausted refugees moving eastward. He finally called for a bottle of his finest Tokay. 'Gentlemen, do me the honour of drinking this old wine, to remember me by.' Among those escapees was the father of Klara Glowczewska, a writer for *Town and Country Magazine*.[46]

3

A Polish General

On the third day of the war, a mud-caked late model Ralf-Stetysz sedan was parked among a thick cluster of birch trees on a high bluff above the Vistula River, where most of the initial battles had been fought.[47]

Sitting in the staff car, along with his driver, was Polish General Wladyslaw Anders, commander of the Novogrodek Calvary Brigade. Stationed at the village of Lidzbark, 90 miles south-east of Danzig and 13 miles south of the East Prussian border, Anders found his command directly in the path of the German attack on the first morning of the war. Since that first onslaught, in those fleeting days of organized resistance against the invasion, he had been given command of all Polish units; at least what remained of the Polish Army, positioned along the Vistula – a last line of defence.

A deep headache throbbed behind his eyes, as Anders looked out through the rain-speckled windshield over the bluff and into the wide valley. Tired and weary, he hadn't slept since the invasion began, except for short naps while curled up in the back of the sedan. A slightly-built man, mostly bald, with a thin moustache, Anders's steady brown eyes sank back into his skull from exhaustion, his face wrinkled with concern about the situation confronting him.

After abandoning Gdansk, the city which controlled the mouth of the Vistula, the Poles viciously fought a withdrawing action at Pomerania, presenting the remainder of the Polish Army with the opportunity to reorganize at the southern bank of the Vistula, where they planned to defend Torun, a key city in their desperate plan. Over four years later, Allied troops moving eastward along the same river would liberate a camp, which was once a Polish artillery barrack, outside at the town of Oswiecim. This killing place became known as Auschwitz-Birkenau, located southward from the bluff where Anders gazed out on the Vistula on that evening of the third day of the war. It was noted that the ashes of murdered Jews, burned in the ovens once they were removed from the gas chambers, were unceremoniously dumped into its waters.

Respected by his superiors as an effective commander, the strength Anders brought to war was the ability to analyze a battlefield, to properly choose and utilize terrain in battle. But as Anders stared down at the Vistula winding like a blue ribbon in the fading daylight, he realized that there would be no such advantages for the Polish army in this war. He wrote later how quickly the German units poured across Poland, and the situation deteriorated:

> The Germans were pressing along the whole length of the line. Fierce fighting was in progress on either side of my sector, which itself was relatively lightly engaged. My regiments were successfully fighting advanced enemy detachments. In the air powerful formations of German aircraft, not one Polish, passed constantly overhead. The radio kept repeating the warning: 'Attention! Aircraft approaching!' News poured in of air attacks, not only in Warsaw but on many other towns far to the rear. Many railway lines were cut. The situation rapidly worsened.

During a moment of reflection on his youth, Anders conjured up dreams of his childhood hero, Krakus, the legendary Polish prince. Closing his eyes, Anders could see the gallant leader charging out of the forest with his men following closely behind mounted on horses, white smoke puffing out from flared nostrils, to defeat armies of the Roman Empire, attacking from the north. On this late afternoon, however, Anders realized it was all a hopeless dream. This new enemy had swept in from the west, powerful and overwhelming, and neither he nor anyone else in the Polish command would have the option to decide battle lines. Any suggestions of prepared openings for an orderly retreat were now impossible, much less the luxury to determine strategic positions from which to regroup the armies. The Polish military simply wasn't in a position to choose much of anything now, and the German juggernaut rolling through Poland was, Anders admitted, unstoppable.

The reason for the rapid German victories along the border was a new warfare tactic – the Blitzkrieg – lightning movements of new fighting vehicles designed for swift actions. The Polish army, locked in a First World War warfare mentality, was simply overwhelmed by this new method of fighting. A comparison between the two armies fighting in Poland, drawn up by Anders himself only the year before, revealed that Germany had eleven tank divisions compared to Poland's one. The German army had just one cavalry brigade. But, Poland still retained eleven cavalry units, which would prove woefully inadequate.

The German strategy of lightning strikes – not along a wide front, but penetrating full force attacks at specific weak spots – quickly created breakthroughs all along the Polish lines. Then came the flush of tanks, motorcycles, and motorized vehicles crashing through the breaches until they fanned out along the Polish rear area. While the German army, the Wehrmacht, rolled through the Polish defenses, the Luftwaffe, the German air force, bombed cities as streams of refugees clogged the streets and roads.

These warplanes represented another impressive aspect of this new war, especially the Junkers-87 Stuka. Developed by Colonel General Ernest Udet, the highest scoring German ace to survive the First World War and personal friend to Hermann Goring, the Stuka was nicknamed the 'terror from the skies' by the frontline Polish troops and the civilian refugees fleeing eastward, the first witnesses to this new frightening weapon.[48] Equipped with a powerful 1,200 horsepower Junkers-Jumo 211 engine for speed and manoeuverability, as the two-seater dive bombers swooped out of the clouds at targeted civilian refugee columns fleeing eastward on the roads, sirens strapped beneath the undercarriage produced a screaming racket which created a wave of demoralizing chaos and confusion at the Polish army's rear.

In the opening days of the invasion, commanders such as General Anders frustratingly found it nearly impossible to move troops between military sectors. Once the German armies had pushed the Polish forces back across the Bug River, Udet, a stunt pilot and famous celebrity in 1930s Germany well known for his mistresses and wealth, visited the front and witnessed the murderous destruction and death his planes had inflicted on innocent Polish civilians. It changed something in Udet, who began to drink heavily and use drugs. Abandoned by Göring, and falling out of grace with Hitler after the Luftwaffe failed to gain air superiority over Great Britain in late 1940, Udet slipped deeper into depression.

On 17 November 1941, Udet committed suicide by shooting a bullet into his head while on the phone with his girlfriend.

∗∗∗

Wladyslaw Anders appeared destined to be a soldier at an early age.[49] In fact, he was one of four brothers – along with Charles, George Edward and Tadeusz – who served in the Polish army as officers at the beginning of the Second World War. His father was of Germanic origin and earned a living as an agronomist, an expert in soil management and field-crop production. Born in the village of Krosniewice-Blonie less than 100 miles west of Warsaw, then a Russian-controlled area of Poland, Anders was raised in a family with strict values with deep religious convictions. As a teenager, Anders was baptized as a member of the Protestant Evangelical-Augsburg Church.

After attending high school in Warsaw, he graduated from Riga Technical University. It was during this time that a visiting Russian general noticed Anders's talent in controlling a stable of wild horses. In 1913, Anders joined the Russian army and served Tsar Nicholas II in the 1st Squadron of the 1st Krechowiecki Lancers Regiment, and during the First World War he was wounded five times. During 1917, Anders studied at the Academy of the General Staff in St. Petersburg, studies that prompted his superiors to assign him to take part in the formation of the Polish Corps, reporting to General Jozef Dowbor-Musnicki. Returning to Poland when Germany surrendered in 1918, he joined the Polish Army and became chief of staff of Greater Poland. When the Russo-Polish war began, he was appointed commander of the 15th Poznanski Lancer's Regiment, was again seriously wounded, but eventually rose to the rank of general. In 1925, Anders entered the *Ecole Superieure de Guerre*, a French institution for military higher education in Paris, returned to Poland, and was later promoted to military commander of Warsaw. At the Nations Cup in Nice in 1932, he headed the Polish equestrian team, a position, according to his autobiography, that gave him pleasure.

In the late 1930s, as the high command recognized his military skills, Anders was given command of the cavalry brigades in eastern Poland, a promotion that placed him directly in the path of the Wehrmacht attack planned to take place in September 1939.

***

After assessing the situation as nearly hopeless, Anders and his driver returned to headquarters from the Vistula River at nightfall. It was after the war, reflecting on 3 September, when Anders wrote in his autobiography *An Army in Exile*: 'The shadow of disaster had already begun to loom.'[50]

Still, prepared to fight on as long as possible, Anders gave orders to hasten the building of fortifications near Plock, which covered a crossing of the Vistula, if the order for a retreat had to be issued. However, at 9pm, after eating a light dinner and as he spent the next several hours studying maps spread out across a trestle table, a message arrived from Warsaw headquarters:

> On the night of September 3, I was informed that the defenders of Mlava, who had held out in the face of great odds, had received orders to withdraw at dawn to a rear position. The next morning, I was ordered to take over the command of the 20th and 8th Infantry Divisions in addition to my own. After explaining the situation to my

second-in-command and telling him to make all necessary preparations for a withdrawal towards Plock, I went by car to Mlava.[51]

It was shortly after dawn the next morning, as Anders was taken by car to Mlava to take command of the two divisions and design a plan for retreating toward Hungary, that he witnessed this *New War,* this total war.

On the way we passed through burning villages. The bodies of many civilians lay in the streets, among them those of children. Once I saw a group of small children being led by their teacher to the shelter in the woods. Suddenly there was the roar of an aeroplane. The pilot circled around, descending to a height of 50 metres. As he dropped his bombs and fired his machine-guns, the children scattered like sparrows. The aeroplane disappeared as quickly as it had come, but on the field, some crumpled and lifeless bundles of bright clothing remained.[52]

Twenty-three months later, the fortunes of two individuals were linked – Anders, this professional soldier possessing both a profound love for Poland and the fierceness to fight for those things he treasured, and Joe Rosenbaum, an innocent child refugee forced thousands of miles from his home. It was Anders who later made the difficult decisions determining whether Joe, as well as thousands of other Jewish refugees, would leave the Siberian camps, or remain to suffer and die.

4

'...And Then into the Forest'

Several mornings later, Joe's grandfather awoke early, and after breakfast he informed the family he was going to the town square to meet with some men. When Joe asked if he could go with him, his grandfather told him that he must stay at home and not to worry because he would return soon.

When his grandfather did return, his face was drained of colour as he told them stories he had heard of the Wehrmacht and the SS troops conducting mass persecutions of Jews. And, he assured them, these incidents were only a warning of the terrible events yet to come. However, he told them there was also good news. The Germans had, at last, announced the border open, and anyone who wanted to cross the border into the Russian zone was free to do so with the provision that once someone crossed the border, he could never come back.[53]

As Grandfather told them all of this, he smiled. 'Things will be better there, I think, when we leave for the Russian side.' He went and sat in a chair by the stove, Grandmother brought him tea, and Joe watched as a shadow fell across his grandfather's face as he stared at the floor. *Things will be better?* Joe asked himself. *If that were true, why did Grandfather look so worried?*

Early the next morning, the family packed their belongings. 'So, now we had to leave.' Joe remembers, 'We had to pack our belongings in under twenty-four hours, and we tried to get a horse and buggy to take us because it was about fifteen to twenty kilometers to a town named Jaroslaw.'

The Russians were reportedly located beyond the river that flowed through the town, and it was an arca that the refugees considered safe. They could only pack small items, *shmates*, some food, a coat or sweater, and only a few necessary valuables and they began walking because there were no horses or wagons for them to ride.

As they travelled along the road, Joe and his cousins became afraid when they heard rumours that, in Jaroslaw, they would have to cross over a big, high bridge. To make matters worse, there were also rumours that either the Russians or the Germans, were going to bomb the bridge just as all the people began crossing, and they would all fall into the river.

That night they slept on the roadside. The next morning, the deportees started again toward Jaroslaw. Joe and his mother took turns as one carried a large suitcase, and the other carried Nelly because she was too small to walk. Then they would switch, and Joe would carry the suitcase. Joe liked his turn with his sister more than hauling the suitcase because he could place her on his shoulders, though he wasn't a big boy at all. Later in the day, as they rested at midday alongside the road, his mother sewed pieces of cloth together, making pouches. 'My mother sewed a piece of cloth to hold something that would hang around our neck, and placed it there to hide. I don't know what it was. It must have been jewellery, or maybe some money, maybe something expensive.' Then she hung the pockets around Joe and Nelly's necks, hiding them beneath their clothes.

An occasional German soldier rode by on a motorcycle, paying little attention to the refugees trudging along the roadside, attempting to reach the bridge. No one was bothering them now. They were simply walking and walking, tired and thirsty and hungry, along with many other people.

After several days of walking, the weather became much nicer; it wasn't as humid, and sleeping on the road wasn't so bad at all. The next morning, they were given a ride on a wagon, which was unusual because the non-Jews all had wagons, and they usually charged a high rate for a ride.

Late in the afternoon, a convertible sedan filled with German officers abruptly swerved across the road blocking their way. The officers jumped out of the automobile, yelling as they always did, 'Everybody gives up what you have, or we'll have to shoot you!'

Joe and the others quietly stood at the side of the road. Besides being obviously very frightened of the Germans, many refugees couldn't understand the orders that the Germans were screaming at them. The people emptied their trouser and coat pockets, then went through their luggage and began passing out possessions to the Germans, hoping that would appease them.

A younger officer, frowning like an angry owl and waving a revolver in his hand, came over to where Joe and Nelly were standing on the side of the road. 'If you have any valuables,' he shouted in a high shrill voice, 'give them to me, or I'll shoot you'. Joe reached to his chest, and felt the pouch his mother had sewed hanging against the inside of his shirt. Instinctively, he stepped back.

Though most of the people didn't understand the officer's orders, Joe understood, and Nelly understood because they were German. Joe was frightened and quiet, as Nelly, who hadn't spoken a word, began to cry softly. Joe's mother's face turned flushed and red. She stepped quickly toward the young officer, 'Look at you such a big brave soldier facing a little child, what could you possibly want from her? She's crying, and you've frightened her.'

For a long moment the young German officer stared at her, stunned at how well she spoke German. The other officers laughed. '*German?*' he finally asked.

'Yes, German', she answered. 'Cologne.'

The officer hesitated for a long moment, and then slowly replaced his revolver in the holster and walked to the automobile.

***

Several hours after the incident with the German officers, they reached the bridge. Joe's heart thumped against the inside of his chest as they started across to the Russian side because of the rumours of planes possibly bombing the bridge. But there were no bombs, and soon they were on the other side, and they slept that night in a farmhouse. Others weren't as fortunate because where they attempted to cross the river upstream, there was no bridge. Both the Germans and the Russians fired at them, and many stayed in the water all night. At daybreak, for some inexplicable reason, the firing stopped and the people crossed the river.

When Joe awoke the next morning, his family discovered that the Russians hadn't yet come to Jaroslaw. 'The Russians were taking their time,' Joe remembers his grandfather telling them. The refugees made their way to a city named Nemirov, a place that his grandfather had often told stories about concerning 'the big slaughter'.

A city in the government of Podolia, Russian Poland, Nemirov was infamous in Jewish history because of a bloody seventeenth-century pogrom.[54] Before this massacre, the city was known as one of the great centres of Jewish learning, and many rabbis with high reputations lived there. The town was fortified, so it was a natural haven for Jews fleeing during the Cossack Uprising in 1648, and in a short time the Jewish population had risen to over 6,000. When the Cossacks arrived in the region sent by Chielnicki, leader of the Cossacks and the peasant uprising against Polish rule, they rode under Polish flags, deceiving the inhabitants. The Greek Christians were aware of the deception and urged the Jews to open the gates. Once the gates were opened, the Cossacks and the non-Jewish people began brutally executing all the Jews – men, women and children. Many Jews changed their religion, and others escaped to the town of Tulchin. But the vast number of Jews, most of the 6,000, chose death rather than 'forcible baptism'.

When Joe and the others arrived in Nemirov, it was very different. The Cossacks were but a distant memory in history, and the town was overwhelmed with Jewish refugees.

There was family at Nemirov to meet the Rosenbaums, which made sense to Joe that this was why they had travelled there. The six of them arrived weary and hungry and joined up with Nachman, his father's brother, and so then there were eleven. Soon another eleven joined them, making a total of twenty-two, once Shmuel and Gitaleh Locker came, accompanied by their seven children who were all older than Joe.

They had little money for food, so Mina split them into two houses. She bought some wool, and knitted sweaters to sell, while Joe lived with a family that operated a slaughterhouse with a big yard full of cows and bulls located behind the butcher shop. In the following days, for the first time in his life, Joe witnessed an animal being slaughtered. It was an experience filled with horrible and brutal sights and smells, and the pitiful bawling of the animal remained with the young boy for months.

Because Joe was eight and so small, he helped with some minimal chores, and in return for his work he earned a big lunch: meat, soup and potatoes – 'a big meal like European people ate'. He sat at the table with the rest of the family. Joe ate such an enormous lunch each day that he was still full at night, and even the next morning when he began work. Late in the day, he went to the house where his mother stayed, and he performed basic chores there six days a week. He stayed home on Friday night and would go to the synagogue in the afternoon after they ate *seudah shlishit*, the third meal. Joe's mother continued her knitting of sweaters, but even young Joe could see they were running out of money. 'Still we managed to live.'

***

On Friday, 17 September 1939, the Soviet Union invaded Poland, a military action initiated without any formal declaration of war, from the east with seven field armies, consisting of over 700,000 troops concentrated on two fronts. Within hours, at 4am, Polish command ordered their troops to fall back and only re-engage with the Soviets in self-defence. What remained of Polish resistance retreated, involved in remote, scattered fighting as the out-manned army fell back before the Nazi and Russian onslaughts. Within days, the Red army had overwhelmed the Polish army, capturing over 230,000 prisoners of war.

***

On 22 September 1939, the German Reich Ministry of Public Enlightenment and Propaganda, headquartered in the Ordenspalais located on the northern corner of Wilhelmplatz at Wilhemstrasse in Berlin, released a wire photo from the battlefront in Poland. The photograph captured the joint German-Soviet victory parade in Brest, Belarus, at the border opposite the Polish city of Terespol, where the Bug and Mukhavets rivers converged.

As an array of military vehicles passed, standing on a makeshift platform was German General Heinz Guderian, accompanied by Soviet General Semyon Krivoshein, in a show of united victory over the Poles. Guderian, recognized for his successes in leading Panzer units in the Polish campaigns, and later in France during 1940, claimed he would break the French defences at Sedan while leading his Panzer units with lightning quick shock tactics.

In 1940, when Germany turned on its ally, Soviet General Krivoshein would play a spirited role in reforming the Red Army tank forces against Panzer attacks outside Stalingrad. It would be Krivoshein who would be instrumental in commanding the crushing defeat of Panzer units (whose strategies were developed by Guderian in 1939) in the Battle of Kursk, the largest tank battle of the war.

With the fall of the city of Lublin, General Anders went about hastily moving his army toward Chelm. That night at his headquarters, Anders and his officers reviewed the progress of the war over their meal, discouragement growing around the table as the officers admitted that further conflict would be pointless. While they were talking, the wireless set was turned on. The news being broadcast stunned them. 'Soviet troops had crossed the Polish frontier and were advancing to the west', Anders wrote.

> I had never thought that Soviet Russia would make what seemed [like] an act of war, not only against us, but also against our Allies— Britain and France . . . Russia had violated the Polish-Soviet pact of non-aggression at a most critical moment and had flung herself like a hyena against the defenceless rear of the fighting and bleeding Polish army.[55]

The day after the victory parade in Brest, *Polskie Radio*, the government-owned radio station in Warsaw, continued to broadcast over the airwaves. Since the beginning of the invasion the station, to inspire resistance to the Polish army and civilians, had repetitively played Frederick Chopin's 'Revolutionary Etude'. With the destruction of the main station, famous pianist Wladyslaw Szpilman, described by his fellow citizens as 'a man in whom music lives', would, on 23 September, play a Chopin recital, 'Chopin's Nocturne in C-sharp minor'. It would be the last live music broadcast from Warsaw.[56]

***

After winter had passed, the Russians arrived in Nemirov. A resident described how he was shocked at the behaviour and appearance of the soldiers:

> The invading Russians were an odd lot. Although their tanks and guns pointed at the citizenry inspired awe, the soldiers' appearance did not. Their clothes were shabby and bedraggled: each soldier lacked some part of his uniform. Some were beltless, their guns attached by mere string; some were without shoes and had their feet wrapped in make-shift rags. The cavalry horses that followed the tanks were in even worse shape than their riders. Covered with blankets instead of saddles, the horses were emaciated and looked as if they would drop from exhaustion.[57]

These conquering troops acted as though they had marched into a wonderland with store windows displaying items that scarcely existed in their homeland. They hastily wandered from store to store and greedily bought twenty watches at a time, armloads of shoes, trunks full of dress material, furniture, pins – 'they cleaned out shelves like locusts'.[58] Many of the soldiers walked down the street with long lines of sausage wrapped around their necks and pockets crammed full of food items. Russian women occupiers were treated with preference and didn't have to stand in the queues the local citizens endured. Shopkeepers who weren't friendly and eager to sell were frequently led away and never heard from again.

When the Russians arrived in a town or village, any aspect of order quickly disappeared. The soldiers wrecked stocks and destroyed crops, and within a short time the towns were unrecognizable. The streets were dirty, as though no one cared to clean any longer now that the Russian soldiers were there.

> The city, neat and pretty before the war, now assumed an eerie appearance: dirty streets full of mud, lawns walked over and covered with mud, lawn fences and small trees lining the streets all broken down. Display windows, unkempt and covered with dust and cobwebs, were decorated with portraits of Soviet rulers. Store billboards were mostly ripped off, with empty spaces left where they were once attached.[59]

Immediately the Russians acted against Christians. They searched homes for holy relics and pictures. In public places, crucifixes were removed from walls and replaced with red flags and portraits of Lenin and Stalin. Officials made lists of religious statues, and then methodically ordered them smashed. Anyone found praying was threatened with imprisonment or denial of food rations.

The authorities were particularly eager to root out religion among the young. A child described his experiences: 'They drilled two holes in the ceiling. The commander (Russian) would say into one: "God, give me a dumpling" and nothing would happen. To the other hole he said: "Soviet, give a candy" and candies would fall down. The commander would laugh and say that God gave nothing.'[60]

Within days, Russian officials began registering Jews, an order greatly feared because if one was found not to have registered, that it meant instant retaliation. So, each Jew, along with the entire Polish population, showed up at designated sites to fill out forms, where they had to state their date of birth, name and where they were staying in the town.

Joe held his mother's hand that morning as they stood in the middle of a large room with a smooth, wooden floor. The Jews were lined up in four rows. Windows opened out over a wide pasture, and glancing out, Joe saw the early signs of spring – the colourful bursts of flowers against a cloudless sky, and tree branches heavy with the first growth and blooms.

There was an awkward silence in the room, and only an occasional sniffle or cough disturbed a still, nervous hush. It was understood that words weren't spoken until one reached the head of the line, and then only when the Russian asked a question.

Grandfather stood directly in front of Joe, his shoulders stooped forward. Those people standing around them were much thinner now from lack of food over the last several months, and Joe felt guilty as he could eat such a big lunch because he worked for the butcher. They wore ragged and worn sweaters and coats, and many of the people stared at their tattered shoes rather than look the Russian officials in the face. Joe's mother wore a worn, paper-thin sweater, not one of the thicker sweaters that she had knitted over the winter. Instead of keeping one for herself, she had sold all of them to feed the family.

The Russian officers conducting the procedure sat at four narrow wooden tables, a sheaf of papers stacked in front of each official, and the refugees lined up before them. When Joe's mother reached the table, the officer removed a piece of paper from the top of the stack, picked up a pencil, and asked her to quote her birth date, proper name and where she was staying. When she had answered his questions, the Russian stopped writing and looked up. 'I'm going to ask you three questions: First, are you willing to become a Russian citizen and live in Russia? Number two, would you like to go back to where you came from after the war? And lastly, if not, would you like to go any other place?'

Joe's grandparents stood one row over. When the officer interviewing them asked where they would like to live, Grandfather informed the Russian that they wanted to go back where they came from. Joe's mother gave a different answer: 'I would like to go to America; my husband is there.'

***

Three months after the questionings, the Russian soldiers came swiftly and without warning on a Friday night, beating on the door. '*Otkriote! Otkriote!*' (Open up!). Then the men burst into the room. An officer read an order of deportation in stentorian tones to Joe's grandfather demanding that they had to be ready to leave immediately, possessing only essential articles.

'So, this is what we did', Joe recalled. Out on the street, Joe saw that squads of soldiers had already cornered many of the Jews by this late hour, and just like Joe's family, they were being led down dark streets to the train station. On the loading docks, people milled about, nervously talking, tightly hugging a travel bag or suitcase, the only possession remaining in their lives.

Joe pushed his way through the crowd following his grandfather, leaving the family members waiting against a wall near the entrance gate. They forced their way forward until his grandfather saw a man he recognized, and the two men began to talk rapidly in Polish. Joe stood by them for a while and then, being such a small boy, he easily pushed his way forward again.

Once he had wandered outside and was beyond the loading shed, Joe stepped over the train tracks and sucked in cold air until he felt as though his lungs were bursting. His hands fell to his side, as it became painfully clear, even for an eight-year-old boy, what was ahead for them. It wasn't a normal train waiting to take them away, not like the passenger train his father had taken when he departed Cologne on his trip to America. The train cars – the old people referred to them as wagons – were made of wood slats with wide cracks open between the boards. Large sliding doors were flung open, a window of darkness. Joe had seen these types of train cars before at the livestock yards located near the tracks in Przeworsk, from where cows and horses were sent to market. He and Grandfather had visited the place many times.

Lined up waiting for the Jewish passengers were cattle cars, a long line of cattle wagons, 'coiled away somewhere in the darkness.'[61]

5

The Trains

The massive transportation of humans across thousands of miles by the German government was conducted without regard to the safety or well-being of the passengers. Beginning in October 1938, 600,000 Jews, labelled as *undesirables*, were deported eastward. Later in September 1939, efficient, full-scale moving operations were in place transporting Jews to concentration camps. It was the German railway system, the Reichsbahn, with its 500,000 clerical and 900,000 manual workers, an example of the methodical perfection of German society, who accomplished this feat for the Nazis with alarming precision.[62]

'Without the railways, the Holocaust would not have been possible', Paul Johnson writes in *A History of the Jews*. 'With their deportation trains called *Sonderzuge*, and their special staff, the *Sonderzuggruppe*, which coordinated the deportation schedules with the rest of the war timetables, the railways made prodigious efforts to get the Jews exactly where the SS wanted them.'[63] Whenever those who suffered through the deportations and the death camps re-experience those dreadful nightmares, they consistently referred to the trains that brought them to the killing camps. Treblinka was an extermination camp built northeast of Warsaw where over 900,000 Jews were murdered, second only to Auschwitz. An inmate remembers:

> The trains left Malkinia station for Treblinka station. It was about six miles. Treblinka was a village. A small village. As a station, it gained in importance because of the transport of Jews. [Every day] Thirty to fifty cars would arrive. They were divided into sections of ten or twelve or fifteen cars and shunted into Treblinka Camp and brought to the ramp. The other cars waited, loaded with people, in the Treblinka Station.[64]

But the Reichsbahn, with its ability to provide Hitler with the tools he needed, also betrayed the claimed innocence of the German people, that being that they had little or no knowledge involving the killing of the Jews. In fact, the German citizens were aware of 'the significance of the huge, crowded trains rattling through the hours of darkness', as one recorded

6. Refugees board a deportation train for labour camps in Siberia. United States Holocaust Memorial Museum, courtesy of National Archives and Records Administration, College Park.

remark suggests. 'Those damned Jews; they won't even let one sleep at night.'[65]

Russian expulsion of Jews and Polish citizens from Poland to Siberia began on the night of 9 February 1940, and was organized into four time periods. A primitive, yet effective tool was selected to accomplish this ambitious goal – that of crude, filthy and unheated railroad cattle wagons. The first action was in February 1940 when over 200,000 departed in 110 trains. In April the largest number at one time, 320,000 travelled in over 160 trains. Thirteen months later, in June and July 1940, 240,000 were forced out. The final deportation action removed over 200,000 in the early summer of 1941.

In the end, over 1,500,000 Poles were deported from their land. Some estimates place the number at closer to 2 million, including not only the targeted military officers and landowners, but farmers, priests, bankers and victims from all walks of life.

Of those exiled, 380,000 were children.

The horror and suffering awaiting them would prove to be unimaginable.

***

Joe and his family huddled against the station wall as the Russian soldiers, bayonets drawn, shouted out harsh orders, forcing the crowd towards the railroad cars. By now it was late into the night, the surreal scene encircling Joe beneath a veiled curtain of light rain and obscure mist. Caught in the swaying beams of arched, glowing searchlights mounted on the roof of large trucks, the mass of people huddled, slowly pushing forward, appearing ghostly, faces drawn, eyes blinking against the lamps' invading glare. Cries and prayers murmured out through the crowd. The bitter smell of coal smothered the air as the locomotive engine discharged murky smoke and rushing clouds of white steam.

The Russian soldiers forced Joe's family away from the wall and onto the loading dock until they stared at the empty, dark doors. White Cyrillic letters – *CCCP* with the Russian hammer and sickle – were stencilled to the side of the wagon. Joe was caught up in the mob of people as children reached out for their mother's hand, so they wouldn't get separated.

As they neared the car, one young refugee about the same age as Joe glanced at a young soldier standing by the sliding door, a grey shirt over riding breeches, and the Red Army badge sewed onto the front of his cap. His breeches were caked with mud and wet snow, and it all struck the young boy as strange that the soldier's black belt and boots were neatly polished, while the rest of his uniform was so filthy. The soldier held a rifle across his chest. The refugee stared at him. Why, he looked to be about the same age as his older sister, he thought, as the soldier stared out over the crowd with long, sweeping glares and then glanced down into his face. For the briefest of moments, there was a smile between them, and then as if to catch himself, the young soldier's face hardened and he stared again out over the crowd.

At the darkened train doors, soldiers hoisted refugees up into the cars. There were so many people crammed into each car, up to sixty, one could only stand. Then the large, wooden doors abruptly slammed closed, and Joe heard a heavy metal click outside the door, as the locks bolted. After a long moment, the refugees awkwardly staggered, yelling out as the train jerked forward.

Zoe Zajdlerowa was on these trains. An Irishwoman, the daughter of a Protestant minister, had married Aleksander Zajdler, a Pole, and was herself caught up in the chaos of eastern Poland when the deportations began. She escaped to England in 1940, and never saw her husband again.

> The trains were very long, and seemed so extraordinarily high. The last was because they seldom stood along platforms, and the whole train was accordingly seen from the level of the ground...the trains, after being loaded, often stood for days before leaving, and the tracks

along which they stood would become piled with excrement and yellow and boggy from the urine running down off the floors.[66]

That first night as the trains loaded with Jews passed through unsuspecting villages and towns, cries of horror drew people out of their houses. In the distance, 'a parish priest stood on a knoll by the church holding out a great cross towards those where were taken past...'[67]

They travelled for hours. By now, many were hungry and suffering from thirst. Children, frantic for water, licked the frost from nails on the car walls.

Joe was stunned at what he witnessed around him. There were sparse piles of hay and nothing else to lie on, and a hole in the floor served as a toilet. Two small windows, 'tiny grated rectangles, the only windows and the only spaces by which air or light could enter', high up on the wall, and secured with iron bars, were also the only views outside the car. Every hour or so, one of the younger men would stand on another man's shoulders, attempting to stare out.

'What do you see?' someone asked.

The young man jumped down with a thud on the wood floor, each time telling the people, 'Snow and trees –nothing but snow and trees.'[68]

***

The train travelled non-stop for two days. Then one afternoon, beneath a drenching rain, the train halted, and the locomotive was unhooked from the cars and disappeared. The refugees soon learned to look forward to when the trains stopped because the Russians gave them bread and soggy soup. It was horrible food, but Joe ate it.

The nights were bitterly cold, and everyone stayed huddled in the car, attempting to keep warm. 'More than once, as a train moved...a few voices first, and then a choir, and then thousands of aching, parched throats, bursting with sorrow, would raise the notes of some pealing Polish song of faith and praise...they are the songs of the Old Republic, the songs of the Polish golden age, the song of the Partitions.'[69] During the day, the mothers let their children out into the open fields to play. Exposure and lack of food and water made people sick, and at night as Joe tried to sleep, the constant rack of coughing kept him awake.

The older people talked of things they had heard. One day a woman came back to the car, and she told everyone who listened about what had happened in a car several spaces back. At one of the many stops, a young couple had been loaded into the car. The woman was pregnant, close to giving birth, as the husband nervously paced around a pot-belly stove in the centre of the car. Finally, a grandmother announced she knew how to birth the baby. This made the young couple worried, until they heard the woman had nine children of her own. Vala Lewicki was a twelve-year-old on that train, and a witness:

> Silence fell among the passengers. Waiting for new life to begin was a most peculiar sensation. There was a holy quality about it, as if one were in the church. The silence was broken, occasionally, by the lady [the grandmother] herself. And then – we heard the baby's first cry… a gasp of amazement came from the passengers. As the new parents' faces displayed a mixture of gratitude and exhilaration for grandmother's courage and skill, a broad grin of pure pleasure crossed her face.[70]

The story offered hope, at least a passing glimmer, to the other passengers on the train.

***

Late one afternoon, the locomotive returned and reconnected to the cars. By now the train stretched out so far that Joe couldn't see the end of it even on a clear day, and he thought maybe the Russians were gathering up every Jew in the world. Joe didn't totally understand, but he was old enough to question why this was happening to them. *Why were they being sent so far away from home? What could they have done so wrong for these soldiers to treat them like this?* In the middle of the cold nights when he couldn't sleep, Joe would lay awake and wonder, *would he ever see his sister, Inez, or his father again?*

Suddenly there was an abrupt surge, awakening Joe from his thoughts, and the train moved eastward again. For hours and hours, there was only the endless clacking of the wheels, the constant blast of the whistle piercing the air, as the trains continued another long journey.

The older people and the weak died first.

Thirst and lack of food haunted the deportees, and the car was so crammed that it was impossible to find comfort, as they sat and slept with their limbs interwoven with each other. The sick among them smelled of an agonizing odour, a constant nuisance to the others. But the worst was the bathroom, because they had to go in front of everyone into a hole in the floor of the wagon. In the beginning, the people were extremely embarrassed with this arrangement, especially the women. As the days wore on, another horrible condition developed – because they couldn't wash, lice soon became a torture.

Soon, all the refugees suffered from foul air, hunger, thirst and filth. The dead lay among the living for days until the train finally came to a halt and their bodies were thrown out, the families praying that perhaps the local people would bury them. Broken-hearted mothers were forced to throw their dead babies through the window bars while the train moved.

Occasionally – and often at odd hours of the night – the train stopped frequently to hook on another series of cars. The glow of lamp lights flashed through the wall cracks. Loud voices and heavy footsteps outside would wake Joe from a fitful sleep.

Joe's mother no longer let him out of the car to play in the snow-blanketed fields because it was too dangerous, and she feared that Joe would be left behind. Suddenly the locomotive would appear, and after additional cars were attached, the train would leave without warning. It was also impossible for the men to go out and forage because one couldn't venture far from the train without papers, and credentials had been taken away at the train station. But still, even with the risk, some people went off and sold maybe a ring or a watch for what little food they could buy.

In the middle of the night, the Russians would abruptly slide open the large doors on the side of the cars, or wagons as they were referred to by the soldiers. 'They would give the people *kipyatokh*, hot water…not tea, just hot water, and *khlep*, bread.' Unlike the experience in other trains moving toward Siberia, Joe remembered being fortunate in many ways: 'Everybody got maybe a quarter of bread, so there was food. We didn't starve there to death. There was no starving. There was food, but not good food. There was bread and water. That's it. No vegetables, no fruits, no nothing.'[71]

The Irishwoman, Zoe Zajdlerowa, writes of the ghastly conditions on the train:

> Bread (sour and black and badly baked) was handed out on most trains at intervals of two or three days … occasionally a few buckets of fish soup with fish heads and bones were distributed, but this was very rare…the water situation was absolutely drastic…in the late spring and summer when passing through the scorching lands of the Ukraine and the central deserts, a pitch of suffering was reached which can never be estimated or described…tongues turned black and stiff and protruded from ghastly mouths and throats…

This punishing life for Joe and his family went on for months, the constant stopping and starting across a vast, strange land as the trains continually deposited train cars, and then returned with others.

Sim Kessel, a Jewish member of the French Resistance, survived for over three years in camps, most of the time at Auschwitz. He survived starvation and torture and remembers when it began:

> The temperature started to rise, as the freight car was enclosed and body heat had no outlet...The only place to urinate was through a slot in the skylight, though whoever tried this usually missed, spilling urine on the floor...When dawn finally rose...we were all quite ill and shattered, crushed not only by the weight of fatigue but by the stifling, moist atmosphere and the foul odour of excrement...There was no latrine, no provision...On top of everything else, a lot of people had vomited on the floor. We were to live for days on end breathing these foul smells, and soon we lived in the foulness itself.[72]

Mercifully, one morning the train halted. Joe climbed up to the narrow window high up on the front wall and stared out beyond the train. Then he understood why the train had stopped and not continued. The tracks ended at a wall of tall trees. Unknown to the deportees, the trains had brought them 2,750 kilometres from Poland, arriving at Archangelsk, at one time in the seventeenth century Russia's only seaport located on the Northern Dvina River near the White Sea.

Considering the long distance and the isolation of their destination, the exhausted refugees feared that they had disappeared from the face of the earth. These worries were partly true in that the world was now feverishly consumed in war. The swiftness and brutality of the Nazi attack eastward had shocked world leaders. The Italians had marched mostly unopposed into Ethiopia, and Great Britain was bracing for an impending German invasion. The 19 May 1940 issue of the *San Francisco Chronicle* headlined 'Nazis Take Paris!'[73]

The British and Polish governments were informed of the mass deportations through reports from the Polish underground, though those sketchy accounts didn't detail the number of refugees sent into Siberia, or the horrible conditions in which they suffered. In the end, both governments felt powerless to respond against such aggressions being played out thousands of miles from the war front.

However, there were two Zionist officials in Palestine who would eventually learn, in August 1942, of the deportees' journey.

David Ben-Gurion was an impassioned Zionist, born in Poland, who immigrated to Palestine shortly after the turn of the century. In 1948, three years after the war ended, he became the first Prime Minister of the newly formed nation of Israel. However, during the war, he played one of his most important roles as leader of the Jewish Agency, the organization responsible for the immigration, the *Aliyah*, of Jews to Eretz Israel. Once he was aware of the Tehran Children, he began negotiations with the Polish government-in-exile to get the children to Palestine.

Henrietta Szold, the daughter of a rabbi who was raised in Baltimore, Maryland, before immigrating to Palestine in the 1920s, was the director of *Youth Aliyah*, a department within the Jewish Agency responsible for the rescue of children out of Hitler's Europe. In the summer of 1942, two long years after Joe reached the Siberian slave labour camps, news leaked out of large numbers of starving Jewish children, among thousands of refugees and recently released Polish soldiers, flooding southward toward the Caspian Sea.

Ben-Gurion and Szold both reacted swiftly.

As the deportees disembarked from the gloomy trains and into a mist-veiled landscape, Joe shielded his eyes from the sunshine. He was glad the train journey was over. He also felt an aching loneliness as he stared at the massive forest of tall, ice-laden trees. Twenty metres away, snow-caked trucks lined up and down along a mud-covered road, the idling of the engines the only sound in the hushed woods, white-smoke exhaust fumes swirling at the rear of the trucks. Grandfather's face darkened as Joe reached up and grasped his rough hand. It was as though the old man's face revealed, at last, a great secret.

How could anyone of our family possibly know where we are? Grandfather whispered, his voice rattling like burned leaves.

6

'A Windowless Cell...'

In the years following the Second World War there was the general belief that the Polish army would be easily defeated by the overwhelming German forces. This assumption was based on the success of the German Blitzkrieg, and the fact that the Germans possessed, along with these new tactics, superior equipment. The outnumbered Poles – over a million and a half German soldiers poured into Poland that September morning in 1939, confronted by only 950,000 Polish soldiers – also faced a vast array of modern tanks and artillery. The German invasion was also assisted by the *Volksdeuthsche*, ethnic Germans living in Poland, armed and trained before the September offensive, ready to fight for the Nazis.

Despite these factors, during the first week of the war, the Poles slowed the German advance, expecting that Allied forces would cross the border and come to their aid.

That support never came.

Left with limited strategy options, Polish commanders then ordered a calculated retreat to the Vistula River. Once the front was stabilized along the Vistula, the generals ordered several successful counter-offences against the Germans toward Romania in the south, resulting in several German divisions being forced to retreat before they were eventually reinforced. The blow that broke the Polish struggle was the Russian invasion on 17 September 1939. Despite now fighting a two-front war, Polish resistance continued until 6 October, when over 100,000 troops escaped to friendly countries to continue the fight later against Germany.

The invasion on Polish soil proved to be costly in both blood and materials for the German army. In 36 days of fighting, the *Wehrmacht* suffered over 50,000 killed and had 1,000 armoured vehicles destroyed. For the Polish army, the eventual surrender would produce devastating results: 66,000 killed, 133,700 wounded and 964,000 captured. Because of the German command determining that the invasion be fought as a 'total war', civilian casualties were much higher, estimated to be over 200,000. In fact, a strategy of the German military was for the Luftwaffe to attack columns of refugees fleeing away from the fighting, to create chaos and block important roads so the Polish military couldn't move soldiers from sector to sector.

During Operation Tannenberg, the codename for German extermination plans directed at Polish nationals, teachers, scholars and former army officers, over 20,000 Polish civilians were shot at mass execution sites.

A month later, in October 1939, the Polish government, exiled and headquartered in England formed a new army in France numbering 75,000 men. After France surrendered in May 1940, 13,000 remaining Polish troops evacuated to Great Britain. During the final week of September 1939, the Polish troops, who fought on with such ferocity and bravery, finally reached the limit of their endurance.

General Anders was totally alone now, cut off from receiving orders from his superiors. After a brief battle around Mlava in north-central Poland, with communications between Polish units severed, Anders ordered his troops southward toward Romania and Hungary. Over the next week, Anders's command achieved several successes on the battlefield following the Jaworow-Krakowiec highway, recapturing the village of Broszki during a surprise attack on the Germans. At Dernaki, however, Anders came upon a superior Bolshevik army of Soviet troops and Soviet tanks blocking their retreat toward Hungary, and ordered his army into a defensive position. Two weeks later, on the morning of 30 September, after a night of violent fighting in the forest outside the village of Zastowka, General Anders ordered what remained of his command to split up. Twice wounded, Anders made his way to the village where he was captured by the Soviets. The event was described in an article, 'The Historic Advance', by Commissar S. Kozhevnikov, published in the magazine *Red Star* a year later on 17 September 1940:

> From the 27th to the 28th September, units of cavalry, in co-operation with an armoured division, surrounded and liquidated General Anders' group to the north of the town of Rajgrodek. This group, whose strength was 3,000 men and 12 guns, tried to escape to Hungary. The outcome of the battle was 1,000 men taken prisoners and big war booty, including 11 guns. Only a small group of Poles succeeded in escaping to the neighbourhood of Przemysl, where they were captured by our troops. On this occasion the following prisoners were taken: Generals Anders and Plisowski, 3 Colonels and 50 other officers.[74]

***

Anders spent the next months suffering through relocation in and out of numerous 'camps' and hospitals.[75] During one of these internments, he was visited by a Polish colonel who mentioned an event that caused Anders great concern: 'How the Russians had broken their agreement and treacherously arrested some thousands of officers after their entry into Lwow, and taken them away to the east.'[76] Despite numerous confrontations with Russian officials demanding answers, and a series of investigations later conducted by Anders' staff, the destiny of these Polish officers remained a mystery, and continued to haunt the Polish general for over three years.

On 29 February 1940, eleven months later, Anders was crammed inside a *stolypinka*, a prison truck without windows. Anders travelled for several days on the truck, and each day he was given a pound of bread, a slice of herring and warm water meant to be tea. He considered himself fortunate; at least it was warmer in the truck than it was in the prison he had just left.

Then one morning, the truck abruptly pulled in front of a large building. Bleary-eyed, Anders was led out of the truck and through a narrow gate. Once his eyes grew accustomed to the sunlight, he found himself standing in the eerie silence of a wide, barren courtyard. Across the way he stared at a familiar scene that brought dread in his heart, a clock centred at the top height of a towering, ornate façade. He knew exactly where he had been taken – Lubianka, the dreaded Soviet prison from where few prisoners ever left. Located in the Meshchansky District of Moscow and originally built in 1898 as the headquarters of All-Russia Insurance Company, the building was taken over as the headquarters of Cheka, the secret police, following the Bolshevik Revolution in 1917.

Ushered into a building and searched along with his belongings, including a bag taken from him, Anders was then given a rug, a piece of soap, a toothbrush and a mug. As the soldiers again searched him, they found a small medal of the Blessed Virgin. In a fit of fury that Anders considered 'a naked spirit of evil',[77] they threw the relic on the ground and stomped on it. 'Let us see if this harlot can be of any help to you in a Soviet prison.' Shortly after that incident, Anders was taken to a narrow, cold room, allowed to shower and handed a glass of tea along with two lumps of sugar. Many times, during his wearisome stay in Lubianka, Anders would think back to that episode. Instead of creating despair or anger, his memories during these dark days turned towards peace and consolation as he remembered how the medal had protected him so many times before.

Anders learned over the next weeks that to give the prison some sort of order, the Soviet guards created strictly observed regulations. No one was to speak except in a whisper. 'Going to the lavatory, serving meals', Anders reflected, 'all had their own times and proceeded like clockwork.'[78] Through a small 'Judas' window in the door, the guards watched as prisoners regularly cleaned the cell floors. Anders was surprised that the prisoners were given haircuts every two weeks, books to read, regular baths and clean shirts and pants. Despite being a thin, tall man, his appearance over the months had turned him into an even more of a gaunt, shallow figure. However, his daily meal of watery soup and two spoons of pearl barley, after months of starving, 'seemed like a royal banquet'.[79]

Within several days, the interrogations began. Led along beautiful parquet floors and pale green walls, Anders found that the Soviets considered these questionings a science. Tea and cigarettes would greet him on some days, when he would be questioned with patience and kindness. And then, on other days, he would be struck in the face and cursed at, with his chair knocked out from under him. On those days when the Soviet officials questioned him without the violence, Anders was struck by their honesty and candour. 'Don't think that we are genuine friends of Germany – we hate the English more', a Soviet officer confided to him. 'But, as soon as the Germans are weakened after the defeat of France and Great Britain, we will push forward and occupy the whole of Europe.'[80]

Astonished at such an admission by the Russians, Anders was even more surprised once his captors openly showed him the dossier they possessed containing his background information. His military life had apparently been fully researched, which was expected. Soviet intelligence also possessed even the smallest details of his personal life, and to Anders' shock, they presented photographs that he wasn't even aware existed – photographs of Anders on horseback at the Olympic Games in Amsterdam and the international horse show in Nice. Noting his astonishment, the Soviets offered that, 'We have such a file for every military and political personage in the whole world. The Soviet Union has long arms.'[81]

Once it was evident that his captors were satisfied with the results of their interrogations, Anders became mostly confined to his small room that he shared with three other men, prisoners who had recently arrived and brought distressing news. France had collapsed, and the Germans had occupied Denmark, Norway, Holland and Belgium. When Anders learned that Paris had fallen, and Great Britain was expected to surrender next, he grew disheartened. Poland's brave and sacrificial resistance during those first weeks of September had provided the Allies valuable time...hadn't they been able to prepare? Despite all the bad news about the war, one thought strengthened Anders's resolve – America certainly wouldn't let England fall to Germany.

As the months grew into his second year of imprisonment, fellow prisoners brought more disturbing news concerning Poles and Soviet political prisoners deported to slave labour camps around Kolyma.

A remote region of the Russian Far East, bordered by the East Siberian Sea and the Arctic Ocean and to the south the Sea of Okhotsk, Kolyma was infamous as the notorious system of Gulag labour camps. Stalin had ordered the construction of this series of gold mining, lumbering, and construction sites between 1932 and 1954, where thousands of prisoners, both political and deportees, were sent to starve and freeze to death as they worked in horrific conditions.

Five decades later, in June 1996, with financial help from the Russian government, the 'Mask of Sorrow', a memorial honouring the prisoners who died in the camps, was erected on a hill above Magadan, Russia, the largest city in the Kolyma region. Standing fifteen metres high, the concrete statue portrays a face with tears flowing out of the left eye, and bears the names on stone markers of many of the labour camp victims. Ernst Neizvestny, the famous Russian-America sculptor, designed the monument. During the 1930s his parents had perished in those camps.

Kolyma was that place the Soviet guards spoke of as the place from which prisoners never returned. All were expected to work, sick or not, and if they refused or were too weak, they were often shot on the spot. During each winter, one in four prisoners died in the camps, and certainly it wasn't expected that any prisoner would survive two winters.

The Soviets running the camps had their own language to describe these prisoners starving and dying. *Fitili* or wicks were terms used by the guards to describe them, as though describing a candle wick, soon to blow out. The Russian verb *dokhodyagi*, meaning to 'reach the end', described the prisoners' bizarre looks and actions they developed in the last stages of starving and suffering from diseases, with eyes locked with a distant stare and often flying into rages, unable to control their bowels or bladders.

Gustav Herling-Grudzinski, a Polish writer, political dissident and underground fighter, chillingly wrote in *A World Apart* of his personal account of life in the Soviet prisons, recalling '…the sight of the night-blind, walking slowly through the zone in the early morning, their hands fluttering in front of them…'[82]

During those long prison days, Anders would sit in the cell and listen as newly arriving inmates told stories about these brutal camps. One day, a prisoner told them about a mine in Komsomoles where there were over 5,000 prisoners of which 436 were Polish. Reportedly, seven to eleven men died each day from either starvation or exhaustion, from beatings from the guards or from thermic shock because temperatures would fall to -70 degrees Fahrenheit. Another camp was Tchukotka, where a boat carrying over 3,000 Polish prisoners, mostly military and police individuals, arrived in August 1940. The Poles were assigned work detail in the lead mines and forced into the worst areas. About 40 died each day from lead poisoning, and the witnesses admitted that by the time they left, over 90 per cent of the Poles had died.

One witness admitted seeing,

> ...A camp at Magadan. It was occupied exclusively by cripples without hands and feet. All were crippled by frostbite in the mines. Even these [the cripples] were not fed for nothing, but had to sew sacks and make baskets. Even those who had lost both hands had to work, pushing large timber blocks with their feet. Others who had no feet worked at chopping wood.[83]

Later, in 1942, as the newly-freed Polish army-in-exile moved southward, Anders gathered reports to establish the number of people involved in the several hundred gold mines around Kolyma. These reports, written from testimonies of Soviet prisoners, assessed that between three to five million people were sent to Kolyma between 1935 and 1940. Further estimates concluded that in 1942, 357,000 prisoners remained working at Kolyma. From these reports, Anders' staff surmised that at least two million people had been either murdered or worked to death in the mines.

Then one day, Anders was told a perplexing report that raised his interest, an account from a man who had survived Kolyma. The story he spoke concerned missing Polish officers whose mysterious fate troubled Anders:

> I worked in the autumn of 1940 on the construction of the Tiangin Road...sixty-four kilometres from the main track, and there I met a Soviet scientific expedition looking for gold and other ore-bearing veins. I spent the night in the same hut as the expedition and learned from them that on the construction of the Yakutsk-Kolyma line, a great number of Polish officers and generals were employed as workers, that they were kept under very strict supervision, and that the escort made it impossible to approach the prisoners.[84]

Were these Polish officers the men who Anders was anxiously concerned about? Was it possible that they were confined to work on the Soviet railways? But instead of satisfying Anders curiosity, the tale heightened his uneasiness. *If these officers were, in fact, out there on the Tiangin Road, why were the Soviets so secretive about their location?*

With the distressing possibility that his officers could be dying as slave labourers, Anders withdrew from his fellow prisoners throughout the remainder of his confinement in Lubianka, staying mostly by himself with his worried thoughts. In those following days, his world became, simply, a 'windowless cell, rather brightly lit...with a bedstead of straw paillasse and a tiny table screwed to the floor...'[85] as any hope of freedom dimmed beneath a heaviness of despair and darkness.

PART TWO

Spring 1940 – August 1942

7

Nightmare

Altajski Kraj, Siberia

Later that morning, the truck convoy pulled away, leaving behind the long line of cattle cars that had brought Joe to this unknown destination. They had driven the deportees through a huge, thick forest. Joe had never seen anything like the mass of tall trees. It seemed as if he had been travelling on another planet.

They rode in the trucks for hours with little food or water, and even though it was now spring, towards evening there was a sharp chill in the air. At times along the way, the narrow road would abruptly end, and seemingly out of nowhere men would step out of the woods, and begin chopping down trees that were blocking the way. Then, the trucks would be on their way again.

At sunset on the third day, the trucks halted in a clearing. 'We arrived in the woods, in a big, giant forest, like the Amazons. It was huge! And there was no end to it.'[86] A hundred yards away, beneath a thick canopy of trees, Joe saw four big camp buildings constructed with logs, surrounded by a scattering of smaller wood-framed structures. The Soviet trucks had delivered them to a camp three hundred kilometres from Barnaul, a city located along the Ob River at the southern point of the Siberian steppe just north of the Altai Mountains. These deportees sent to Siberia, and not into northern or central Asia, were fortunate in that there was at least accommodation waiting for them – labour camps built in the 1930s to quarter the first inhabitants, *kulaks*, undesirables, mostly wealthy citizens purged by Stalin.

Men stood alongside the trucks staring at the cargo of starving, weary deportees as the Jews were unloaded from the trucks and were directed down narrow paths towards the structures. Joe and his family were led to one of the long, narrow log cabins referred to as barracks. The interior was divided into 20 or 30 rooms and, upon their arrival, they had to sleep on the floor. Over time, each person would find materials and build his own primitive plank bed. The first night, the woman and children woke up in a panic as mice bigger than cats ran across their blankets. Even when the mice were frightened away, the refugees had to contend with bedbugs, gnats and fleas. Another deportee recorded that, 'there were such bedbugs in the barracks and so many of them that at night if you struck a match [lighting up the room], your body was black and the wall [was] gray with bedbugs.'[87]

Several months later, as winter approached, to keep away the brutal cold, *mech* – a green moss like weed that grew in the swamps – was stuffed between the logs. Each living space inside the cabin was elongated, about ten feet by fifteen feet, with several double windows on two opposing walls. An iron stove for cooking, built into a dividing wall between the two living areas, also provided a little warmth. At least, Joe thought, it would prevent them from freezing to death. Several days into their stay, the deportees discovered that there was another strange aspect to this peculiar and different land. Darkness fell at about three o'clock in the afternoon, and sunrise didn't come until after ten o'clock in the morning.

After a time getting settled into their new homes, the deportees ventured out into the camp, mingled with the people already living there, and were told that no one had lived in the place before 1936. These people, Russians, were all labelled anti-Communists, so they were considered criminals. Joe thought it strange that there were no guards or soldiers, until several of the older boys told him there didn't have to be guards because there was no place to go. If one escaped into the huge forest and attempted to walk the 300 kilometres to Barnaul, he would get lost and freeze to death or be eaten by the bears or wolves that roamed the thickets.

Those who already lived there, designated as political enemies, possibly five or eight families with children, supervised the camp – the bakery, the wash house – all aspects of basic daily living. Basically, Joe's family worked for them.

The camp had an overwhelming feeling of confinement and sorrow:

> All around the horizon stretched the dark wall of the forests. The paths through the camp zone were made of two planks laid side by side; they were swept every day…cleared away the snow with large wooden shovels…outside the kitchen stood a queue of ragged shadows, in fur caps with flaps over their ears, their feet and legs wrapped in rags and tied about with string.[88]

The deportees were given one day of rest before they were instructed in the work of harvesting *jivyitzeh*, a thick juice from the trees in the surrounding forest. Joe didn't know if it was sugar or rubber, but he quickly learned a simple rule of the camp: 'If you worked you got 60 grams of bread, or maybe 90 grams. If you didn't work, you got 30', Joe recounts. 'My mother and I, and my little sister got 30 grams per day. I had to go out and find some mushrooms and some other food in the forest.'[89]

To gather the *jivyitzeh*, a worker would take a knife and slice a vertical cut on the tree trunk and then carve two slanted cuts to the side. The procedure would then be repeated three or four times around the tree, each time placing two pieces of wood along the cuts that funneled the *jivyitzeh* into a cup. An adult who was a strong worker could perform these tasks on as many as ten trees at a time. Then the next day, they would move either up or down using ladders on the same trees, creating the same incisions only at different heights. The final step in harvesting the juice was to take the cups and empty them into a bucket.

A Russian overseer would then weigh how much *jivyitzeh* the worker brought in, and that determined the amount of food he received. The expected amount harvested daily was fifteen pounds. If a worker brought in less, maybe ten pounds, then he received less food. If a worker brought in more, maybe twenty pounds, he was considered a *stachanovitz*, a good worker who received more bread.

The smaller children, Joe and Nelly included, were too young to work. Joe's mother didn't work either, so each day they received only 20 or maybe 30 grams of bread for the three of them. That wasn't much to survive on, only about four per cent of a pound, about one small loaf of bread. Most of the family members living in the barrack room with Joe and Nelly worked, including 'cousin Shlomo, who was 17, and could earn 60 grams of bread. And cousin Paola, she was tall and strong, and she could work every day to earn food for the family.'[90]

It soon became clear to Joe that the distribution of food was the most significant happening each day. He noticed that first the old and then the youngest dwindled away from lack of nourishment. Because of the rigid rules on receiving food, many children begged for food because their mothers and fathers were starving to death, and there didn't seem to be much they could do to stop it. Starvation was the first misfortune the deportees dealt with upon arrival in the cruel camps. Working in such conditions and limited caloric energy intake with such poor foods to eat, created a severe deficiency and led to widespread malnutrition. A person's body fat and condition of general health, which was considered poor by the time the deportees arrived in the Siberian camps, determined how long they could survive without proper nutrition. The average adult facing starvation could live only eight to twelve weeks. The first signs were diarrhoea, skin rashes and oedema, and the victims often appeared irritable and lethargic. One young deportee admitted that he went from cottage to cottage and sang, shaming myself a lot but it couldn't be helped. One had to go because mama and brother were dying of hunger. The urgency to obtain food even forced the children to steal if they didn't want to perish.

Then another harsh enemy arrived at the camps.

The Siberian weather came as a brutal cold force in October and would stay until late May. Because of the geographical location, the deportees would experience long winters with brutally cold temperatures of four degrees Fahrenheit in January. Unfortunately for them, the next two years proved to have even more extreme Siberian winters, frequently producing temperatures plunging to -49 degrees Fahrenheit.

Snow fell in early fall. When the winds stirred, Joe experienced a cold bone-rattling chill that clung to the skin on his face, tearing at his hands and feet. Snow storms, *bourans*, would later blast across the landscape, making going outside a futile, suicidal act. By May, the snow would melt away, and, briefly, there was spring. Then summer arrived. The once brutally chilly winds turned into a hot furnace of stirring dust, delivering sweltering heat from which there was no escape. By July, the nights were airless and intolerable; the deportees were covered in a film of sweat as they tried to sleep.[91]

The weather was one thing to endure, but the most dreadful situation was the starvation, the constant pain of hunger after they had been in the camps for several months. A letter dated 8 March 1942, written by a Pole stranded in Siberia stated: 'Bread is running out and stealing has started.'[92]

Joe was soon hungry every day, the pains knotted his stomach as he began losing weight. He witnessed bodies being carried out of barracks every day. The old were the first to die in their sleep from starvation. Witnessing the mud and filth that each of them were forced to live in, Joe no longer questioned anything because there was no reason to wonder anymore. As the suffering began, it was no longer important to ask why they were forced to come here and suffer, ashamed of the life they now were forced to live, as if they themselves were the criminals and not the Russians.

As winter dragged on and the weather worsened, snowfall was deep and unending, and as the temperature dropped to a certain level, no worker had to go to work because the cold was too dangerous. Joe remembers that if you went outside with the temperature at -50 degrees, within two minutes an ear, or a nose, or a finger would freeze off.

An older child remembered the brutality of their existence.

> We went through a fierce winter in this white hell they called the Re-education Camp. The snow piled up in the forest. On days when it was impossible to leave the camp we huddled shivering in the hut, binding our legs, which were prone to freezing, with every scrap of

cloth we could lay our hands on. Frost collected on the windowpanes, creating strange shapes. Looking at them, I remembered how I loved to look at these scenes as a child, sitting in a heated house, content with my lot, observing enchanted worlds in the making. I found it hard to detect the magic now. The scenes on the hut's windowpanes looked nightmarish to me.[93]

There were no winter clothes among the Jews to fight off the extreme cold during the long, dark days, only a thick sweater if one could afford it. People either sold whatever valuables they possessed, or they froze to death. The Russians in the camp were only too willing to buy articles if the Jews wanted to sell them because they established the price to pay. Several months after their arrival, Joe's mother sold several possessions for bread, and for several weeks they had plenty of food.

Joe had also, by now, dismissed any thoughts about his older sister, Inez, whom he loved so much. And his father? America was a land too far away from this thick, vast forest to imagine it any longer. Joe's thoughts simply turned to those of finding a way to guide his daily life through all the hunger, sickness and total despair he witnessed.

Perhaps, Joe's thoughts, his dreams, his hopes changed when he realized that, as a young boy, he no longer determined the life he was to lead. He hadn't chosen his fate, the Germans had. And for that, Joe allowed one powerful emotion to build somewhere inside – hatred for the Germans for bringing him there. Hatred for having to witness all the dying. He hated the Germans most of all for making his mother sell her ring.

All because they were Jews.

That act of sacrifice, of having to sell something so precious to her, stirred something inside Joe's heart. Soon he would be big enough, he thought. He would, after all, be nine years old soon and he swore to himself he would help to bring bread to their barracks. He never wanted to see that look on his mother's face, again.

***

The Poles and Jews being deported out of Poland faced two types of camps. By late 1939 and into 1940, Jews found themselves on trains delivering them to concentration camps. The ones located in Germany were mainly designed for slave labour. The camps in Poland were built for one purpose – to murder Jews and enemies of the state.

The Soviet camps were very different. In the initial deportation out of Germany and Poland, the situation in which Joe found himself, the deportees ended up in remote, barren Soviet camps where dying was a slower process. Hunger and disease were the enemies because there were no SS guards to brutalize the Jews, to randomly murder them. There were no crematoria to burn away the victims' bodies. In Siberia, because the land was so vast and isolated, there weren't even barbed-wire fences. For these prisoners, the enemy was the loneliness as described by a captive:

> We found only unending forests and marshlands – areas upon which no human foot had ever trod before. For us nothing was prepared in advance. We were brought into the woods and told to build barracks and enclosures, to find water, to cut roads…that was how the northern camps came into being. For months on end we slept in holes dug in the ground. We subsisted on a diet of dry rusks made of black bread and, in the summertime, on wild berries. We were unarmed in the struggle against harsh nature. The biting cold, the strength-sapping labour, disease – these left alive only a few of the original prisoners here. Even among our guards the death rate was catastrophic…I can recall numerous cases of the 'white death' – when a prisoner simply remained alone in the snow, not being able to muster the strength to get up.[94]

***

The thousands of Polish refugees flooding into Siberia arrived at different camps in this region of northern Asia. Not all the *posioloks*, settlements or penal colonies, were like Joe's camp, located deep in the dense forest. There were *posioloks* located in Vologda *oblast*, an administrative division in Russia in Novosibirsk in the Seroi region, and in Krasnouralsk in the Sverdlovsk *oblast*. As the war dragged on, and the German army fought its way deeper into Russia, the Soviets moved entire factories to Siberia to protect them from enemy attack as part of a systematic plan to protect the Russian industrial complex. The number of refugee camps remained unknown, however, because the Soviets didn't keep effective records, and the migration of thousands of displaced persons had taken place during such a short period of time that it had created confusion. In each *posiolok,* living conditions, the work demanded and the structures were different.

In each place, though, one aspect was common, and that was the suffering and humiliation suffered as the Jews were mistreated by both the Russians and non-Jews in the camps. David Laor, older than Joe and located in a different camp, described the conditions he found in Siberia:

It was nightmarish. Inconceivable. Too absurd to be true. I, a young man whose consuming wish was to emigrate to Palestine, a person who always tried to do what was honest and correct, had been transported to the ends of the earth in order to be re-educated. Found guilty of a crime I had not committed. Deprived of my liberty. Human rights cancelled and dignity lost, trampled. Palestine was receding from me. I knew this was only the beginning, and my heart was very heavy...

...Suddenly, amid the sighs and laments of the prisoners and the commands to organize the lavatory parade, the sound of singing suddenly broke out. The singer was Rij, a young man with a tortured face, who was deeply in love and had left his beloved far away. Who knew when he would see her again? He sang sweetly and tearfully in Yiddish, as the emotional words spread and echoed over the vast body of water, in the white northern light. A night that was illuminated with a golden light, that never went out all day and night, a light that was in sharp contrast to my feelings.[95]

David Laor survived the Siberian camp, and the harsh task of going out into the forest each day and toiling at woodcutting. He fell in love with a girl, Rachel, months later in the Tehran tent camp, and was later director of the Tehran Children's Refugee Station.

Some of the refugees arrived at camps very different from those where David Laor and Joe Rosenbaum were forced to live. Eliot 'Lonek' Jaroslawicz, a ten-year-old Polish Jew, described arriving at Sverdlovsk, an *oblast* located in the Urals Federal District and north of the Ural Mountains:

We were sent to a little village. And there were already prisoners from the time of the czars, from a long time ago. The communists took them to Siberia during the revolution, the new Russia. It was a labour camp, where there were towers outside, and we saw a couple of guards with dogs. I remember the towers, I don't remember the surroundings.' He went on to describe a landscape like the Poles had never seen before: 'This was like a desert, not a hot desert, a cold desert. It was a wasteland; the whole thing was woods. You could go through miles of woods and you [could] get lost in the woods. When you fall down, you cannot get up. Like sand.[96]

The camp were Joe and his family lived in a series of long barracks in the forest, like many other camps with log barracks which held up to 200 people. In other camps, the Poles lived in a series of small shacks. One *posiolok* was located 2,000 kilometres away from Vladivostok where winter lasted ten months there, and one could only reach the camp during the two months of summer. The camp commandant sternly informed them that no one was ever released from this camp because there was no way back.

Work conditions differed from camp to camp, depending on location.

To the Russians running the camp, neither age nor sickness should keep the Jews from conducting their work in harsh, cold conditions. Children were marched for kilometres to work that included driving machinery, sawing timbers and delivering them to the local sawmill. One camp ordered the smallest children who couldn't saw logs to walk ten kilometres to an area where they were expected to clear roots from the grounds Because there wasn't a river close to Joe's camp to float timbers to sawmills, workers didn't cut trees; instead, they gathered *jivyitzeh*. Even with the deplorable conditions in which they were forced to live, Joe and the others were fortunate. Cutting timbers in freezing temperatures was a brutal work, the woodcutters toiling under slave-labour conditions, were forced to work twelve hours at a time. The men cut down the trees, as the women loaded the timbers in train cars. Small children as young as eight and nine collapsed and died from exhaustion in the forest.

Accidents caused many deaths, especially among the elderly men and the young boys. Falling trees or branches, snapping loose from above, crushed many to death or broke arms and legs. Someone who was injured and couldn't work, received only half pay, usually bread or a few *kopecks,* a Russian unit of money.

Although most refugees worked cutting timber, in other camps they performed equally harsh tasks. Some cleared forest areas and planted potatoes, beets, cucumbers and onions. Men and woman were forced to build railroad embankments. Refugees living in camps located closer to the White Sea worked in brick factories hauling clay. Farther south, the men worked in coal mines or quarries, earning only 110 rubles a month.

Starvation and freezing temperatures took the weakest first. Joe's grandfather died of starvation within several months after arriving. He gave his food away. One deportee later wrote about how his mother and one of his brothers went on a two-day trip, trying to exchange some of their last belongings – their own badly-needed clothes – for some flour to bake a little bread. Day after day those family members who remained behind waited and worried about what might have happened to their mother and brother.

> On the fifth day one woman comes over and says that one woman with a boy froze to death. We all cried at once, Dad walks around the

barracks like crazy.' The father asked the camp authorities for a horse and wagon to bring back the corpses, but is denied. After a day or two, 'Dad comes back…and says that Mama is frozen, [and] we started crying worse. Older sister fainted…two kilometers away from the village Mama was sitting on the sleighs and holding my brother in her arms. Both had frozen to death.[97]

Within months after the refugee's arrival, malaria and dysentery spread throughout the camps. One of the most feared symptoms among the deportees were the first signs of dysentery, an inflammation of the intestine caused by bacteria, viruses and parasitic worms. The sickness first appeared with a fever followed by severe abdominal pain, and a feeling of incomplete defecation, followed by mucus, pus and blood present in the faeces. Without proper treatment, which was practically non-existent in the poorly-equipped camp hospitals, one's body simply wore down.

For the deportees, being placed in the middle of a vast, freezing land far from their familiar homeland of Germany and Poland, created waves of depression and impossibility. Their dreams and fears haunted them as they lay down on board beds, scratched at gnats and bedbugs, somehow trying to sleep perhaps for an hour, or two. But the basic human nature of survival, continued to burn within them, a glimmer of hope.

As they toiled and suffered and died in the *posioloks*, the refugees found ways to keep that simmering faith alive in the camps. One deportee reflected that in the camp near Sosva, they painted one of the barracks blue and white…to remember Palestine.

***

During his second summer in Siberia, Joe went to work picking mushrooms and berries to earn money for bread. By this time during their captivity, the deportees were starving and trying anything to get food. They planted onions, potatoes, and sunflowers and gathered berries from the forest. While observing the older boys, Joe discovered another way to make money. When the men cut the trees to harvest *jivyitzeh,* Joe noticed that not all the juice ran into the cups, but dried, turning thick on the side of the tree. Joe began cutting away the hardened *jivyitzeh* and placing it in a bucket. His idea turned into a worthy chore, because one bucket of dry *jivyitzeh* was worth four buckets of wet juice because it was condensed. The problem was Joe was so short he could only scrape from the lower part of the trees, and he couldn't carry a ladder. Because of Joe's small stature, he was only strong enough to carry a half-bucket back to camp.

There were, among the brutality of the slave labour camps, moments of humour. One morning, after he and cousin Shlomo gathered firewood, they loaded it on a sleigh and began making their way back through the snow to camp. They took turns pulling the rope at the front of the sleigh as the other pushed from behind. It was cold that morning, and Joe's hands and feet felt frozen. When it became time for Joe to pull at the front, 'he noticed how the sleigh suddenly weighed more. When he turned, Shlomo was riding on top of the wood pile.'[98]

Later in the summer, Joe also learned that mushrooms were just as valuable a product as dry *jivyitzeh*. After he learned which mushrooms were non-poisonous by watching the older boys, he ventured into the forest and collected the mushrooms, and his mother would string them on rings and thread and hang them up to dry. These valuable mushrooms could be eaten later the next winter, when the days were so cruelly cold and food was even scarcer. Joe's mother also put a portion of the remaining mushrooms to good use; she would buy an onion for a penny and cook them with a potato to make a meal.

Along with the mushrooms, the young boys gathered blackberries and strawberries and *klukva* – a sour fruit that women used to cook with. This work took place near a dreary swamp. His mother would have complained, of course, if she had known they were in such a dangerous place because she knew her son couldn't swim. The first spring the refugees were in the camp, the bigger boys had pushed Joe into the cold water as he walked along the bank near a log, and he quickly learned to swim.

In the summers, the water warmed up and was more pleasant. There was the dread of leeches that would attack the skin, and they could only be cut off with a knife. But Joe soon learned that even these dreaded leeches could turn a profit, and he would catch them alive to be sold for medicinal purposes.

These things Joe learned because he had a quick mind and the ability, even as a young boy, to adjust. One lesson he learned quickly was not to make friends.

Even though they were all Jewish, Joe and his cousin Shlomo were the only children from Germany. All the other children were from Poland, and they didn't like Germans. Shlomo was bigger and stouter and he could fight off his attackers, but Joe was too small and not strong enough to fight back, which made him an easy victim. When the boys went into the forest to gather mushrooms, the bigger boys waited until Joe had gathered a small sack, then they would jump on him and take away his mushrooms. He would have to go back home empty-handed.

Many times, Joe returned to camp without any mushrooms, and he would see the sad expression on his mother's face as she was forced to sell possessions for food. 'It was a big deal for her, my mother', Joe recalls. 'She gave up her gold watch, and she sold it in Siberia. We got some money, and we got food for a couple of weeks, maybe for a couple of months.'[99]

But two months later, Joe watched his mother sell her most prized possession, her wedding ring, to the Russians. He saw the 'the deep pain on her face as she gave up something so dear to her. Some people had money, so they got it for a bargain', Joe remembers. 'So, we did survive.'[100]

Never again did Joe want to see his mother so unhappy. But there was something else going on, another image that haunted him. He had noticed several mornings before, as his mother got out of bed and wrapped the blanket around her shoulders, how thin she looked. In the morning light through the windows, her face was scrawny and pale. Joe decided right then that it was up to him to take care of his mother and Nelly. He had a plan.

He would go out into the thick forest by himself. It would prove to be a mistake, of course, such a child going out into the forest alone, one innocent miscalculation on the part of a small boy who simply wanted to help feed his family. 'So, I decided to go out on my own', Joe remembers, 'and that was a problem, because if you go out on your own, you have to come back also on your own. And where do you go? How do you know where to go and how to go back?'

It was a mistake that still haunts his thoughts today, all these years later.

8

Lost

Joe stood at the camp's edge the next morning, staring out at an early fog hanging like smoke at the base of the trees surrounding the camp. A knot churned in his stomach. Standing there all alone made the forest appear more frightening and gloomy than it ever had before.[101]

He had a problem, and there was only one solution, so it wasn't as if he wanted to go into forest alone. He had come home too many times with his buckets empty, saw the disappointment on his mother's face, and although she hadn't ever said a word, he knew it hurt her. He was determined to never again allow the hateful action of the older boys to disappoint his mother.

The previous night had finally convinced Joe even more that he couldn't turn back this morning. As was their custom, established soon after arriving in the camp, each night before they went to sleep his mother would divide the bread and what mushrooms or onions she could gather, and they would eat. That way, she explained, they wouldn't wake up hungry the next morning, which wasn't exactly true because Joe woke up hungry every morning. Each night he and Nelly sat on either side of mother on the small, narrow bed. She would divide the bread into three parts and place them in a tin plate. Then she would count out mushrooms, berries or onions, if they had any, and place them in the plate. Several weeks ago, however, Joe noticed that his mother had stopped eating the late meal herself, meaning she mainly ate only one meal at midday. 'I'm not very hungry', she had tried to explain, but Joe knew better. How could she not be hungry? When he stared into her face, her eyes were different – dull and distant. Was she sick? No, she smiled, hugging Joe. 'I'm just tired and ready to go to sleep.'

That expression on her face convinced Joe that he must pick up the two buckets and walk alone into the forest. Every step drew him into darkness beneath a web of thick branches that, this morning, seemed much murkier than when he went into the trees with the other boys. After walking several yards, as he planned, Joe glanced back towards the camp, reassuring himself of the path he was taking, and more importantly, the way he would take back. He would simply remember a certain tree, noticing that the vines hung down a certain way; maybe several branches lay at the base of the tree where they had crashed to the ground, broken by the weight of ice the last winter. Finally, after he turned back one last time, the camp was out of sight, but Joe wasn't concerned, he was confident in what he was doing.

When Joe came to the creek, swollen with late spring rains, he knew where he was, and grew even more confident. He knew that if he stayed close to the creek, he would find his way back to the camp. Turning right at the creek bank, Joe followed a familiar trail worn down by others when they came out to gather mushrooms. After making his way along the creek for several hundred yards, Joe stopped where a log lay out into the water, the place where he had learned to swim. His heart jumped. He knew that beneath the thicker grove of trees there would be mushrooms to take back to the camp. His mother would be so proud.

Turning away from the creek and towards the trees, Joe became excited because he quickly saw that he had guessed correctly. In the moist soil there were hundreds of mushrooms sprouting out after last night's rain, everywhere, like small gifts to be picked.

Joe glanced around the silent forest. Not a movement or sound other than the occasional stir of the morning wind through the top of the trees or a large black bird swooping through the branches. He had done it, he had overcome fear, and now the mushrooms were his to gather. Satisfied, he hurriedly went about gathering mushrooms and tossing them into one of the buckets. When the bucket was full and the other bucket almost half full, Joe decided, as a big surprise for his mother, he would fill up the remainder with berries. To get to where the berries were located he had to go farther along the creek, but he was confident now as he headed along the bank.

What he walked upon several minutes later was surprising. Where several days ago the berries had been picked over, there was a whole new crop to pick. Blackberries were everywhere.

Beneath the looming canvas of the tree Joe worked hard, and soon the second bucket was overflowing with mushrooms and blackberries. He came back under a large tree where he had left the first bucket and rested, satisfied of what he had done this morning. Joe couldn't wait to show his mother that he had outsmarted the larger boys.

Taking the buckets in hand, Joe hesitated and then walked to the left where he expected to find the creek, where he could head back to camp. After walking for a while, though, he hadn't reached the creek. What could be wrong? But – he was sure – no, the creek shouldn't be that far. Certain that he was close, but with his heart beating quicker now, Joe back-tracked to the larger tree, then headed farther to his left.

He walked through thick, tangled underbrush that didn't look familiar at all – then stopped. Joe sat the buckets down and stood still, listening for the waters rushing through the creek.

Nothing.

His heart beat against the inside of his chest…the trees, the dark forest, began to close in around him. Without the creek he was lost.

He panicked and ran. The bucket in his left hand racked against a tree, spilling mushrooms, and as he spun, Joe fell to the ground as the other bucket overturned.

How could he have allowed this to happen?

Quickly he was at his feet, running again. Branches tore at his face, and his legs began to ache, until he couldn't go any longer. He collapsed on the ground, the air burning in his lungs.

Resting on the forest floor, Joe's breathing slowed. And then he heard it – the distant running of water.

The creek!

He jumped up, running toward the noise. Then he saw the creek. His buckets were only half full now, but he didn't care. He would find his way back to the camp. He wasn't lost.

Slowing his pace, with his confidence growing, Joe followed the creek to the big tree with the vines that he had used as a landmark. Then he headed back down the trail beneath the familiar thin gathering of trees – and froze.

Directly ahead of him was the gray, sketched outline of the barracks in the morning fog.

Joe broke into a run as fast as he could go, the buckets flailing at his side, tears of relief filling his eyes. He felt ashamed that he was crying because during his ordeal, since leaving Cologne, he had never cried. Many times, he had been scared, but he had never cried. And now that he was so close to home emotions overtook him, and he ran faster.

Just as he entered the clearing of the camp, Joe tripped and fell, the remainder of the mushrooms and berries spilling out in the mud from the overturned buckets. Tears blinded Joe as he tried to place them back in the bucket. He couldn't even find the other bucket.

Then he was on his feet, running across the yard as several women stared at him from an open fire. Joe ran as hard as he could to the barracks, pushed the door open and ran inside.

A strange woman sat in front of the stove, her hands open to the heat. She stared up quickly, her face filled with surprise. Then she yelled at him in Polish as two children stuck their heads out from under thin, worn covers. She jumped to her feet and yelled again, much louder now. He had entered the wrong barracks. Joe ran out of the door, the bucket bumping against his hip.

The fear of being lost in the forest rushed back at him.

Never! Never again! Joe promised himself.

Finally, outside in the air, Joe stopped. But he was in the camp. He wasn't lost any more, and he forced himself to calm down. Realizing he was only several barracks away from where his family stayed, he ran to the door.

His mother immediately saw Joe was disturbed, and she came to him and hugged him close. 'What happened?'

'I…I was lost in the forest', he told her.

Her face changed. 'But why did you go alone into the forest?'

'Because the older boys steal my mushrooms and berries', Joe admitted. 'If I went alone then they wouldn't bother me…they couldn't steal our food… and we would have more to eat.'

She led him to the bed, went and got a cloth she had dipped in a cup of water from the container and sat beside him. 'I think you were very brave to do such a thing', she said as she dabbed the scratches on his face with the cool cloth.

His mother reached into the bucket and took out two mushrooms – all that remained of everything he had gathered that morning. Two small, miserable mushrooms. Joe wiped tears away with his shirt sleeve. Now, instead of mother being happy, she would be disappointed just as when he had allowed the bigger boys to steal his gathering.

From that experience in the forest, a deep fear of getting lost stayed with him the rest of his life. Even 'driving in a big city like New York with people all around', Joe admits that dread at times grips him.

After a moment, his mother cupped his cheeks in her hands and turned his face toward her. She looked so weak, her frail eyes staring into his, much weaker than she had looked only days ago. She drew him to her, and Joe found her skin cold. Something was wrong, he thought, something was very wrong.

Then, that worried thought slipped into the back of his mind as his mother kissed him on the cheek. 'Thank you for the mushrooms, Yossi.'

9

Fear in Belgium and Palestine

By early 1940 Simon Rosenbaum was established in New York.

Since arriving in 1938, he had connected with his cousins and worked at a good job earning fair wages and had recently rented a small apartment. In fact, events had unfolded just as he and Mina had planned two years earlier sitting at the kitchen table at 23 Alexander Strasse. Now Simon would be sending for his family, and as soon as they arrived in America, Nelly could have the operation on her mouth that Mina so badly desired for her daughter.

There was a problem, however, Simon had absolutely no idea where his wife and two children were; it was as if they had simply vanished from the face of the earth. The only clue of their fate was from the war reports printed in the newspapers, describing how thousands of Jewish refugees, unfortunately living in Poland when the war began, had been deported eastward. Instinctively, Simon knew his family, except for Inez who had been sent to Belgium in October 1938, was with those poor people torn from their homeland.[102]

By the winter of 1939, to escape Nazi oppression, over 400 refugees a week were entering Belgium, at Merxplas and at Marneffe, a castle that had previously served as a Jesuit college and where the Belgian government set up 'isolation camps'. From these camps, the refugees were allowed occasional visits into Brussels. Before the war, the Jewish community, numbering over 70,000 with 55,000 in Antwerp and Brussels, had assimilated into Belgian society, becoming successful university professors and business owners. Jewish political organizations were active in the country, holding fund-raisers for Yiddish schools in the *Maison des Huit Heures* and hearing lectures by Angelika Balabanoff, a Russian-Jewish Communist activist, on her favourite subject, 'Fascism and the Working Class'. By 1940, though, as Simon worried for his daughter, the dominating topic on the streets was rumour of a threatening and expanded war. The Belgian government was aware through British intelligence reports that, with Poland conquered, Hitler's armies would soon advance to the west into other countries. What was uncertain was the fate of the Jews who had fled there.

Heartbroken that he had no idea of whether Mina, Joe and Nelly were alive or dead, Simon urgently wanted Inez, now fourteen, with him. He sent a telegram and money to his brother-in-law instructing him to secure passage for his oldest daughter on a ship to America. When she was informed of the telegram, Inez was at first hesitant. Finally, encouraged by her aunt, she wrote her father that she would come and live with him. His brother-in-law immediately began making plans for Inez to travel to America.

Operation *Fall Gelb* (Case Yellow) began on 10 May 1940, and was a massive military action of Hitler's invasion of Belgium, the Netherlands, and France. With overwhelming military power, the German army swiftly defeated King Leopold III's forces in just eighteen days, with the king capitulating, accepting Hitler's terms of 'unconditional surrender' at 11p.m. on 27 May. Once the occupation of Belgium was completed, the German government acted swiftly, and by October had liquidated all Jewish businesses and ordered all Jews over the age of ten to wear the Star of David. In August 1942, using as a ruse the benign expression *Arbeitseinsatz*, 'recruitment for work', the Germans began deporting the 70,000 Jews living in Belgium to concentration camps, mostly to Auschwitz. The Nazi ploy worked so well that almost half of the Jews to be deported went voluntarily.[103]

Uncle Philman and one son, Alfred, escaped from the Nazi oppression and eventually ended up hiding in the Italian hills throughout the duration of the war. His wife and three daughters, swept up in the deportation, were murdered one morning alongside a rural road in France.

For Inez, the decision to join her father in America would prove to be a fortunate choice.

Around 1 May Inez obtained passage on a ship. It was during this journey on a late afternoon, as the sky turned a pale red at the horizon full of ocean, that Inez heard the announcement over the loud speaker – the Germans had invaded Belgium.

***

In the following months, as Joe wandered through the camp begging for food, he often overheard the older people as they spoke of Palestine. Their conversations made this place sound almost a mythical place, a land where they should all pray to live – if they should ever leave Siberia. Yes, Palestine was where they'd go, the old men insisted, once the war was finished.

Joe didn't completely understand everything he heard about this place called Palestine. He didn't even know where it was, really. Several years before, when his family still lived in Cologne, Joe would listen to his mother's conversation with a relative or neighbour as she told them, 'My husband is in America, and I have a brother living in Palestine.' Joe naturally believed that America and Palestine, because they were spoken of in the same sentence, were very close to each other. It would be years later that he would realize that his geographical theory was all wrong.

Palestine hadn't escaped the war as the old men talking in the Siberian camp believed. In 1940 the *Yishuv*, the Jewish community in Palestine, lived in a land where there were constant attacks among Jewish and Arab villages. Several times, in the 1930s, Arab strikes had created violence in the streets and hills. Now, as Germany invaded Belgium, Luxembourg and the Netherlands, and as Italian troops marched into Greece, the war edged closer and stirred a wave of anxiety in Palestine.

The 29 July 1940 issue of *Time Magazine* reported a dozen casualties during the first attacks on Palestine by Italian SM82 aircraft bombing Haifa, targeted because of its importance as a port and refinery controlled by the British.[104]

Just over a month later, on 9 September 1940, a squadron of Italian Air Force bombers swept through the skies over Tel Aviv dropping bombs and creating widespread destruction and death. One hundred and thirty-seven people died in the bombing. One stray bomb killed seven people in an Arab town north of the city including five children. The *Palestine Post* reported the carnage: 'In one street alone, fifteen people lost their lives. Of two bombs falling together, one wrecked the wall of a synagogue where four people were killed, while the other crashed through two stories of a building.'[105]

Remarkably, with only a small, poorly-equipped force to protect them, the people's resolve stiffened as the Axis armies reached deeper into the Middle East, and with the bombing of the two coastal cities. The destruction and death brought out an unbending perseverance, compared proudly to that of the British civilian determination during the London Blitz by the German Luftwaffe. The day after the Italian bombing of Tel Aviv, a *Palestine Post* sub-headline read: 'The public preserved complete calm during and after the raid.'[106]

Still, hidden beneath the calm and encouraging appearance of life going on in the streets, there was an invisible vigilance among Jews regarding the approaching peril. A Tel Aviv writer for the weekly *Palestine Review* described his personal, and genuine, perspective: 'Drawn features would first betray the feelings of the people about him. Then he would note the piles of sandbags and burrowing of workmen in basements and trenches. Finally, at night he would find the country reduced to utter darkness.'[107]

By then, he would know that Palestine was a land ready to meet the worst, should it come.

10

Exodus

'Through their actions, the Germans would indirectly be responsible for saving hundreds of thousands of Poles from certain death in the Soviet camps.'[108]

'And, on that day the Lord brought the people of Israel out of the land of Egypt like an army.'

Exodus,12:51

TOP SECRET. The Führer's Headquarters. 18 December 1940

The German Armed Forces must be prepared to crush Soviet Russia in a quick campaign before the end of the war with England. For this purpose, the Army will have to employ all available units with the reservation that the occupied territories will have to be safeguarded against surprise attacks...Preparations are to be completed by May 15, 1941. Great caution has to be exercised that the intention of an attack will not be recognized.'[109]

On the morning of 22 June 1941, Sunday morning newspapers, delivered on shaded sidewalks and watered lawns throughout America, told of shocking reports that Hitler's armies had crossed over into the Russian plains, attacking his allies in the east. The *San Louis Obispo Telegram Tribune* edition declared: 'Russian Army braces, Counters on South Front – Red Army Stands off Nazi Drive.'[110] The apparent sweeping success of catching the Soviets totally off guard prompted Goebbels to record in his diary at 3:30a.m., 'Now the guns will be thundering...may God bless our weapons.'[111]

The invasion was an action no one, not even the Soviets, expected. Exactly one year to the day after France had surrendered to Germany, Hitler's armoured, mechanized, and hitherto invincible armies poured across the Niemen River and various other rivers and penetrated swiftly into Mother Russia. Operation Barbarossa, the codename of the German invasion, had been planned for over seven months in meticulous detail at various stages of the invasion. Over four million German soldiers, 600,000 motor vehicles and 700,000 horses swept into the Soviet Union along an 1,800-mile front, catching the Soviet forces in total surprise, successfully capturing large sections of land eastward throughout the Russian plains. This was all part of Hitler's 'expansion' as he had outlined in *Mein Kampf.*

Despite the brutal, victorious sweeps towards Moscow, Leningrad and Stalingrad, the German advance would, within a year just as the Nazi army approached the gates of Moscow, bog down under harsh winter conditions, staggering beneath massive Soviet counter-attacks. As historians wrote after the war ended in 1945, Operation Barbarossa's eventual disaster was noted as the high watermark of Hitler's Third Reich.

***

On the morning of the invasion, David Laor and other men knelt and stood around the camp clinic radio, a large brown box with a golden light illuminating the half-pie dial. Only moments before a prisoner-doctor had run into the room yelling that they should turn on the radio because an important message was being broadcast. Vyacheslav Molotov, the Russian Minister of Foreign Affairs, was announcing that the German Fascists had crossed into Soviet territory and their planes were bombing Kiev and other cities. The radio announcements concluded with the call: 'Death to Fascists!' Then patriotic songs began playing. The message stunned the refugees, and Laor thought: *what would the turn of events bring to us?*

In slave labour camps throughout Siberia, there was measured awareness of happenings among the Polish deportees concerning the German invasion of the Soviet Union.

Soon rumours began to surface of the possible release of the Polish army troops held in Soviet camps, which many took to mean that at some point, the deportees would be released also. The question then became, where would they go?

Six months later, in December 1942, a refugee group, with permission issued by a *kolkhoz* administrator, could travel to Barnaul, a two-hour trip by horse and buggy, located on the Ob River in the West Siberian Plain. When they returned late that afternoon, the news they brought back, at first unbelievable, created a wave of excitement in the camp.

An amnesty notice for all Poles – soldiers and all civilians – had been posted on the front window of the post office. Since Germany had attacked Russia, Poland had become a part of the Western Alliance along with England, France, and the United States and had declared war on Germany.

One of the men who had travelled to Barnaul told the refugees huddled around that within weeks trains would be organized for 'Polish deportees' to leave for the south of Russia, where Polish army camps were being assembled.

The man also told them that they had learned that the Polish army, held in Russian prisons, would soon be released and sent to military training in camps at Kirghizstan and Uzbekistan.

From those locations, they would be transported to the Middle East and Egypt where they would fight with the British in North Africa. All Polish refugees would be free to travel within Russia with the released soldiers, with one rule – they couldn't go back to Poland.

***

News of the anticipated release of the deportees didn't reach all the camps in the Siberia because of the lack of communication and the immense distances between the camps, especially the camp where Joe was because of its isolated location. Instead of joy and hope and believing that the news would bring the Poles freedom, their camp continued as a place of barely surviving, of enduring the freezing cold, without any hope of getting out, as the long dark nights drifted into morning. 'We were living in Siberia for more than a year, I think', Joe remembers. 'The situation got worse, and for my mother, she gave us [Joe and Nelly] more food than she gave to herself.'[112]

As the summer brought, at long last, welcome warmth to the camp, Joe found himself dealing with demands on his young life without any knowledge of the amnesty agreement, of the forming of freed Polish forces, or of refugees already making their way southward. Even as Joe gathered berries and mushrooms in the forest to help feed his family, the vast German Blitzkrieg swarmed eastward over the Russian plains.

When, finally, the refugees in the camp were made aware of these events unfolding, they believed the German invasion was a blessing, which it was in the beginning, if for no other reason than it gave them hope. Soon, however, they suffered the ruthless wrath from the Soviets because of Russia's losing the war against Germany. The exiles were forced to work two hours longer, with less bread, which meant twelve-hour days. Rations in most camps were reduced to 600 grammes per day for adults and 400 for children.

Within a month after the war broke out, the refugees were informed that they had to work two days a week without pay for, as they were informed, the defence of the country. Because of the additional work and less food, disease, exhaustion and death soared among the refugees. Many, who had been filled with hope when the amnesty news reached them, now wouldn't live to see the freedom just ahead.

There was no way for the deportees to realize the effects the approaching events would have on their lives that morning, for it was six long months before they began an exodus out of slavery in Siberia and toward Persia.

Ironically, Hitler, with his calculated betrayal of the Soviet Union, had unintentionally set free thousands of Jews, the very people he desired to eliminate from the face of the earth. Hitler's betrayal of Stalin would also shift world events and the alignment of warring allies from the Pacific to Eastern Europe. The implications were felt in every world capital throughout the globe, and even to the deportees struggling to exist in the Siberian camps.

For Joe Rosenbaum, languishing in the camp and trying his best to support his mother and sister, his life was about to drastically change again because of the release of a single Polish general from a Soviet prison.

***

At 4p.m. on the evening of 4 August 1940, General Wladyslaw Anders was led up a short flight of steps and then into a lift. The prison commander walked with Anders in a non-menacing manner. This struck the general as odd, for the other times when he had been led out of his cell often his arms were pinioned behind him.

Another twenty meters and the corridors 'became more luxuriously furnished'. When they were met by several NKVD officers and they acted courteously, then Anders knew that what he had suspected for over a month now was, in fact, true.

In mid-July the prisoners had heard bomb explosions in Moscow, followed by heavy anti-aircraft firing. The prison officials assured Anders and the others that these had only been an air defence exercises. But when the exercises continued day after day and the fifteen minutes of exercise allowed daily in the prison yard, was discontinued, Anders 'was overcome with emotion.'

There were even disagreements among the prisoners about whether the planes were British or German. Optimism quickly grew throughout the prisoner cells, but Anders knew.

'My experienced ear had not deceived me', Anders wrote. '...For the next day they started painting all the windows blue and sandbags were put into the prison corridors.'[113] For Anders, it could only mean one thing, but he dared not believe in it too much or speak of it with the men.

Anders was led down the hallway and into a large room where there were several NKVD officers standing against the far wall and typists working busily at their desks. After a brief wait in this room, Anders stood and was told to follow one of the officers. It was then that the very thing Anders had prayed for, but also considered impossible, was about to unfold. His heart quickened.

'Then, after a short wait, I was shown into a big, beautifully furnished study, full of carpets and soft armchairs. Two men in civilian clothes rose behind their desks.'

'How do you do?'

'Who am I addressing?'

'I am Beria', and 'I am Merkulov', they answered me one after another. They asked me if I would like a cigarette or tea. I asked whether I was a prisoner or a free man' – the answer was:

'You are free.'[114]

***

With the headline 'Agreement between Poland and USSR' in the 31 July 1941 issue of the *Polish Daily* published in London,[115] the world soon learned of the Sikorski-Maisky Agreement.

Since the attack on the Soviet Union, the Polish government-in-exile, now headquartered in London, and the British Government, mainly through Prime Minister Winston Churchill's intervention, had been in negotiations with Stalin to release over 60,000 Polish soldiers imprisoned in camps across Siberia. Anders would lead that army, known informally as Anders' Army, into Persia for just that purpose. Operation Barbarossa not only saved Joe Rosenbaum and the Polish exiles, but the attack on the Soviet Union also probably spared General Anders from an eventual firing squad at Lubianka Prison.

As Stalin showed signs of agreeing to the releases, the newly-formed Polish army was originally organized to fight with the Red Army retreating across the vast Russian plains towards Moscow under the swift, fierce attacks of the German armies. It didn't take long, though, before Anders and the Polish government realized there political issues which would confuse the situation. Churchill, convinced that the Poles and Soviets would never fight side-by-side, adamantly argued that, instead, these men should be equipped, trained and transported to frontlines in North Africa in the fight against General Edwin Rommel's famed Afrika Korps. As a final point to the Soviets, the British Prime Minister reminded the Russian leader of how bravely and furiously the Poles had fought against the superior German invasion.

The responsibility of forming the prisoners into an army was placed under the authority of General Wladyslaw Sikorski, Prime Minister of Poland's government-in-exile in London. Sikorski, born and educated in Austrian Poland, served as war commissioner of the Polish Legion fighting with the Austrian army against Russia during the First World War. Later, in 1921, he was named chief of the Polish general staff after distinguishing himself in the Polish-Soviet War. After serving as the Polish Prime Minister between 1922-1923, he served for two years as minister of military affairs, directing the reorganization of the army.

A man very popular with the Polish people, nonetheless, when the government changed Sikorski was dismissed and resided in Paris in the years before the Second World War. He spent most of his years writing about the future of warfare. His book, *War in the Future*, made him the first military mind to suggest the theory of Blitzkrieg warfare. In 1938, as Hitler came to power and the political landscape of Europe shifted, Sikorski returned to Poland and once again was asked to serve.

Sikorski formed the Polish government-in-exile located in Paris after escaping to France during the invasion, travelling through Romania. When France capitulated in May 1940 after German armies swept over the French forces, Sikorski ordered Polish forces to evacuate to ports in southern France. Seventy-five per cent of the Polish Air Force and over 20,000 ground troops escaped to England. London, already the location of five Nazi-occupied nations, welcomed Poland as the sixth. Sikorski immediately appointed Professor Stanislaw Kot as the new Polish ambassador to the Soviet Union. Born in 1885 in Ruda, Austria-Hungary, Kot studied philosophy at the University of Lwow, earning his PhD. He escaped to France in 1939 and assisted in forming the Polish government-in-exile, serving as Minister of Internal Affairs.

He then shifted his attention to whom he would appoint to command the 70,000 Polish soldiers and transform them from a group of emaciated, sick prisoners into an effective fighting force.

General Anders was his man.

Sikorski believed that Anders possessed great strength, resolve and unwavering courage on the battlefield, inspiring his soldiers. The main reason he chose Anders, however, was his organizational skills that would be badly needed if the exiled Polish soldiers were ever to be an effective fighting force. Anders and Kot never got along, and Anders considered his appointment as ambassador as unfortunate because Kot knew nothing of the Russian people, he couldn't speak their language and he had no any diplomatic experience.

On 3 December 1941, Sikorski, Ambassador Kot and General Anders flew to Moscow and met with Stalin. Anders thought that the talks, which lasted for over four hours, went well as Stalin and Sikorski discussed the past wars between their countries. 'We always used to fight each other', Stalin offered. 'We ought to be done with the past.' The Russian leader then agreed to allow some Polish units to move to Iran, and suggested a Soviet loan to help hasten the transfer. The leaders then agreed on another meeting.

But Anders had one more item to discuss, and he brought up the missing 20,000 Polish officers. Stalin hesitated for a long moment, and then shrugged. 'They may have escaped to Manchuria.'[116]

In the following months, Anders utilized his administrative expertise to prepare to evacuate his army from Soviet territory through the Persian corridor to Iran. Accompanied by over 76,000 civilian refugees, the shortage of food, clothing and weapons to supply the newly- formed army proved to be overwhelming. The Poles were issued *udostovierenyas*, internal passports that allowed them to travel within the Soviet Union territory. From these harsh labour camps and settlements deep in the vast forests, the deportees made their way south, searching for this Polish army that they had heard of, an army organized and trained to fight with the British Army in the North Africa campaign and later into Italy. The last of these deportees departed the camps on 24 March, reaching the army camps throughout April 1942, their hearts gladdened to be out of the slave labour camps.

Happy to be free again, regaining his health to a good degree, and working with purpose, Anders set about his new task. He writes:

> About September 10, 1941, I flew with my hastily organized headquarters to Buzuluk, sending on by rail the fine Zis car with which Stalin had presented me. [During the meeting in December 1940, Stalin aware of Anders' career in the cavalry, had presented him with two thoroughbred horses and an old Packard limousine.] We flew very low over fields in which half the crops did not seem to have been harvested and over poor and dilapidated villages. On my way I landed at Kuybyshev, where I was received with the utmost pomp, and treated to much vodka and caviar – the usual routine with foreign guests.

In addition, another sight Anders witnessed that day as he was flown to headquarters in Buzuluk south of Russia, saddened him. 'It was a typical Russian town with wooden houses and poverty obvious everywhere. The mud was several inches deep in many of the streets…Polish headquarters was located in a big brick building, over which, I saw, with great emotion, a Polish flag was already flying proudly.'[117]

Seeing the Polish flag flying over the command centre had briefly lifted his spirits, a beautiful sight after two years of prison. It was when the general reviewed his troops that his heart sank. What would later form the 6th Infantry Division of the Polish II Corps, approximately 17,000 soldiers, paraded by the officers. The soldiers were dressed in just-delivered British Army overcoats and many carried wooden guns because there simply weren't enough weapons to go around. As much as he had prepared himself, the condition of these soldiers still stunned him. Deplorable was the only description:

> There was not a man who was not an emaciated skeleton and most of them were covered with ulcers, resulting from semi-starvation...but to the astonishment of the Russians, including General Zhukov (the Russian commander assisting in the transfer), they [the troops] were all well shaved, and showed a fine soldierly bearing.[118]

By November 1941, 40,000 Polish soldiers were bivouacked in the camp, over half without boots. They lived on insufficient rations and slept in Soviet-made summer tents, 15 to 20 men per tent, as at night the temperatures dropped to below freezing. Many of the soldiers reached the camp proud to have the opportunity to fight the Nazis but arrived in terrible shape.

Zygmunt Tadeusz Rymaszewski was only twenty years old when he was arrested in 1940, accused of talk against the Soviet government. He was sentenced to five years of hard labour in Vorkuta, a slave labour camp in Siberia. Released among those granted amnesty, Rymaszewski joined the vast flow of soldiers streaming southward to find any method of transportation.

7. Six members of the Anders Army pose in front of a railcar prior to departure for Iran. February 1942. United States Holocaust Memorial Museum; courtesy of Dr Joan Ringelheim.

Many travelled on horse-driven sledges across snow fields or rode on crowded, freezing cattle truck trains. He spent three weeks suffering from hunger as there was never enough food to go round, and bitter cold. Waiting to catch the next train, the soldiers sang Polish patriotic and military songs. Rymaszewski finally reached Buzuluk, and then his garrison was transferred to Guzar past the Urals. His brother writes of his happiness, then tragedy, when receiving information through the wartime Polish Red Cross in London, 1944: 'Zygmunt was very happy to wear the uniform of a Polish soldier but his body was so weakened by the labour and prolonged starvation that he soon died on 4 June 1942, aged 21.'[119]

By 19 March 1942, General Anders ordered the evacuation of Polish soldiers and civilians, establishing new headquarters at Yangi-Yul, New Roads, near Tashkent, Uzbekistan. Between 24 March 24 and 4 April, over 33,000 soldiers, accompanied by 11,000 civilians, including 3,100 children, a thousand of which were Jewish orphans, departed the Soviet Union and began making their way south to Iran. To Anders and his officers, there was the lingering question of how not to leave anyone behind, if possible. What of the ones who didn't leave with his army? For many the Soviet Union became their final resting place before the war's end. According to the 1943 report, Document D:

> ...about 200,000 Polish citizens, both children and adults died during the period of deportation.' Another quarter of a million – including, no doubt, some deportees – were repatriated to the recovered territories of western Poland during the massive population exchanges following the Second World War. As for what happened to those who never got out, God only knows. Some, no doubt, are still there.[120]

Five months later Anders's troops numbered 67,500, most being sickly and ill-clothed. Anders also received a report that an estimated seventy thousand refugees – men, women and children – were flowing southward. He couldn't begin to imagine the condition they were in as they exited the Siberian camps.

In a letter dated 17 July 1942, Churchill and Stalin finally agreed to allow the Poles to move to Iran as part of the Allied occupation force. Over the next two years, the Polish soldiers proved to be a valuable part of the Allied fighting forces. Their reputation would be formed in North Africa fighting with the British against General Rommel's famed Afrika Korps. A year later, they accomplished much more than were expected of them during the fighting in Italy.

At this point, though, a plan had been set to prepare for that future battle, as was the route Joe Rosenbaum and thousands of weary Jews would take out of Siberia.

***

Joe watched helplessly as his mother physically drifted away from him.

Her deterioration had begun a month ago, and it was now obvious to Joe that his mother was growing weaker and thinner, her face terribly drawn and pale in the morning sunlight. With his mother's frailty, Joe instinctively began to turn to his sister who was constantly lonely. The other children had little to do with Nelly because she had no teeth in the front, and they couldn't understand her. From the beginning Nelly refused to go outside because she sensed that she was different from the other children.

Joe had changed also, suffering through these months in Siberia.

Although Mina had many nights given her share of food to Joe and Nelly, Joe had lost weight, and Nelly languished on her cot during the day. Even though he was now only ten years old, Joe was no longer a child. The stress of hunting for food, of watching his mother slowly become silent and drifting away was too much. Sometime after arriving in Siberia, though he didn't remember when, Joe realized that he could no longer afford to feel anything. He couldn't remember the last time he had cried or laughed. There was no desperation, no hope, no fear, only the will to survive. He had also watched the change in families. The inner circle of father, mother and children, that caring, helpful outlook that all families had arrived with, was now simply gone, replaced by a stern stance each had taken, that hidden will in the human soul to survive. Joe, sensing that, turned away from other family members, and didn't hate anyone for that. He understood. Life had become too harsh, and he emptied any emotion from his mind and turned towards his sister.

'I got very much involved with Nelly then…my mother, once the war broke out, she realized that the chance of us going to America was very, very small. Once she thought that we might not be able to make it, she went into a deep depression.' Mina lost her voice, and on those few occasions when she did speak, it was in a hushed, quiet voice, even a whisper. 'And later on', Joe says, 'she talked even quieter. Nothing…because of being…I don't know what. And so, that's why I got more involved with Nelly, my little sister.' Several months after they arrived at the camp, Joe's mother suddenly couldn't understand her daughter, and she would ask Joe, 'What did she say? What does she want?' Joe could understand Nelly, however, and that drew them closer together. 'I liked her a lot, and I took care of her.'

During this time, camp officials confirmed that the rumours of an exodus out of Siberia were true. Joe listened to the older men gathered in the opening between the buildings talking of trucks that would take them to a train station many miles away, and that soon they would all leave the camps and travel southward with a new Polish army.

Of course everyone was excited about this news, and Joe couldn't imagine how it would be to get away from this bitterly cold camp. Even though the men wondered out loud if living conditions would be much better, Joe thought at least it would be warmer.

The promised escape from the camp drifted back in his mind over the next two months, as the warm weather returned, but his mother's appearance worsened and, for the first time, Joe was haunted by the fact that his adoring mother might die. The thought froze him. Grandfather had died from hunger three weeks before, but he was an old man, and old men were supposed to die. Still, whenever Joe allowed himself to think that Grandfather wouldn't tell him stories anymore, it made him sad. It was different with mother who was so young and besides, Joe wondered, what would become of Nelly and him without their mother?

That fear drove Joe to work harder gathering more mushrooms and berries, spending as much time as he dared in the forest. Once he found blackberries, which was fortunate because it was nearing the end of the season, and he sold them for three onions. He couldn't remember the last time his mother possessed three onions. When he gave them to her, she gave him a big hug, but that afternoon she ate only mushrooms, leaving the onions to divide between Joe and Nelly.

It was the lowest point in Joe's young life. Frustration and depression for a nine-year-old boy aren't easily recognizable because a child shouldn't have to deal with the problems that Joe was facing every day. The anxiety of what would happen if his mother were gone drove Joe deeper into despair. He would work harder to bring in food – but he could only do so much. His small, frail body was slowly wearing down from lack of food and constant worry. Joe decided that he would not eat also, and that he would give his food to his mother until she regained her strength. Even with the best of intentions, when she divided up the food at night, he and Nelly received the largest portions. With the gnawing hunger in Joe's stomach, his best intentions were forgotten, and he ate all that she gave him. For many years after he would feel guilty. 'We made it to summer', Joe admits, 'but my mother began drifting away, and I'm sorry I didn't see it'.

One morning, about three weeks before the refugees could leave the camp and begin their journey to the south, Joe came into the barracks. Nelly was on the floor wrapped in a blanket, where she stayed most of the day.

Then he saw his mother, lying across the bed at an odd angle, twisted into a strange position. Joe knew something was terribly different and dreadfully wrong.

He ran to her and knelt beside the bed. He placed his hand on her cheek. She expelled air from her lungs, a deep raking cough that sounded from somewhere deep inside of her, a strange sound that Joe had never heard before. Her breathing slowed, and at times she would gasp and breathe rapidly for several deep breaths. Air rattled like dry leaves from her throat. She would bury her face in the covers and then would go quiet and still.

When she finally turned her face, and looked up at him, Joe pulled back. Her eyes were wide, disoriented, but strangely not afraid. They were soft and clear and full of love for her beloved son, he was sure of that. Then Joe fell on her, hugging her thin body with a tender panic, certain that he would never be able to let go.

***

Later, his uncle came to get Joe and Nelly and took them to his room. Joe didn't want to go, but his uncle convinced him that he would sleep with Mina and look after her.

Joe, deep inside, knew better.

At sunrise, his uncle and the family woke Joe up and told him that during the night his mother had died.

Time stopped. He sat very still for a long moment and then went and sat by Nelly on the floor. Joe wanted to cry. His mother was gone forever, but the tears wouldn't come. Something inside of him wouldn't allow any emotion to break. Maybe it was the heavy responsibility placed upon a boy so young, knowing that he and Nelly were all that was left of their family, at least his immediate family. His father and sister were gone and had no idea where they were, and how would he ever find out.

Later – he wasn't aware how long – Joe stood, took his little sister by the hand and walked to the door and then outside. He had to be where there was sunlight and warmth. Some of the fear of the future went away, and was replaced by the fact that there was still family – not brother, sister or mother – but family that would look after them. After all, his uncle was wise enough to know that Joe was too young to look after both him and his sister alone.

The next day Mina was buried, as Joe and his family stood beneath the long shadows of a solitary tree on a hill just beyond the camp. Her grave, like that of so many refugees who perished in Siberia, remained unmarked. Strangely, Joe remembered back to the day he and Nelly and his mother had left their Cologne apartment and started this long journey. He thought of the apartment key she had carefully placed in her pocket and how he had, at that moment, believed that they would one day return and live the happy life he remembered. He had believed, but if that wasn't true, then there was nothing to believe. He wondered if she had kept it all this time? Joe's uncle told him that the son should say the *Kaddish*, the mourner's prayer, over her grave. Joe didn't know how. 'So, one of my cousins taught me how to do it.'

> *May His Great Name grow exalted and sanctified*
> *in the world that He created as He willed…*
> *He Who makes peace in His heights,*
> *May He make peace,*
> *Upon us and upon all Israel.*
> *Amen.*

According to Jewish tradition, sons are required to recite the prayer at the funeral and for eleven months after the death of a parent.

'I said it once', Joe admits.[121]

11

Tashkent: Death Lingers

Joe's uncle was kind enough to help bury their mother, but after that, over the next several days, it became clear to Joe that he was on his own to face new responsibilities. Amidst the stinging hurt of losing his mother, Joe realized that he had learned a hard fact of suffering in the camp. When the goal was to survive, brother, sister and mother meant everything; the immediate family always came first, a hard and fast rule. As conditions worsened, outside the inner family circle, other family members were held at a distance. An incident several weeks after Mina's death made that fact painfully clear.

When their mother died, Joe's uncle suggested that Joe and Nelly would one day eat with the aunt, and then the next day they would eat with the uncle. So, the first day after they had eaten with the aunt the little amount of food that she had, Nelly and Joe walked out into the hall, and they looked at each other. 'We agreed that we were still hungry, so what we can do?' Joe came up with a solution, so they went to his uncle and Joe told him, 'that they hadn't eaten'. He stood up and yelled at Joe 'You are lying. You ate there today; you weren't to eat here today.' Then he back-handed Joe. Nelly cried, but Joe fought back the tears because he would have been embarrassed to cry. The strike hurt very badly, but in a way Joe couldn't blame him. Once Joe understood that he and Nelly were on their own, he vowed that he would never ever again depend on someone else to survive. 'Besides', Joe thought, 'if the old men's discussions were true, they would be leaving the camp and going south and that could mean better times.' Soon the deportees found out that this hopeful road they followed southward only led to more disappointment and even crueller hardship.

For the moment, though, Joe had all the problems he could handle.

He and Nelly were together but all alone. 'After my mother died, I was older than nine, not ten yet, and I felt like I'm a grown-up person because, nobody...nobody in our family was taking care of me when my mother died.'

Freedom was a distant dream if Joe even dreamed about it at all. For a boy so young, burdened with responsibilities even adults shouldn't carry, Joe tried to live one day at a time, unaware that more desperate trials were just ahead.

'And here I was…with me, and Nelly to take care of, which wasn't easy.'[122]

***

During those months preceding the evacuation out of the Soviet Union, Anders established headquarters in Buzuluk with his newly formed Polish 5th Infantry division camped in Tatishchevo and the 6th Infantry Division in Tockoje. In the early spring of 1942, a Polish military photograph was distributed to the western press showing Anders sitting in the snow, hands on knees, his exhausted eyes hidden behind sunglasses. Around him sat a group of his new Polish soldiers wearing British helmets, listening intently as the general discussed the evolving aspect of their purpose in the war. In the background, Soviets officers solemnly observed the conversation.

Besides facing the seemingly impossible task of evacuating so many soldiers, Anders had personally witnessed the deplorable conditions in which these civilian deportees lived in the camps surrounding the army camps. This had compelled the general to persuade the Soviets to allow as many refugees as logistically possible to accompany the military convoys. 'Conditions were appalling and training conditions primitive', one deportee wrote:

> The pledged rations of food, clothes and armaments rapidly diminished, leaving the Polish soldiers famished and in tatters. Forty thousand food rations were provided for up to one hundred thousand people….soldiers were reduced to roaming potato fields barefoot, gathering whatever was left in the ground. Polish children gathered, begging and searching through the military garbage for food.[123]

General Anders reported that staff doctors, medical orderlies and nurses worked with 'great self-sacrifice', struggling under awful conditions, without medicines, hospital accommodation, linen or suitable food. Accordingly, Anders issued orders that any Polish citizen who reported to the army camp would be included in the military transportation and nurseries and orphanages.

At the start, thousands of released Jewish prisoners and exiles gathered at the collection points, anxious to join the Polish army. The number was so great that within six months, Anders estimated that Jewish soldiers constituted 60 per cent of his army. As the merging of refugees, deportees, and Polish soldiers increased, anti-Semitism became as evident in Anders' army as it had been in the regular Polish army. Hesitant to express his view on the subject, Anders still felt compelled to write that considerable problems arose for while the army was being gathered when members of racial minorities, especially the Jews, began to pour into the camp. The problem existed within the ranks of the Polish soldiers because it was believed that some Polish Jews had welcomed the Soviet troops in late September 1939 as liberators instead of invaders. For many of the Polish soldiers who had suffered so much and lost friends and brothers in the fighting, this was 'difficult to overcome'. To deepen Anders's quandary, some Jewish politicians expressed their desire that the Jewish deportees be handled 'independently of the general Polish cause'.

It was rumoured that Anders had issued a secret Order of the Day, stating that he 'understood' his officers' concerns. He asked that they realize the sensitivities of Poland's allies and promised that after the war 'we shall deal with the Jewish problem in accordance with the size and independence of our homeland'. When the text was released several years later, Anders dismissed the document, calling it a forgery.[124]

Anders understood that this anti-Semitism reflected badly on his army, especially considering political relationships with Britain and America. Using his sharpened organizational skills and military precision to protect citizens, Anders saw that he could redeem himself, in the eyes of the Allies, concerning the deportees once the need arose. Unexpectedly, in late March, Anders received a telegram from the Polish government in exile ordering him to discontinue co-ordinating civilians to evacuate Russia along with his army. Anders reflects: 'On March 26, 1942, I received an unexpected and most unwelcome telegram from [Professor] Kot: "Information on evacuation of civilians with the army has spread causing a violent flood of people from the north and an uncontrollable movement southward. I request that you issue instructions for the evacuation to be organized as discreetly as possible in order to hamper the spreading of the news. Kot, Ambassador."'

Even when several days later he received another personal telegram from Ambassador Kot demanding that all families could be left behind, Anders made his decision.

> There was no time for long explanations and arguments by telegram: either I could save the civilian population or leave it to its fate. Evacuation might mean that some would die in Persia, but if they stayed in Russia, they would soon all be dead. I decided to take full responsibility, and that the evacuation of civilians should proceed as planned. Therefore, I did not cancel my orders and instructions.

This angered Anders because he realized that any Polish citizen who didn't leave Russia then would probably never do so. It was the only way to save them from starvation, and he had watched proudly as his soldiers, with limited rations, shared their portions with the deportees, a people who had 'gathered under the wing of the army for protection, aware that it was their only avenue of survival'.[125]

Soon, another disturbing situation confronted Anders. The Russians wanted to exclude Ukrainians, White Russians living in the eastern part of modern-day Belarus, and Jews from the ranks of those to leave with the Polish army. On 1 August Anders had a conference with Jewish authorities, advising them that the Soviets had limited the number of Jews who could leave with the army. However, in the end, over 4,000 Jews left Russia with Anders' army. For many years afterwards, Anders received letters from rabbis, Jewish leaders and Jewish citizens thanking him for saving their lives.

Aware that there was only one solution, in late October Anders realized just how important a moment like this was in his career. If it was within his power, no one would be left behind. He strongly expressed his decision that 'we were creating an entity which was the continuation of the former Polish army, all citizens; without distinctions of faith or nationality – should find a place in it'.[126]

With those decisions now behind him, Anders turned his attention to achieving the evacuation of soldiers and deportees as soon as possible. However, one worry continued to haunt him – he had secured information he considered inadequate concerning the disappearance of the 15,000 Polish officers who had vanished while prisoners of the Soviets. While organizing the Polish army, Anders found (in the Griasovietsk camp) only three officers of the units who had been under his command in Poland, though these three told Anders that many of his officers were located at the Starobielsk camp, and had been held until spring 1940.

Most the Polish officers captured after the invasion were confined in three camps located within Russian territory: Kozielsk to the east of Smolensk, Starobielsk near Kharkov and Ostashkov near Kalinin. Anders, in *An Army in Exile*, reported that:

> At the beginning of 1940 there were 5,000 men at Kozielsk (4,500 among them officers); 3,920 men at Starobielsk (all of them officers, with the exception of about 100 civilians, cadet-officers and ensigns); 6,750 men at Ostashkov, among them 380 officers and the rest N.C.O.'s, frontier guards, priests and public officers of Courts of Justice. Of all the above 15,000 prisoners of war, only 400 were released after the Polish-Soviet Agreement of July 30, 1941.[127]

To Anders and his staff, there was no obvious reason for the Russians to not let them know where these missing men were located. Fearing this unknown about his men, Anders initiated an investigation: 'On my own initiative', Anders writes, 'I sent Captain Jozef Czapski, a man of fine character who had been known to me for a very long time, to carry out a search for them throughout Russia, a most delicate mission. He had been a prisoner of war himself in Starobielsk and had a thorough knowledge of the problem of our officer prisoners of war.'

Anders was confident he had chosen in Czapski the best man to head the investigation. A Polish artist, author and critic, Czapski became an excellent officer in the Polish army. Raised on his family manor of Przluki, near Minsk, he began his military career in 1915 when he joined the cadet corps. He had served in both the 1st Krechowce Uhlan Regiment and the Polish I Corps. After the Russian Revolution in 1917, he moved to Poland and studied at the Academy of Fine Arts in Warsaw. In 1920, he joined the Polish Army and, being a pacifist, asked for duties that wouldn't involve fighting.

Later, he studied at the Academy of Fine Arts in Krakow until 1924, when he moved to Paris and shifted his work to writing essays on philosophy, art, and literature. Returning to Poland in 1939, Czapski re-enlisted, was captured by the Russians, and interned in prison and labour camps, where his health suffered. After the German invasion of the Soviet Union, he joined Anders and worked tirelessly at his new task of investigating the mysterious disappearance of the Polish officers.

Even Czapski failed to uncover any information on the officers. 'Alas, his long search was completely in vain', Anders conceded.

> …His long and painstaking enquires produced nothing. Nor had the Poles reporting for service in the Polish army from all parts of Russia been able to tell us what had happened to the missing officers…All we knew for certain was that there had been no news of any one of the 15,000 missing officers since the spring of 1940.' From the officers who had been held in the Griasovietsk camp, Anders learned that that the three camps were broken up in the spring of 1940, the prisoners from them 'taken in batches to an unknown destination'.[128]

***

One gray, overcast morning two months after his mother died, Joe Rosenbaum looked out the barracks window. People were walking out of the camp, a long line of exhausted refugees, trudging along on foot and covered with rags as though each step took the last bit of their strength. They were gray-faced, uncertain of their destiny, and covered in sores, and most of their hair was gone.

No one came for Joe and Nelly, no one approached their section of the barracks and told the young children to come with them, and that they were all going to freedom. Joe knew that he and his sister should go with them also, and he went about gathering what food morsels he could find as Nelly stood in the middle of the room watching him as he wrapped the food scraps in a rag and placed them in his jacket pocket. He found two blankets; he wrapped one around Nelly's shoulders and then one around himself.

Then he took Nelly's hand, and they simply walked out of the camp following the refugees. Later, as they were down the road, one of the older men told them that they were walking to a town where they would catch a train.

After several days they came to the town the old man had told him about. The misery that they stumbled into was bleak, and many refugees wondered if maybe they would have been better off staying in the Siberian camps. There were thousands of refugees and hundreds of Polish soldiers who had been released from prisons without food or water.

Eugenia Huntingdon, the daughter of a Russian White Guard officer whose husband was a Polish prisoner of war, was deported from her home and elegant lifestyle in Warsaw during 1939 and had lived in the camps outside northern Kazakhstan. Released during the amnesty, she boarded a train that spring in a small town crowded with soldiers and described the appalling scene:

> What I saw was a collection of skeletons covered in rags, their feet wrapped in newspaper or dirty cloth kept in place with pieces of string, although many had nothing on their feet at all. There was not a normal face to be seen. They were either very thin, the colour and texture of yellow parchment, or bloated and shapeless like the face of a drowning man. Their eyes were sunken and either completely lifeless or glowing feverishly. They all looked old and shrivelled although some of them, at least, must have been young.[129]

While the train journey that brought them to the brutal Siberian forest remains a vivid memory many years later, for a depressed and sick Joe those weeks in which he travelled southward out of Siberia remained an obscure shadow in his memory.

These refugees' journey would take them south in conditions that were all too familiar. Little food and no facilities were a shock to many because they thought that once they departed Siberia things would become better.

Instead, the food supply was terrible with only a half loaf of bread for each person. Sick people were littered throughout the cramped train cars, and lice covered everyone. Typhoid and dysentery plagued the refugees and with no restrooms other than a hole in the floor, or outside while waiting for the train, one had only a moment to jump outside and relieve themselves. Each time the train halted, Joe would stare out the window as dead children were brought off the train and tossed to the side of the tracks.

It was on the train where Joe again heard the men talking about now that they were free to go anywhere they desired, where were they to go? Poland was torn apart with the war, and Germany was out of the question, of course. Many of the younger men had left the camp once amnesty was announced to join the Polish army, leaving behind mainly women, old men and children, most of whom were ill.

Fear and anticipation swept through the refugees, not knowing what lay ahead at the end of the train trip, and because of their living conditions – cold, hunger and filth – travelling was horribly slow. Often the trains were pulled aside to make way on the tracks for long lines of flatbed cars loaded with thousands of Russian troops, clad in summer-issue brown cotton tunics, heading toward the advancing German army.

Several of the men discussed meeting up with the Polish army somewhere to the south. Other men said they would all go to Iran with the soldiers. Joe thought this was good because once they were there maybe he and Nelly could get to Palestine, where his uncle lived, or maybe even America, where they could find their father.

Other than the few conversations Joe could overhear, he didn't pay much attention to the world going on around him, just like when they first arrived in Siberia. Now, his life was worse. He was hungry and he was watching over Nelly. 'Where we go, why we go…if we go, I didn't care.'[130]

***

Tashkent, meaning 'Stone City' in Russian, was in the South Kazakhstan region near the Syr Darya River. This was Joe's destination although, of course, he had absolutely no idea when he left Siberia or exactly where he and Nelly would end up.

Known as the centre of Islamic culture, the capital of Uzbekistan in the late 1930s was an educational oasis with theatres, museums and universities. By late spring of 1942, however, Tashkent had descended into a hellish place flooded with destitute, starving refugees without a place to live and where very little food was available. 'The Uzbek part of the town had probably once been beautiful, but now it was in ruins. Dilapidated houses, with Eastern arches and canopies, courtyards with mulberry, almond or bread-fruit trees, and half-demolished mosques decorated with a few blue enameled tiles, bore witness to the old culture.'[131]

For those new arrivals who had money, street vendors offered *shashlik* (mutton cooked on iron grills dripping with fat), *uruk* (small fruit similar to olives) and *kyshmysh* (raisins and walnuts). For those arriving without any money, there was a diet of nettles, hog-weed, stolen fruits and even lizards and crows.

For the Jews like Joe and Nelly, there were no assistance or government programmes in place, mainly because the agencies that would normally assist people with such needs were simply overwhelmed. One witness described what the refugees appeared like as they entered the city:

> ...in rags, impoverished, covered with sores, louse-infested, with hair...resembling rather some strange creatures more than human beings. Death and disease smothered the city. Crews rode through the streets and picked up corpses with a pitchfork, tossing them on sleighs, and drove them outside the city. Then they threw the bodies on a pile, poured crude oil on them, and burned them. Many of the Jewish men tried to enlist in the Polish army, but they weren't accepted. Instead, they wandered the streets filled with despairing refugees with no hope of shelter, very little food and water, and disease. Large pictures of Stalin were painted on the buildings, the dictator staring down on those lost souls.[132]

As Joe led Nelly off the train, he instantly knew from the scene around him that life in Tashkent wouldn't be any better. Fear rose up in him that surviving there would be even harder. There was an endless parade of refugees wandering about, the throng so thick that it shocked Joe. 'When we came there, we got off the train and it looked like a billion people. It was endless, and it was so thick that in the whole city there was not a place to walk, or stand, or to lie down. So many people came here.'[133]

However, this wasn't the first time Tashkent had faced such disasters. In 1219 the city was destroyed by Genghis Khan, the military leader of the Mongol Empire. Rebuilt in the following years, Tashkent was conquered by the Russian Empire, and under Soviet rule witnessed growth in both economy and population. Shortly after Hitler's attack on the Soviet Union, Tashkent, located in a key position in central Asia, became a gathering place for evacuees from various war zones, increasing its population to well over one million persons.

Joe wandered through the overcrowded streets, Nelly holding tightly onto his hand. He heard that they should register, but Joe didn't know where or how to register, which meant that they wouldn't receive any food. Within days after they arrived in Tashkent, typhoid broke out on the streets, 'as if a wind came through bringing the disease, and everybody got sick.' Joe quickly assessed the situation that he and his sister were in. 'So, when you have no food, and you have no money to buy food, you're in big trouble.'[134]

The United States and Britain provided supplies, but many items were scarce – blankets, clothing, and medicines were limited. Some found shelter in stables and barns, others in cellars, lean-to-shacks and mud huts. Officials reported that many of the deportees 'lived under open skies and slept directly on unpaved alleys in freezing weather. Whole families were emaciated by outbreaks of malaria, dysentery, and typhus.'

Although the refugees died from an assortment of diseases, typhus was one of the most feared because it spread so quickly. The disease killed thousands of the Polish refugees, among the victims hundreds of the Tehran Children, not only in Tashkent but until they reached the safety of Palestinian camps where medical facilities could help treat the malady. During the war, millions died from typhus. It was prevalent in the German POWs who surrendered at Stalingrad, in the ghettos where there were no hygienic conditions and in the Nazi concentration camps. After the liberation of Bergen-Belsen Concentration Camp in late 1944, mass graves of those who died of typhus were uncovered. Those who died included Anne Frank, the fifteen-year-old girl from Amsterdam who attained fame when her diary was published in the 1950s, along with her nineteen-year-old sister, Margot.

The refugees were forced to fight these threatening illnesses without physicians or medicines. They struggled to make their own version of basic medicines, such as penicillin, by soaking a piece of bread in cold water and placing it on the sick person's forehead. The loss of teeth, brought on by malnourishment, was also rampant, and any tooth that became diseased was pulled, without anesthesia most of the time, to prevent further infection.

After several days, Joe eventually found who remained of his family, left Nelly with them, went out into the streets, and instinctively did what now was natural for him – roaming for food. He searched for any food scraps thrown away, anything edible, because by then many of the refugees lived on collecting peanuts and boiling them for soup. An elderly refugee remembered the chaos of the city:

> I went to the city park, where men, women, and children slept on and under the bench...children both with and without parents. The orphans, or those who had been abandoned, were concentrated in

institutions specifically established for that purpose, until some solution could be found for them. Poles were given absolute priority in the orphanages: I saw sick and hungry Jewish children wandering abandoned in the streets. It was a heartbreaking sight. I saw one of the local inhabitants gathering a few destitute children and teaching them to pick pockets. With the agility of hungry wolf cubs, these children spread out in the marketplaces and bread depots, snatching and grabbing food from other unfortunates. Turmoil and confusion prevailed in the city, everyone trying to survive, sometimes at the expense of others. Virtually the only government aid extended to the thousands of refugees was soup kitchens set up at various points in the city. The portion of bread and soup they handed out was only enough to prevent death by starvation.[135]

Non-Jewish Polish refugees and those who still had money fared much better, finding their way outside of Tashkent where their new home would be a Polish camp. At Dzael-Abad they were met by Polish soldiers, many dressed in Russian uniforms. Each family lived in a small tent and was given two meals a day consisting of soup, bread and milk for the children. They slept on the ground, with only a single piece of clothing for a pillow. Because many of those in the camps were Polish, and the Polish army had been released from Soviet prisons, the men were encouraged to join the army.

As rough as it appeared for the refugees, no one complained. These refugees had been informed by the soldiers that a ship was coming soon to take them out of Russia and deliver them to camps in Iran. Some of the men had travelled into the city and came back reporting the deplorable circumstances in which the Jews were suffering and dying. Many of these men simply couldn't describe the conditions and the sorrow they witnessed.

Conditions worsened.

For the Jews in Tashkent there was little opportunity, but some fortunate ones were sent out of the city to collective farms, only endless dry fields. As these refugees heard of the Polish army being assembled in Tashkent, and the rumour of civilian transports leaving Russia, they made their way back to the city.

***

Joe 'hunted for food like a dog', scrounging for scraps and anything for him and his sister to eat to keep their strength up. When he wandered down the streets, he would glance in the windows and see the most amazing sight – people seated in restaurants eating their meals! Joe couldn't believe people had money and all the food they wanted to eat, while just outside the window the Jews were starving to death.

It was in Tashkent, more so than in Siberia, where at least there were mushrooms and wild fruits to gather, where Joe truly learned the basic instincts of survival. On the sidewalks in front of the restaurants, Joe honed his art of begging. He, along with the other children, also learned other valuable lessons. Reading through discarded newspapers, they found the addresses where birthday parties and wedding receptions were being held. Aware that extra food was simply tossed out into back ally trash cans when the celebrations were over. 'Everybody got sick and there was no work', Joe recalls of those days in Tashkent, 'so I had to go out and steal a little bit, beg a little bit, find a little bit in the places where they had food. When other children my age, between seven and eleven, went to school, I hunted for food – I was like an animal, looking for food.'

For months Joe and Nelly were able to eat and survive on these food morsels that Joe was able to gather. It was never enough to eat, though, and Joe was hungry all the time, every day, every morning, and every night when he went to bed.

Because of that hunger, a selfish habit began to creep into Joe's mind, a self-regarding blackness that would live with him for many years after his journey was over. He never meant for it to have the results that this greediness finally caused. When he did come across scraps of food, a piece of meat, perhaps a remainder of a slice of cake, a bread crumb, he would take it back and he and Nelly would divide it. At least in the beginning. But as the portions shrank, and the food became scarce, there just wasn't enough. In time, Joe ate the food when he found it – in an alleyway, curled up behind a trash bin – not taking Nelly her half, but instead maybe only a small portion.

Several weeks later, the family decided to go farther north into Kazakhstan. Grandfather and Joe's mother had died in Siberia. Now there were Joe and Nelly, along with Yechen and Paola and Shlomo, and there was the grandmother and some aunts and uncles, making nine. There were also members of the Locker family who had joined them.

Once they made their way to Turkistan, 'the Land of Turks', they signed up with the Russians who sent them to a commune, a *kolkhoz*, a large farm community outside of the city where everyone worked together. They paid the government with the food they grew, and the workers got the leftovers to live on. The large farm was divided into a European side containing the caucasian people and the other side containing Asians, Mongolians and Chinese. The latter didn't like the Poles because to these people they were like the Russians, people who wanted to rule them. They didn't help them but they didn't bother them, either.

At the *kolkhoz*, the family could live in a round building, two families, about twenty people, lying on the floor with little room around them. Because all of Joe's family was registered, they were able to work for food, usually a rationing of wheat kernels. Joe learned quickly the basic rule of the *kolkhoz*: if one arrived without money and for some reason couldn't work for money, then he died. The family was allotted an amount of wheat for the entire family, so he didn't know, being so young, what his portion should be. All he knew was that he and Nelly were given wheat. Joe took their portion, learned how to grind it and cook it with water and maybe a little salt, making it into porridge.

Still, it wasn't enough to eat, and every day Joe watched people leave the *kolkhoz* searching for food. Joe remembers that one family of a doctor, his wife and a child simply disappeared one morning. The Locker family decided, also, that it was best if they left for Turkistan, a city where other refugees hunted for food and work. The problem was that they hadn't told anyone else in the family of their plan, and several weeks later, they simply slipped away in the night without letting anyone know.

This all was happening around *Pesach*, or Passover. Amidst this confused scene of hunger, death and suffering, an incident unfolded that haunts Joe to this day.

Joe didn't pay much attention to *Pesach*. He was busy living from day to day, simply getting his portion of flour, cooking it for Nelly and himself to eat. To supplement their food, Joe went into the village and begged, but no one ever gave him anything to eat. He would hunt the alleyways and the garbage for any food scrap. The hunger pains were terrible, and he saw Nelly getting weaker also. Early one morning before sunrise, Nelly reached over, touched Joe's arm, and told him that she was very hungry and wanted Joe to get up and cook the wheat he had ground the day before. Joe insisted that it was too early, that if they ate now they wouldn't have it for later. Besides, everyone else was still asleep. He told Nelly to go back to sleep, and when they woke up, then they would eat. They both went back to sleep.

Joe jerked fully awake.

The room was too still. An awkward silence hung in the air.

Looking around the room and seeing that everyone was still asleep, Joe tried to go back to sleep. But the room was too quiet. He looked at Nelly, and she was on her side, bowed up in an odd position. She always slept on her back, her small hands curled up on either side of her face. Joe got up, poured the wheat into water, and built a fire so he would cook the wheat, while he remembered that she had awakened him in the middle of the night.

Well, now she could eat. Once the water was boiling on the fire, Joe went over and touched Nelly's face to gently awaken her.

Her skin was ice cold.

Joe pulled back in horror, the reality of the unkind touch of death slamming in his mind. He remembered how his mother was so cold the morning she died. Joe sat back on the bed, and the thoughts flooded over him. She had been starving to death, and he hadn't recognized it. Why hadn't he seen it? Why hadn't she told him that she was more than hungry, that she was sick…he would later recall that in this room full of death, after Joe had awakened everyone telling them that Nelly had died, none of the older people spoke to Joe. Instead they whispered among themselves as Joe sat in the corner, alone and dazed. He began blaming himself, but how was he to know that she was starving?

Then the older people decided. They didn't discuss it with Joe, didn't ask his opinion and if they had, could he have said anything to change their mind? Instead, they made a choice concerning Nelly's death, one that would burn a painful scar in Joe's soul that would take many years to even begin to heal.[136]

***

That night, for the first time since Joe could remember, he dreamed of home, the apartment on Alexander Strasse. He dreamed he went back there, and only his father was there to greet him. When he awoke from the dream, Joe realized that Cologne didn't matter anymore, both Mother and Nelly were gone, Father was far away in America, and he was all alone. Going home meant nothing. Besides, he admitted to himself, it was the Germans who had killed his mother and sister. It was the Germans who were responsible for the pain and sorrow in his life. He hated the Germans.

It was then that Joe swore to himself, that if he did somehow manage to survive to see Palestine, he would never go back to Germany ever again.

12

Journey to Pahlavi

If Air Marshal A.T. Harris, commander-in-chief of the Bomber Command of the British Royal Air Force (RAF) had any say in the matter, there wouldn't be a home in Cologne, Germany for Joe to return to after the war.

Arthur Travers Harris was known as 'Bomber' Harris and 'Butcher' Harris within the ranks of the RAF – nicknames well deserved. Harris was appointed Officer Commanding the RAF, assigned to carry out Churchill's policies and to implement Britain's shattering bombing of German cities. Harris, urging the British government to be open and honest with the English people, spoke of the purpose of the bombings:

> The aim of the Combined Bomber Offensive...should be unambiguously stated [as] the destruction of the German cities, the killing of German workers, and the disruption of civilized life throughout Germany...The destruction of houses, public utilities, transport and lives, the creation of a refugee problem on an unprecedented scale, and the breakdown of morale both at home and at the battlefronts by fear of extended and intensified bombing, are accepted and intended aims of our bombing policy. They are not by-products of attempts to hit factories.[137]

Three thousand and five hundred miles from Tashkent where Joe struggled to survive, allied forces had begun pounding Germany unmercifully with bombing raids co-ordinated with American and British warplanes as early as the second week of May 1940. Within two years, as the Luftwaffe lost control of the skies, the Allies stepped up their bombing campaigns against the Third Reich.

On 30 May 1942, Cologne fell under the bombing of over a thousand British bombers. Delivering 1,500 tons of bombs in a 90-minute raid, the attack delivered a troubling shock to the morale of the Germans within the medieval city. Once the British bombers had turned back westward over the channel and to England, officials assessed the damage. It was devastating. Over 600 acres sustained heavy damage, 45,000 citizens were suddenly homeless, 5,027 were wounded and 469 were killed. More importantly to Air

Marshal Harris, *Operation Millennium* had delivered the desired results from the attack. Machinery and chemical industry locations were destroyed to the point that they were useless to the Nazi war effort. The British cost of the raid was 43 aircraft.

Harris had warned, quoting the Old Testament of the Bible from Hosea 8:7, of such destruction upon the German population:

> The Nazis entered this war under the rather childish delusion that they were going to bomb everyone else, and nobody was going to bomb them. At Rotterdam, London, Warsaw, and half a hundred other places, they put their rather naïve theory into operation. They sowed the wind, and now they are going to reap the whirlwind.[138]

Amid the smoke and fire of destruction, the smouldering rubble and the swollen bodies of the dead, the giant cathedral that Joe and his father had often admired stood practically undamaged after fourteen hits. The stained-glass windows had been removed months earlier by German officials, and stored in a safe place with plans to replace them after the war.

The twin spiral towers, easily recognizable as navigational landmarks utilized by British bombers, still stood pointing skyward.

Before the war ended, Cologne was bombed in 262 separate air raids, causing Martha Gellhorn, American novelist and war correspondent, to write when she visited the city in March 1945, two months before Germany surrendered: 'Cologne felt like one of the great morgues in the world.'[139]

***

Almost six months after Nelly died, during those two to four weeks surrounding the time of *Rosh Hashanah* (Feasts of Trumpets celebrating the Jewish New Year), the Lockers came and gathered their older parents and the young children, and took them to the city 30 kilometres away. They left without telling anyone. 'My Uncle Nachman was very upset. They were in another hut, like we were, but farther out, maybe two hundred feet away, and they were gone.'[140]

Uncle Nachman designed a plan where he would go to the city and find them. 'Nachman was a 34-year-old man, and Paola was a 19-year-old beautiful, tall young woman', Joe says, a fact he learned later. 'He liked her.' But Paola insisted that she wouldn't go without her brother, Shlomo. So, Uncle Nachman, Chana, Paola and Shlomo left, promising that they would return with a wagon and horse and get Joe and the others whom they had left behind. Now, there were four weak and sick people in the hut: Joe, his grandmother, Yechen and Chana's husband, Avraham. How long Uncle Nachman and the others were gone, Joe had no idea because he was sick, fading in and out of consciousness with a high fever. Also, it was about this time that a profound depression came over him because of Nelly's death. All he knew was that he was very ill, and the others had promised to come back for them in a few days.

The first to die was Joe's grandmother, and then a few days later, Yechen. Joe, as weak and sick as he was, dragged himself out of the hut and hunted for some food, for he knew he would die also if he didn't. He didn't bother bringing food for Avraham because he was religious, and he wouldn't eat it anyway.

Then one morning, Joe was simply too weak to go out and search for food. His grandmother and aunt were dead in the same room, and Avraham was dying slowly. Joe faded in and out of consciousness, losing track of time. He was bleeding when he went to the bathroom because of dysentery. He had a fever also, from typhus. For the first time since leaving Germany, Joe honestly thought that he was going to die. 'I was a kid. I just know that me and Avraham were lying in the same hut with two dead people. We might have been there two days; we might have been there two weeks.'

Joe jarred awake, fever racking his frail body. His eyes were swollen and he couldn't see past several feet, but he sensed a shadow, someone moving around in the hut. 'I was awakened by Nachman, and he looked around and he saw what he saw. He saw his mother dead. Yechen was dead.' Joe didn't remember what his uncle did with the two bodies, but later he took Joe and Avraham, placed them in a wagon, and they left the *kolkhoz*. They reached the city in just over a day, and his uncle took him to a house where some of the Lockers now stayed because as a family they now lived in two different places. Shmuel, the father, instructed one of his daughters, nineteen-year-old Rivka, to take Joe to the hospital. Because Joe was so emaciated, Rivka lifted Joe in her arms and walked three kilometres carrying Joe to the hospital. 'All I remember is that they lived in the new city and near a railroad track. And that Rivka dropped me off at the hospital.'

Gradually from his hospital bed, Joe began to improve because of the medicines given to him. 'In the hospital, I was put in a bed, and I was treated, and I came to myself again.' It had now been eight months since Nelly had died, and Joe hardly remembered a day since that time. Except for Avraham, Joe didn't see much of the family as he gradually grew stronger. Now Joe realized that he had a problem, however, because if he was determined to be well by the doctors, he would have to leave the hospital, which meant he would leave a bed with sheets, food and a place to stay. The hospital was very well organized, people walked around, and one couldn't separate who were patients or visitors. Among this confusion, Joe started walking around, and met some other Jewish boys and girls. They discussed how Joe didn't really want to leave the hospital, and the comfortable bed and food. If the doctors thought he was well, then he would have to go to a camp that wasn't so comfortable. So, his new friends gave him something to drink that made him violently sick, though Joe would never know what it was.

In the spring of 1942, amidst these crowded deportee centres, there was very little access to news, so people learned of the war situation from a constant swirl of rumour. People talked, but one never knew how much to believe, such as the rumour Joe heard that soon every child who was living in an orphanage nearby would go to Tehran, Iran in Persia. They were also told that soon they would travel from Tehran to Palestine, a place of interest to Joe. As a child, he didn't know much about Palestine except that his mother's brother lived there. From what Joe remembered as a small boy, it was all confusing. When his family still lived in Cologne, Joe, hiding under the table, would hear his mother tell people that her husband went to America and that her brother Anschel went to Palestine. Joe had no formal education and didn't know reading, writing or geography, so he had to make his own assumptions. With all the talk he heard those years ago, Joe figured Palestine was close to America. That was why it was important to Joe to figure out a way to get to the orphanage and go to Palestine. Then he would be near America and his father.

This opportunity to leave Tehran presented Joe with another problem. To be in the orphanage, a child had to be Polish. Joe spoke a little Polish but spoke Yiddish well. There were Jews, especially in rural areas that spoke very little Polish, but spoke Yiddish. They didn't speak Yiddish at the orphanage because they were Christian. They wrote in Polish, though, and that was the opportunity Joe needed to make his plan work to get into the orphanage.

Joe, along with three other boys, slipped over a hospital fence with broken glass placed along the top and went to the orphanage. The officials wanted as many children as were available, so they took them in. Joe was horrified to learn that the reason the orphanage wanted Jews was to convert them, and that's what they tried to do with Joe from the day he arrived there. They thought that if these Jewish boys were young enough to influence and weren't educated yet, they could be converted to Christianity without much problem.

To the orphanage officials, Joe was an excellent candidate because they saw he didn't read or write, spoke Yiddish and knew only broken Polish, so they started at the beginning. Joe remembers those prayers taught to him in the orphanage to this day, learning them by heart because he knew he had to stay in the orphanage and go to Palestine. He learned the hymns, too. 'This was a Catholic orphanage run by priests, which meant you didn't get food until you crossed yourself and sang the hymns', so Joe played the game, amazed that some of the children with a deeper background in religious Judaism refused to. Joe told the nuns, 'I'll do anything you want me to do; I want to eat. I'll do anything. I'll praise Jesus. I'll do anything as long as you give me food.' Joe got his food, which wasn't that good, but it kept him alive.

When within two days the children had not started towards Tehran, Joe grew restless and upset, thinking maybe he'd made a bad decision. The hospital had been, after all, a good deal with better food and a good bed and everything he needed. Here at the orphanage, besides the bad food, a religion he didn't want was being forced on him. Joe was disappointed, but he decided to stay.

During the next two months in the orphanage, while everyone waited for the trains that would take them to Persia, Joe again lost track of time. He had always kept an internal calendar in his mind by co-ordinating events with holidays. He knew his mother had died five weeks before *Rosh Hashanah*, and he knew Nelly died during *Pesach*. To Joe, what was important was that during those two months he learned some Polish, sang the songs and said his prayers, and the priests fed him three meals a day. No matter where Joe was, however, he found that he couldn't escape the prejudice against him and the other Jewish children. Life in the orphanage was just as in the camps where the other boys knocked him down and took his berries and mushrooms. 'There were some rough kids who didn't like me because I was Jewish, and they came behind me and hit my plate from under my hands.'

In early August there was a sudden announcement that created a stir of excitement that finally they were all going to Persia. Priests, adult helpers and the children hurriedly prepared themselves to leave. One morning, just that quickly, the orphans were herded on foot to the train station, and many were brought in carts.

When they got there, Joe was pleasantly surprised. Somewhere in the back of his mind, he feared they would again travel in the dreaded cattle cars, ones like they had travelled in to Siberia, and relive the deplorable conditions of no food or water. He was surprised when he saw that real trains awaited them, and his heart lifted at the sight of deportees loading into the cars, laughing and crying, as they scrambled to find a seat.

Everyone was so excited, though the train cars were packed with a lot of people. Persia was a place that had been promised them, and from there Palestine and home. Why wouldn't everyone be excited?

But there was a problem, a big problem.

Since being forced out of Poland, most of his travels had been on trains, mostly the cattle trains. Joe was experienced with trains, and even as a young boy, he knew a train needed one thing to be sure to travel. He had noticed the thing missing when they loaded them. Without it, a train went nowhere. That meant that today they weren't leaving for Persia, Joe was certain of that.

There was no locomotive.

Despite this situation, the authorities promised the deportees that soon they would leave on the train. Instead of being excited like the others, Joe tried to remember everything that had happened in Siberia, where even as a small boy, Joe realized his life, if he survived, would be full of trouble for a long time. He remembered all of that, because Joe thought he should. If he closed his eyes, Joe could see a single, barren tree on a hill outside the camp, where his mother was buried. And finally, sitting on the train that wasn't going anywhere, at least for the moment, a deeper sadness came to his heart again, as he realized that, as he moved southward with thousands of other homeless refugees, he was leaving behind little Nelly.

***

Because there wasn't a locomotive, between meals and school classes on the train, Joe left the train to see his family. He found Shlomo and convinced his cousin to join him, that he would fit in. 'You speak Polish like me', Joe told him, 'and you can learn the crossing of yourself and the Catholic prayers. You can come to Persia, and then to Palestine.' Joe also told him that there were rumours that once in Tehran they would be placed in a Jewish orphanage. Shlomo wouldn't leave his sister Paola who was alone and very ill. She couldn't walk and was swollen, suffering from dysentery and typhus. Also, there was now a man in her life who cared very much for her. Much later they would marry, so Paola convinced her brother to go with Joe.

When Joe and Shlomo arrived back at the train station, at last a locomotive had arrived, and confusion swirled through the crowds. Joe and his cousin quickly learned that orders had been issued that the Jewish children were going to be left behind. The children wept openly, and a priest stepped in and convinced the authorities to take all the children who were at the station. From that one incident, the Jewish children learned not to take freedom for granted and to stop speaking Yiddish.

Several days later, the train, packed full of refugees including Joe and Shlomo, took them to Krasnovodsk on the Caspian Sea. There, Joe witnessed Polish soldiers being loaded on Soviet oil tankers like the *Agamali Ogly* or packed on ramshackle cargo ships. When it was apparent that there wouldn't be enough ships, officials put the civilians on with the soldiers, and in many cases the soldiers only had enough room to stand. Both soldiers and civilians, despite what they had lived through in Siberia, were stunned at the conditions in Krasnovodsk. An older refugee remembered:

> There, without protection from the intense sun and heat, we waited all day to board the ship. Heaven and earth created such intense heat that it became painful to breathe. Instead of a cool sea breeze, our lungs were filled with the foul odour of oil from the Baku oilfields. We could not even reach the water itself because the shoreline and sea were covered in oil.[141]

Despite the conditions, Joe understood that the trip across the Caspian Sea meant freedom.

One Polish soldier wrote of the first sights he watched upon reaching Port Pahlavi, a city that Joe would soon look upon:

> The first most exciting sight to me in Port Pahlavi was the Persian flag on the ships in port, showing a Lion and Sun. For the first time I saw a different flag, not the hated and feared hammer and sickle symbol anymore!! It convinced me that I was definitely not in the USSR. I was so happy that I was now in the normal, human world again, where people were free – not in the Soviet world of lawlessness, violence, hypocrisy and hatred to human beings.[142]

The next morning Joe departed across the Caspian Sea aboard the *SS Zhdanov,* accompanied by other children who were looked upon by the crew as a pitiful sight.

> They [the children] were pale, gaunt, and famished. They had a haunted expression in their eyes…they were like little battle-weary soldiers, exhausted by gunfire, expulsion, imprisonment and wandering across Siberia's endless, forgotten wastelands…dragged through like beasts in cattle trucks. A rheumy-eyed horde, bleary with the inflammations that were wreaking havoc with them; riddled with boils, ringworm, scabies – defecating in public, unable to control their bowels because of intestinal and stomach diseases….standing in long queues for a piece of bread, a little soup.[143]

***

The largest group of refugees arrived in Pahlavi on 31 August 1942.

Until 1935, the harbour town on the sea was known as Bandar-e Anzali ('bandar' meaning port) where Anders' Polish army disembarked in an operation that began in April and ended in October 1942. During the two-week stay, the housing was basic; the children slept in tents, and as with most of their other journeys, food and medical supplies were scarce.

Anders had travelled from Tehran to Pahlavi several days before, and his memoir didn't mention the horrid conditions the Jews suffered on the beach:

> On August 28 I went from Teheran to Pahlavi to visit the military and civilian camps there, and I saw the arrival of new transports from Russia. It was heartening to see these emaciated men, women, and children express their joy at being free again, [and to] dash down to bathe in the sea, and splash gleefully in the water. All showed the effects of starvation, misery, and disease. As Pahlavi was in the Russian zone of occupation, we could not avoid seeing Soviet soldiers, but we were outside the boundaries of Russia, and the people could express themselves without restraint. It was a most moving experience to share their new happiness with them, and one I shall never forget. I consented to take a march past the troops on the beach, a parade probably unique of its kind.[144]

That morning, Anders gazed upon strange sights along the beach. Naked Polish soldiers, stripped of clothing and squatting, were waiting to be deloused. Farther down the beach, soldiers who had passed through the process milled around dressed in new uniforms.

Within the next week, wire services distributed an encouraging photograph dated 5 April 1942, from that part of the war zone where news correspondents, it seemed, were constantly dispatching bad news. The picture showed a priest standing before a communion table positioned in an open area on the Pahlavi beach. On three sides were formations of Polish soldiers, showered, deloused and dressed in crisply-starched British uniforms. In the foreground, neat stacks of backpacks, helmets and weapons were lined out in the sand. It was the first Easter service for the Polish soldiers since the invasion of their country in September 1939.

Anders was inspired by what he witnessed along the beach. His spirit lifted, he wrote upon leaving: 'I returned from Pahlavi by the most beautiful road I have ever seen, the Shah's road connecting Pahlavi with Teheran.'[145]

Upon his return to headquarters in Buzuluk, Anders had a visitor. Eugenia Huntingdon, the wife of a missing Police officer, had arrived in Buzuluk several months before in the brutal cold. She had written about the 'collection of skeletons' she had seen at the village as the refugees flooded southward. 'His office was situated outside the perimeters of the camp in a building which in the past must have belonged to a local bigwig and, although neglected, preserved traces of former elegance,' she wrote. 'There was a lot of activity in the building, and the sight of the Polish uniforms made my heart beat faster.'[146]

Eugenia explained to Anders, who she had known in Poland as the commander of a cavalry regiment, that she was seeking information about her missing husband. When she explained that he was an officer and had been missing since the September Campaign, Anders' expression changed. It was the first time that Eugenia heard of the 15,000 missing officers, as Anders explained that he had conducted a thorough investigation and had uncovered no evidence of where his officers were located.

Seeing the disappointment on Eugenia's face, Anders assured her that he wouldn't give up until the officers were returned. In fact, his men were working on the last information that the Soviets had given, that of the officers had been transported to camps in the far northern part of Siberia, and the brutal weather prohibited them travelling southward to meet his army.

***

The refugees departed Bandar-e Anzali by boat overnight from Russia to Persia. Joe and the others were assembled on deck where they were given some food. It was so cold that Joe climbed down a ladder and went to where the engine was, curled up next to the engine to find warmth and slept there for the night. 'In the morning I came up [on deck] and I was black from the engine's soot.'

The ship's journey lasted twenty-four hours.

Joe was standing at the rail when the ship docked at Port Pahlavi in Persia, watching small boats crowded with tanned, well-dressed, smiling people waving as they circled around them. He overheard several of the older children discussing 'it all seemed so unreal, like a wonderful dream. We are out of the hands of the communists and finally free.'[147]

The children disembarked from the boat onto wide moorings once it had docked where officials met the managers and the counsellors assigned to direct them from there. First, they were led to a transit camp near the port. They were placed in straw huts and worn tents that were brutally hot inside. The poorly-clothed and barefoot children were told to lie under torn rush-mat roofs on the beach where the sun was blazing, and there were only small amounts of drinking water. So much for wonderful dreams, Joe thought, as he lay in the hot sand among a line of other half-naked children. All they had done was to go from a harsh, cold Siberia, to a brutally hot Persia. They could all die here just as well as they could have frozen in the forests.

Conditions improved that afternoon as tins of cold bully beef, corned beef and concentrated milk, along with several truckloads of clothes arrived from America. Joe attacked the pile of food and came out with several cans, one of which was quickly hidden in his pocket. The Jews were always treated badly, always last on the list for any assistance; here in Persia the situation was no better. Always, no matter where they were, Joe saw the Jews as hated. In the Siberian camp, the Polish Jews didn't like him because he was a German Jew. In Pahlavi, it was no different. They were insulted and humiliated by both the Polish soldiers and the Russian soldiers assigned to guard the port. As always, the Jews waited. For the Polish refugees who weren't Jewish, however, arriving in Persia seemed like that wonderful dream of freedom from Siberia.

There was a hospital tent in the camp, but not one ill Jewish child was treated there. The Christian children wore better clothes, were medically treated and many were accompanied by their parents, while most of the Jewish children by now were considered orphans. As a last insult against the lingering heat, the Christian children were allowed to cool off by swimming in the sea near the camp. The Jewish children were kept at a distance.

One diary written by a deportee described:

> We were stripped naked in the baths – children and adults without exception. We were shaved in all areas where lice could lodge and multiply. Warm water was poured over us and we were punished with birches. Following such a bath, we emerged as God had made us. While we were bathing, all our clothes were burnt. We were given a blanket each with which to cover ourselves, and driven back to the beach…all our possessions, other than those in trunks, were burnt. Documents, photographs, other memorabilia…gone.[148]

After Joe and the children were showered and shaven, they were given clothes that often were too large for their emaciated bodies. Dysentery was still widespread throughout the camp, and then to make matters worse, a mysterious eye problem spread among the children, making their eyes sensitive to the sunlight. At night they filled with pus. Each morning their eyes had to be washed out so that they could open them.

From the spring until autumn 1942, over 25,000 Polish refugees arrived in Pahlavi from Russia and over 2,000 Jews, half of them children. They arrived hungry, bewildered, dirty and aching. Pahlavi was considered a gateway of liberty for thousands of Poles, and it was the first city on their route where Poles and British assisted in caring for the refugees. Relief camps were set up throughout the area attempting to save human souls, especially the children who arrived in complete exhaustion, to prepare them for the Tehran camps.

Within the camp were some young people, members of the Zionist youth movement, who assisted in making conditions as best they could for the children. Even with the clothes sent to the camp, the Jewish children always stood in line and received last, and remained barefoot and ragged. When food was freely passed out, even to the Jewish children, many simply ate too much and became violently ill after the long famine.

All along the beach patients were hospitalized, and corpses of those who had died during the day were removed just before dark. Diseases struck everyone, regardless of age, sex, status or religion, but the first victims were the weak and the helpless.

Eighteen children in the camp died in the first month. Joe found himself surrounded by children not any better off than himself – walking skeletons suffering from any number of diseases rampant throughout the camp: typhus, scabies, ringworm, tetanus and dysentery. Lice swarmed throughout the camp, totally beyond any kind of control by the administrators.

Still, wave after wave of refugees poured off the boats, over-running the hospital at Pahlavi. Thousands of starving, ill, broken people. One nurse described a sad story:

> The boy in the last bed on the Children's Ward was one such patient [received sick]…I never saw his name but day after day I saw him fighting desperately hard to stay alive. Each day when I came on duty I expected him to have gone, just another corpse in a body bag, but each day he hung on, little more than skin and bone, but with eyes that burned with the intensity of his struggle. Then, one day he made signs to me that he would like a biscuit. I took one and crumpled it into tiny pieces for him. I know that if he had asked me then I would have baked a mountain of biscuits for him. I put the crumbs gently onto his tongue. The sun was in his eyes and I got up for a moment to lower the blind. When I looked back he was dead.[149]

By now Joe had lost faith in adults, and constantly hid food from them, afraid that it would be taken away. He would readily steal to live; lie to live, or do whatever it took to live. Joe, along with the others, never believed what was told to him. Therefore, when news spread that trucks would be coming for them at the end of August and that Polish authorities had granted permission to transfer the children from Pahlavi to Camp 2, where a Jewish orphanage would be established, Joe and the children hid their bread and refused to believe what they were told.

To the children's amazement, the trucks did come!

Early the next morning over 100 British army lorries arrived. The rears of the trucks were covered in canvas so the children couldn't see the dangerous twists and turns they'd be making. The sheer cliffs were so tall that they blocked out the sunlight, and, on the other side of the roads were deep canyons. The children were quickly loaded, and there were immediately problems for the counsellors to address. Children wanted to travel with friends, or sisters, or brothers, and not be separated. Some feared the journey, and suspicious of the adults, and they grasped their bundles of bread and jellies so they couldn't be taken from them. Eventually, each child was loaded onto a truck, and the convoy took off following the narrow, winding road through the Elburz Mountains. In the distance was the extinct volcano Damavand.

The trip to Tehran would last several days, following the narrow roads along the Caspian Sea coast, past clusters of palm trees and sand dunes which served as a shelter whenever planes were spotted.

Tents were tied to the top of the trucks and unloaded at night as the children washed themselves in the sea. What little food had been brought along, and what the locals contributed to the children, was quickly consumed. Once this trip would have been considered a great adventure for the children, camping out under the stars, by a mirror-lit sea. But, this was the second year in which the children had suffered greatly, waking up in a different place and then herded off to the next location. For the children it was a miserable dream. Still, they were the blessed ones, although they wouldn't realize it until much later, for they would arrive in Tehran, truckload after truckload, amidst huge swirls of dirt and sand.

Numerous refugees, the unfortunate, were destined to stay forever in Pahlavi.

Today, if one walks down a narrow road southward out of the city of Pahlavi, they will come upon a cross and sign atop a set of blue-painted metal gates bordered with lush green trees. The visitor can read '*Cmentarz Polski,*' which is the Polish war cemetery in Bandar-e Anzali.

Buried in that cemetery are 639 Polish soldiers and civilians. The gravestones of each are all marked with one common date: *1942.*

***

At dawn, 21 August 1942, General Anders departed Tehran, where he was overseeing the organizing of the Polish army. He was flown to Cairo where he met with Prime Minister Winston Churchill the next day at the British Embassy in Cairo in the presence of General Sir Maillard Wilson and Colonel Jacob of the British Army.

The men discussed at length the structure and order concerning the Polish army. Stalin, apparently true to his word, had allowed all troops to be released and transported southward. Anders then brought up several points that seemed to disturb Churchill. Anders' staff had estimated that the Polish army had lost over 4,000 soldiers to hunger and exposure while waiting for evacuation orders from Stalin. The second issue was, as Anders presented it, the mysterious disappearance of 'a large number of our best officers in Russia'. Churchill assured Anders that the issue would be studied.

Lastly, Anders informed Churchill about a large group of Polish children, possibly as many as 4,000 who, if they weren't evacuated, couldn't possibly survive the winter. Churchill told him that decisions had been made that his army would eventually leave Iran, transfer to Iraq, and then be considered under 'British command for further training and equipping'. As for the children, Churchill assured him, he had already given orders for the women and children to be received from Russia together with the Polish troops, but, only as far as Iran.

Even as news of the Polish Children later reached the world press, there was a total disbelief and shock at the thought of such atrocities, at what the Nazis were capable of inflicting on the Jews. Five months later, on 9 January 1943, *The Nation*, an American weekly newspaper, would publish an article titled 'The Jews of Europe: Seven Ways to Help Them' and mentioned the children. The article shared the author's thoughts through several recommendations:

> 1)That the Jews would have a hearing in the United Nations, 2) to let Jewish regiments be formed, 3) open the doors of Palestine, and 4) frontiers should be open for transit purposes wherever possible; where necessary they should be forced open. Then, the writer went on to write: 'The plight of the 500 Polish Jewish children now in Teheran is a case in point…governments [should] guarantee to neutral countries the cost of maintaining escaped Jews during the war…Save the children. Let every technical barrier be set aside…Even the Nazis are reluctant to shoot children in cold blood.[150]

***

The undeniable truth of the devastation consuming the European Jews arrived on 16 November 1942.

Sixty-Nine Palestinian Jews – kibbutz members, Zionist activists, and scientists – held in Europe, were exchanged for German nationals living in Palestine. Eliyahu Dobkin, head of the immigration department of the Jewish Agency responsible for rescuing Jews from Europe, was sent by Ben-Gurion to interview the exchangees. Dobkin, born in Babruysk, Russia, had immigrated to Palestine with his wife and daughter on 6 June 1932. A leading figure in the Labour Zionist Movement, he became involved in the Jewish Agency. In May 1945, when Israel became a nation declaring its independence, Dobkin would be a signee of the Israeli Declaration of Independence.[151]

At Athlit Detention Camp north of Haifa near the Coastal Road along the Mediterranean Sea, Dobkin, along with other Jewish Agency members, spent two days questioning the exchangees. Built by the British in the late 1930s as a military camp, Athlit was transformed in 1939 to function as an incarceration camp for illegal Jewish immigrants. Sadly, as Jews escaped from Hitler's Europe, they arrived in Palestine only to find themselves prisoners once again behind barbed wire. Three years later, on 9 October 1945, Athlit was the site of a daring rescue operation as Jewish underground commandos broke into the camp and freed the prisoners, creating pride in the fight for the right to come to Palestine.

In 1942 as the war raged on, what Dobkin and the other Jewish agency interviewees were told was, in so many ways, so shocking that there was a general air of disbelief so strong that one of the survivors would write: 'They did not believe me! They said I exaggerated. They asked me questions and subjected me to an interrogation as if I were a criminal inventing a story in order to cause somebody harm, in order to deceive people deliberately and for ulterior motives...They tried hard to weaken my certainty, so I should doubt the veracity of my information.'

Eventually, faced with so many witnesses, Dobkin did believe, telling his associates that apparently the Germans were 'operating something like a [murder] apparatus', something 'that was going in the direction of total extermination'. Later while filing his report to the Jewish Agency Executive, JAE, Dobkin related the words he had heard as 'blood-curdling descriptions' and 'the dreadful details'. It was obvious to him, that 'the Jews of Europe were being systematically wiped out'.

Dobkin reported certain assumptions that were soon considered true: 'the slaughtering of young and the old *en masse*' was happening in Poland's cities. Secondly, from all over Europe, there was in motion the mass deportation of Jews. For the first time, they learned of 'large concrete buildings' on the Russian-Polish border where Jews were being gassed and cremated.

On Friday 27 November 1942, after Dobkin had completed his interviews at Athlit, the exchangees were released, *The Jewish Standard* led its daily edition with bloody evidence of the *Shoah*: 'Germans try to Exterminate European Jewry – Mass Murder in Eastern Europe.'[152]

Within a month, Ben-Gurion spoke out:

> We do not know exactly what goes on in the *Nazi Valley of Death* or how many Jews have already been slaughtered, murdered, burned, and buried alive and how many others are doomed to annihilation...only from time to time does news of atrocities break through to us...the screams of women and children mutilated and crushed. But we do know what Hitler had in store for our people and what he wrote in *Mein Kampf* and what he has done and is doing to us...before the war...during the war...We do not know that the victory of democracy and freedom and justice will not find Europe a vast Jewish cemetery in which the bones of our people are scattered....[153]

Three months later. Eliahu Dobkin travelled to Jerusalem and attended a meeting with the JAE sub-committee responsible for 'the absorption of the children and for their welfare'. He informed the sub-committee that the British mandatory government had notified the Jewish Agency Executive that 'it would allow the entry of four thousand children, to be accompanied by five women from Bulgaria, into Palestine'.[154] During the meeting, plans were made for absorbing this large number of children and the financing needed for such an undertaking was discussed.

An attendee in the meeting was Ben-Gurion. He sat at the head of the long table, wearing a crumpled black suit, and a white starched shirt open at the throat. He appeared older than his years, a short, thick man with a tangled nest of uncombed gray hair, a dark face and gazing, penetrating eyes.

It was during this meeting that, for the first time, Ben-Gurion was made aware of an estimated 1,000 Jewish children, mostly orphans, making their way toward a makeshift camp consisting of 2,000 tents hastily constructed by the British Tenth Army on the Caspian Sea. From Pahlavi, Ben-Gurion was told, the children would later travel by truck to Tehran. Among those refugee children heading southward out of Siberia was a young German Jew who was now ten years old, ill, alone and dreadfully homesick.

PART THREE

September 1942 – January 1943

13

The Jewish Agency Reacts

'Never has childhood been so assailed and tormented since the beginning of man.'[155]

'To kill the Jews, the Nazis were willing to weaken their capacity to fight the war. The United States and its allies, however, were willing to attempt almost nothing to save them.'[156]

'Ten months in Iran gave you a feeling of complete isolation from the world', an American journalist wrote during the war while stationed in Persia. 'No other capital city was completely cut off from the war, except perhaps Lhasa in Tibet.'[157] That may have been the case when Sydney Morrell wrote the description, but it certainly wasn't the fact by September 1942. Tehran had overnight, because of its geographical location, become the epicentre of military activity in Persia. British troops were stationed outside the city. Polish troops, exiled from Siberia, were being organized and trained under Anders' watchful eye, soon to be deployed to Palestine for additional training, and then to North Africa to fight with the war-weary British units.

Despite its growing importance in the Allied war effort, conditions in Tehran were found by the arriving refugees to be deplorable. The water supply remained poor, in summer the heat blazed down on unsuspecting visitors to the city, and in winter the cold rattled one to the bone. Remarkably, despite these obvious disadvantages, the Iranian capital remained a centre of culture. By the 1940s, half of its citizens, numbering 700,000, could read and write. *Luk* (luxury) hotels possessed heat and running water, cafés flooded with music, a focus on nightlife, and especially, for the British, there were the sound-film cinemas.

Horse-drawn carriages shared the streets and roads with a growing number of double-decker buses. However, Tehran was two distinct and different cities. Workers, beggars and artists inhabited the southern part, and travelled narrow, deceitful streets, vastly unlike the northern part which

8. Tehran Children in Iran. Joe is on the far right. Courtesy of Rina Rosenbaum.

resembled a nineteenth-century Russian provincial town, with broad roads and avenues, one and two-storey houses.

***

During those first days in Iran, Joe no longer hunted for food with the other children. Afflicted with a high fever, all he could manage to do was to remain on a bed of rags in a makeshift hospital tent, grieving over his mother and Nelly. On the crowded train southward out of Tashkent several weeks before, the fever and dysentery had again racked his small, frail body, and Joe's memories slipped behind a dark veil of grief and sickness. 'I had no memory', Joe recalls upon his arrival in Tehran. 'No memory…it's totally blank. Like a black hole there. I just remember in Tehran when I was with the Jewish group…I slept in a tent on the floor.'[158]

There remained, however, the constant ticking in his mind of *could he have done more for both?* There was the constant drum in his fevered mind that he was, even at the fragile age of nine, the one who could have prevented their deaths if he had just known what to do. For the other refugees pouring into Tehran, any hope born on the train southward of something better, quickly faded away once they saw the conditions of the fly-infested camps. Facilities were simple, with no running water and limited sanitary toilets. Sleeping on straw mats, the children were warned that when winter came, the brutal night temperatures would drop to below freezing which meant more children would die. Still, there was at least some food, with meals of butter and jam spread on bread with tea. But, sadly, the children again lived with hunger, cold, unimaginable filth and over-crowding, and with many of the same diseases that had killed their family members and friends.

Located on the outskirts of Tehran, these camps were within sight of minarets and mosques domes, encircled by tall buildings and row after row of huts and the military barracks of the Persian Air Force. At Doshan Tappeh, several miles east of the city, red-brick adobes were scattered about the vast landscape, and in their midst were row upon row of pitched tents. Next to the airfield was a machine gun factory that was offered as shelter by the Iranian government and converted into crude housing. There were no beds, and the refugees slept either on the concrete platform or the cold floor. A total of five camps were built, four for civilians spread out in various locations in the city area. Commercial and government buildings were committed as shelters, along with sports stadiums and swimming baths for the refugees. Camp 2 was the largest, consisting of nothing more than a collection of tents outside the city. Camp 4 was a deserted munitions factory. Camp 3 was situated in the Shah's own garden, surrounded by flowing water and beautiful trees. There was also a Polish hospital in the city, a hostel for the elderly, an orphanage run by the Sisters of Nazareth, and a convalescent home for sick children, Camp 5, situated in Shemiran.

In Isfahan, in the mountains close by, a Polish orphanage was established for over 2,600 Polish children. It was a two-storey building which faced the garden, with French windows giving access to a balcony. It stood in the shade of fruit trees including apples, pomegranates and many large bushes. To this idyllic place, many Polish families came searching for their missing children.

Along with the Polish soldiers, thousands of refugees who had followed them out of Siberia continued pouring into the camps throughout August and into September, overwhelming the officials. There simply wasn't enough food, or shelter, or medicines, making the situation appallingly desperate within weeks. Tehran became a place of refugees desperately searching and asking for relatives and friends, seeking any information they could so they could be reunited with loved ones. But the vastness of the camps inhabited by so many deportees, were too overwhelming for authorities to organize any information. Finding a relative, perhaps not seen for months or years, within the camps was simply left to fate. In the following days, rumours swirled among the refugees. One story often told was about Anne, a Jewish woman, whose small girl had arrived in Iran very ill. As the child lay dying in the one of the makeshift hospitals she looked at her mother, 'Mummy, Jesus is here, and He says He loves me.' Weeks later, as the Jews refugees made their way to Palestine, Anne would stay behind and convert to Catholicism.[159]

A British officer, Colonel A. Ross, who later became a liaison with Jewish officials sent to Tehran to assist, filed an account titled 'Report on Polish Refugees in Persia', describing the horrors he witnessed as he attempted to detail the conditions of the refugees pouring out of the Soviet Union:

> The physical and mental state of the refugees on arrival in Tehran was generally very bad. The most prevalent diseases were dysentery, diarrhea, deficiency diseases due to prolonged malnutrition, many malarias imported from Russia, and typhoid: forty per cent of the refugees were malaria cases. A visit to any of the hospitals at the beginning of the first or second phases of the evacuation was sufficient to create on the mind an indelible impression of unmerited hardships and physical suffering.[160]

General Anders, upon his arrival to Tehran from Russia and upon witnessing the conditions of the refugees, rushed off a report to the Polish government-in-exile in London that 'he expected twenty-five per cent of the refugees to die after their arrival in Persia.' Still, he knew among his ragged and starved soldiers and the refugees there was 'not one who would not have said: "God had delivered us from the house of bondage".' Anders told his officers that 'the summer of 1942 was the dawn of freedom'.[161]

Several weeks after arriving in Tehran, Anders received orders that he would be transferred to the army headquarters at Quizil Ribat, and that the remainder of his command would be relocated to Palestine for training to fight in North Africa against Rommel's Afrika Korps. Plans were managing nicely now, and Anders was proud of the way his exiled army was coming together. But, still there remained the mysterious question surrounding the fate of his 15,000 Polish officers. Along with the suspicions came the rumours that the prisoners had been deported to an Arctic Island and drowned in the Arctic Ocean. But rumours didn't mean anything to Anders. All he knew for certain was that 15,000 of his finest officers had been missing since the spring of 1940. Without a trace.

Once the Polish army crossed the Caspian Sea into Iran, the forces instantly came under the authority of British Commander Lt. General Sir Henry Pownall, Commander of the Persia and Iraq Force (PAI) headquartered in Baghdad. Pownall had been Chief of General Staff to the British Expeditionary Force in France and Belgium until they fell to Hitler in late May 1940. He wrote to Anders, having kept up with the Polish army as it moved southward, informing Anders that he, Pownall, considered that the Polish soldiers needed battlefield training.

The 26 British Liaison Unit, commanded by Brigadier Eric Frith, was assigned to the Polish Army to establish training units. This position, established by British Command, turned the Polish troops' stay in Tehran into one of a position of waiting until they were transferred to either Iraq or Palestine.

To many of the Polish soldiers, and civilians who weren't Jewish, Tehran was a paradise, especially compared to the Siberian camps:

> We arrived in Tehran in April 1942…The streets were lined with people who had gathered to welcome us. We looked into their faces, as they waved and cheered us, and we saw that they were beautiful, free and happy. We were taken to the Persian University, nestling in the foothills of the mountains, which had been converted to receive us. As our convoy drove through gates which closed behind us, we saw magnificent buildings, lawns, and trees with ripe apricots…As we disembarked, to be met by Polish soldiers, we were warned, do not eat the fresh fruit. We will give you fruit in the dining room – eat only that. Do not buy anything from the hands of local traders. We learned later that this later precaution was because of the venereal disease that was endemic in this country. We were even warned not to sit on seats that were still warm…[162]

***

Towards the end of 1942, the Polish Minister of State, Professor Stanislaw Kot, met with the Jewish Agency to discuss several issues of importance. Among the first subjects discussed was the situation, which was growing more precarious under Soviet influence, of the civil rights of the Polish Jews after the war had been won. Several days before Kot had stayed in Haifa for a brief rest. But while residing at the Carmel Pension, high up on Mount Carmel amidst breathtaking views of Haifa Bay and the Mediterranean coastline, the minister broke away from his holiday to discuss other issues with Zionist officials. The talks centred on 'doing whatever was necessary to get the 400,000 Jews out of Russia'. Kot proposed a Polish-Jewish collaboration to succeed at such actions, but refrained from making a direct commitment. Kot then sent a letter to Moshe Sharett, who would become the second prime minister of Israel, and who was at that time head of the Jewish Agency. Sharett promised that he would follow up with Kot on the matter as soon as possible. Sharett, in turn, shared this with Ben-Gurion. In a meeting a week later, Sharett brought up the situation surrounding the Tehran Children. When Kot delved deeper into the subject, Sharett suggested that Kot assist them by transporting the children by sea, especially after the fact that Iraq would not allow them to travel through their country.

Once Ben-Gurion was informed of the suffering children in camps outside Tehran, the Jewish Agency leader would confidently call upon Henrietta Szold and the *Youth Aliyah,* an organization whose purpose was to rescue Jewish children from Nazi-occupied Europe.[163]

***

Within days, word of the children arrived at Henrietta Szold's Jerusalem office at Pension Romm, a two-storey cottage of pink Jerusalem stone at No. 11 Ramban Street. Aware now that over 450 children of Polish Jews had arrived in Pahlavi and transportation to Tehran was already under way, she immediately understood the danger confronting the children.[164]

At 81, Szold was weary. She was tired of the bureaucratic burdens she had carried over the last several years, and longed to retire and go home and spend her last days with her sisters in Baltimore. But this wasn't the first time she had entertained ideas of walking away from the problems of the struggling *Yishuv* in Palestine. Strangely though, every time she had made the decision to return to America an event interrupted her plans. In 1916, there was the First World War, with the influx of wounded and Jewish refugees from other countries. She simply couldn't leave then. Now, it was this war, the trials confronting the European Jews, and specifically the knowledge that there were a group of Polish children making their perilous way across Persia.

Youth Aliyah had been founded on Monday 30 January 1933 by a rabbi's wife in Berlin, Recha Freier, on the same day that Adolf Hitler came to power in Germany. She foresaw what Hitler had planned for the Jews, and was especially worried about the future of Jewish children. Freier decided to set up a programme for them to travel to Palestine, where they could work and study. At first her idea was rejected by Henrietta Szold simply because there was no funding available. But finally persuaded, Szold took control of *Youth Aliyah,* placed it under the authority of the Jewish Agency, and applied her skills at organizing the efforts. It is estimated that as many as 20,000 children were immigrated from Nazi Germany by the end of the war. Szold then turned to the group she had founded in New York, Hadassah, and guided their efforts to organize funds for the children's cause.

Started as a Bible study group in New York, after Szold had travelled to Palestine and witnessed the sickness, poverty and lack of medical facilities, she decided that her group should turn their efforts to a worthier cause. Named the Hadassah Chapter of the Daughters of Zion, taking the Hebrew name of Queen Esther, the group was formed on 24 February 1912, at New York's Temple Emanu-El. Its purpose was to promote 'Jewish institutions and enterprises in Palestine, and the fostering of Jewish ideals.' By late 1942, Hadassah had grown to a nation-wide organization in America and had connections to business leaders and politicians.

Szold stared for a long moment out the back window of her office that opened out over a small garden. Reports had described how the children had been travelling since 1939, which she considered horrible. But, now that she knew the children were within reach of the Jewish Agency, it was a time for action. To accomplish the rescue, Szold realized that she needed a staff of experienced leaders to guide the children through their suffering, and prepare them for the trip to Palestine. Unable to find anyone in Iran, Szold managed to obtain a single official visa, and sent Mrs. Zipporah Shertok, wife of Moshe Sharett, who headed the Jewish Agency political department, later referring to her friend's achievements in Iran as 'an angel of mercy with a good head on her shoulders'.

Her husband, who would become the second Prime Minister of Israel, gained assistance from the British High Commissioner, and Zipporah soon departed for Palestine, unselfishly leaving behind her two sons and a small daughter because there was a group of Jewish children in Tehran who needed her help.

Several weeks later, another report came to Szold's desk increasing the number of children to over 1,000 refugees, prompting her to then report to the Jewish Agency: 'They had been sleeping in the woods, half-naked, exposed to disease, eaten by vermin, starved, guiltless.' Szold, also through the proper channels, informed the Palestine government that she was willing to assume responsibility for bringing the children to Palestine.

Two hectic months later, on 16 October, Henrietta Szold, prepared to approach British officials on the subject of obtaining travel certificates for the children, would write of her commitment to the children: 'My sole interest at the moment is the children of Tehran. The more I enter into the details of the task, the better I realize the difficulties we are facing...'[165]

Szold shifted her agency into action. From Palestine, she dispatched Reuven Shefer and Avraham Zilberg, two of her associates who opened the Palestine office in Tehran. After several telephone calls and meetings, more food and clothing contributions began flowing in, and were dispersed to the children.

The situation in the Middle East was complex. Jewish immigration to Palestine was a major obstacle, and Iraq had made it painfully clear that they wouldn't assist in any way 'to allow one Jew to reach Palestine'. Szold was also aware that the British government wouldn't allow immigration for the Jewish refugees to be altered because they feared antagonizing the Iraqi government who obviously controlled vast gas and oil fields. However, Szold surprisingly found that the British government sincerely wanted to help the children. Any concerns Szold received were regarded as truly heartfelt on the British officials' part. Numerous 'letters, memos, telegrams and personal notes' reflected the conscience of many officials in the British Foreign Office in Whitehall, London.

Through a series of cables, Szold learned the exact number of children now in the camp and immediately requested, through the chief immigration officer, travel certificates. A depressing mood fell over the Jewish Agency's offices. As the Iranian and Iraqi governments turned their back on her efforts to get the children to Palestine, Szold realized that her final chance now fell on a group of women – Hadassah.

This Women's Zionist Organization of America, founded in 1912 by Henrietta Szold, had donated thousands of personnel and raised millions of dollars to improve health and medical conditions in 1920s and 1930s Palestine. But, more importantly concerning the problem facing her of getting the children out of Tehran, Hadassah officials also had connections in Washington D.C., which might allow for such a rescue.

As the situation became more desperate, Szold suffered deep anxiety. Her fears were based on past events, when freedom appeared so close for Jewish refugees, only to have it end in disaster. One such story haunting Szold was of 1,200 Jewish refugees from Vienna, Danzig and Czechoslovakia, who had embarked on a journey to freedom down the Danube on three boats. The boats became frozen in at the Yugoslav border. When British officials were asked for assistance, only 200 certificates were issued for the children, and not the entire group. The children were sent forward and eventually ended up in Palestine. After the war, the Serbian government found the bodies of over 1,000 adults, frozen to death where they waited for freedom – their passports in their pockets.

Szold also remembered two ship disasters – the *Patria* and *Struma* – so haunting that she refused to think back on them.

After contacting a Hadassah representative first in London and then America, Szold could now only wait; constantly whispering to herself her true belief for the children in Europe: 'Lost to Yishuv, lost to Jewry.'[166]

***

Arriving in Tehran on 28 October 1942, Zipporah Shertok undertook the supervision of the entire operation for the duration of the children's stay. Among the refugees there were a few *halutzim*, who had served as leaders of diverse European Zionist youth groups.

Realizing that a disciplined daily life needed to be maintained for the children, Shertok instructed the *halutzim* on what she expected until the children departed, and then enlisted the financial aid from Jews living in Iran to provide badly-needed medical care and toiletry items. 'An educational programme modelled after Israeli orphanages was established. Hebrew courses, lectures, popular discussions, choirs and dance groups were organized.'[167] Even with the lack of books, papers and pencils, and with the staff over-worked in poor conditions in a difficult climate, the children slowly began to flourish. One concern painfully obvious to Zipporah was that religious authorities were attempting to convert the children away from Judaism.

One counsellor remembered this stranger, this woman from Palestine hurrying about the camp with her dark hair drawn back in a knot:

> She spoke to counsellors and children, trying to lift their spirits and give them the feeling that she was their direct link with Palestinian Jewry, who cared about us, wanted us, and were doing everything in her power to help us. She did not confine her activities to weighty matters, but tended also to many small, practical details…She moved around the camp with her flit pump, spraying everything against vermin and insects. She gave the little ones special care, checking to see which were in greatest need, washing, binding, applying ointments. Her devotion was endless, although she was missing her own children.[168]

Of course, the Jewish camp was separate from the other Polish areas. The Jews lived in the tents suffering through the brutal heat, and were occasionally struck by rocks thrown at them by their Polish neighbours. Sick Jewish children, described by one of the nurses as 'exhausted and feverish', were forced out of their beds to be present at roll call, as lines of tanned and healthy Polish children laughed. If any of the Jewish children cried, security people would angrily yell out 'Quiet, Zhids', a degrading name.

***

One morning in October 1942, Zipporah Shertok traveled from her hotel to the camp wearing her best hat and coat. There, she had a photograph taken with a group of the children with counsellors gathered around her. Shortly after the photograph was taken, she escorted Nachum T. Gidal, chief reporter of the British 8th Army magazine *Parade,* through the campgrounds. In his notebook he later wrote, 'I saw hordes of children, half-starved, in rags, recovering in the care of the American Red Cross and of a small group of Jewish workers sent from Palestine. Moshe Sharett's wife led this group. She told me the story of the children, and took me to the camp.'169

Later that afternoon, Mrs. Shertok sat down at a writing desk after returning to her Tehran hotel room. She stared out the window looking out over the capital, lingering for a long moment, searching for the exact words to write, realizing the gravity of what she was about to relate, and then composed a report to the Aliyah Department of Jerusalem:

> The children are housed in one big hut and six big tents. In the big room, sleep 98 small children up to age eight. They sleep on the floor, on thin mattresses and cotton cushions. Each child has three woolen blankets. Under the mattresses are spread mats…in the isolation room children, too, sleep on the floor. There are few white sheets, but mostly they sleep on dark blankets. The children over age eight sleep in the tents, but they do not have any mattresses or cushions but only blankets and mats. The tents are torn and cold and rain penetrates and the children are often sick. The autumn has already set in and it is chilly. The children complain that it is cold. The children receive food from the kitchen three times a day. In the morning, ½ kg. bread per child for the whole day, a dab of butter, a bit of jam and an apple. At noon: soup and cereal. At five: tea and an egg. Some get extra rations by medical prescription. They eat in the tents, without table or a cloth, on the blankets. Some children built themselves tables of brick. The children are shorter than their age, underdeveloped and pale, some of them very pale…twice a week they take a warm shower and one of their blankets is disinfected. Some of them have skin rashes and sick eyes and one child has pneumonia. Some two hundred children go barefoot; other have worn-out shoes and very shabby and insufficient clothing.170

With this report, she let Palestine know that under no uncertain terms, if the children weren't pulled out of Iran, many would perish. Several days after this report reached the desk of Henrietta Szold, Joe would slip into another bout of fever. This small boy, broken and sick without family, simply existing as were the other children, was completely unaware of the enormous effort underway to vacate the children out of Tehran.

***

Szold, with all efforts in Persia exhausted, through the Jewish Agency in Palestine contacted the Hadassah office in New York. She requested that they establish contacts with both American and British officials in Washington D.C to secure transportation for the Tehran Children out of Persia. Three women learned of the drastic situation unfolding, and immediately dedicated themselves to this cause. Tamar de Sola Pool was the Hadassah national president, a visionary born in Jerusalem who had immigrated with her rabbi father to America in 1904. Gisela Warburg, chairman of the National Board of Hadassah, was born in Hamburg, Germany, and was herself a refugee leaving her home in 1939. The third woman, New Orleans born Denise Tourover, was Hadassah's first Washington representative. She had lived in the nation's capital since 1920, had made herself familiar with the political leaders of both parties, and the political maneuverings since the beginning of the war.

By 1943, Washington was very much like any other boom town during the war – its population had doubled since 1940, decent housing was impossible to find, uniforms were everywhere, gasoline was scarce, buses were over-crowded and living costs were high. Most of the newcomers were women, searching for jobs as typists and clerks in the burgeoning federal bureaucracy, which had spread its offices into every available space, into ugly temporary buildings, old schools, apartments and homes, gymnasiums and skating rinks. They were called GGs, or government girls; they came on buses and trains with their suitcases in their hands, to live in huge dormitories specially erected for them, and with their help journalist David Brinkley wrote 'the federal government created more records in the four years of war than in its entire previous history'.[171]

Washington's population had swollen to over a million people, 'temporary wooden housing began to clutter the Mall, destroying the artistic beauty of the reflecting pool graced by the Washington and Lincoln monuments'. Real and wooden anti-aircraft guns, addressing the fear of additional attacks, decorated the White House. 'Secretary of the Treasury Henry Morgenthau, Jr., haunted by visions of the London Blitz, dispatched an army of Secret Service agents to blacken the mansion's window, to fit bulletproof glass in the Oval Room windows, to install special General Electric outdoor floodlights, and to pour a concrete "bomb barrier" along the west wall of the Executive Office Building.'

Having been kept updated on events unfolding in Persia, Tourover had begun a campaign of reaching out to her contacts in the State Department making them aware of the children's plight. For Tourover, the most appalling roadblock was the unshakable attitude of Iraq and Turkey, both of whom were receiving Allied aid, and refused to open any door on the rescue operations. She understood this angered Zionist leaders in Palestine, as it should she reasoned.

Attempting to establish contact with anyone who would assist them on the 'Tehran Children issue', Tourover, along with de Sola Pool and Warburg, forged ahead, following new avenues such as calling on oil companies tied to oil interests in Iraq. Tourover wrote: 'We called on the Turkish Ambassador but made no progress. We called on companies that had major oil interests in Iraq. That too failed and I was really incensed that a two-by-four government which was getting lend-lease from us should set its will against a humanitarian effort such as this.'[172]

On 28 October 1942, Gisela Warburg wrote a letter intended to prompt action by the Under Secretary of State, Sumner Welles. Then, two days later, Warburg directed a memorandum to Tourover, stating that she felt some progress had been made, but she did 'not want to let the day go by without my daily resumé on the Tehran front'.

Any efforts to get the Tehran Children out of Persia seemed secondary against American and British efforts to not offend Iran or Iraq if the outcome of the war was in doubt.

Tourover, the political mind in Hadassah's effort, and del Sola Pool, whose strength was possessing the charm and energy to charge ahead no matter how bleak the future looked, refused to give up.

Then Tourover, who had heard the President wanted to assist them in the situation, was able to arrange through Mrs Henry Morgenthau, wife of the U.S. Secretary of the Treasury, Henry Morgenthau and friend to the President, a meeting at the White House. Tourover's argument was that Iraq was receiving aid from the Allies, and couldn't anything be done to pressure them to assist in this rescue?

As the two women waited for answers,[173] Warburg wrote, 'Denise, I wonder about something else. The State Department did say that there were no American planes in Persia. But I don't think they really know. I suppose only the War Department knows. Could you find out authentically where there are any [planes]?' Tourover scribbled back: 'Even if there were some [American] planes there, I doubt if they would use them on their [the children's] behalf.'

What had started as a fruitful avenue soon turned to one of disappointment. 'I went to the White House', Tourover later wrote. 'The meeting there was arranged through Mrs Henry Morgenthau [wife of the Secretary of the Treasury].' After pleading their case, Hadassah leaders anxiously waited. Two days later, the White House response was received.

The Iraq government wouldn't budge.

14

A Bucket of Eggs

Eighteen children died in the camps during the first month.

It was a frustrating situation for those in charge because there was only a small amount of money available for medicine. Rooms that were set aside for the sick that should have held eight, often sheltered up to 80 ill children. There were no professional nurses available to care for the Jewish children, so *halutzim* and *halutzot*, Jews waiting to immigrate to Palestine, were hastily trained to care for them.

To care for the over 800 children, a group of 58 older Polish Jews were carefully chosen. The head counsellor was a former Polish military school officer candidate, David Laor, who ran an efficient camp, created units focusing on specific needs: food, cultural works and storerooms. It became obvious more counsellors were needed, but the Persian government denied visas to Palestinian Jews who were trying to reach Tehran to assist Laor and the others.

Being a counsellor didn't mean that one lived any better. Most of them were themselves without shoes and proper clothing, food was scarce, and they slept without mattresses or sheets. Upon their arrival, they found the children frightened; many were wild and disruptive, almost animal-like and ill with numerous diseases. There was a constant battle with nightmares, or the children hiding their food, afraid that it would be taken away.

Gradually, some conditions did improve and the seriously ill were sent to hospitals in Tehran. Large huts were constructed as an infirmary for those children chosen to stay but who remained ill.

***

In the morning Joe stirred beneath a bath of soft sunlight through the open window. As he awakened he realized that the fever had broken, and that the breeze felt cool on his face.[174]

He drank a swallow of water from the glass on the table beside his makeshift cot, and it felt good on his dry throat. Maybe, he thought, maybe he wasn't going to die in Tehran after all.

Then he drifted back off to sleep.

It was later in the morning when Joe again awakened. The sun was high up in the sky, and now the breeze through the open window was warm and dry. A dark-haired *halutzot* came to his bed. She checked his pulse, inspected his mouth and playfully scolded him with a smile for not making sure the damp cloth on his forehead stayed in place. Then she tapped his shoulder, 'You are better', she told him. And quickly she was gone to the next bed.

Joe's thoughts turned to the girl who had been lying in the bed next to him, and how she had groaned terribly throughout many of the nights he was in the sick tent. She appeared to be Joe's age, maybe a year or two older, and her hair was cropped close to her skull with pale skin and terribly weak eyes. But despite the constant groaning at night, each morning she would turn to him, offer him a weak smile, waving at him with her fingers sticking out under the cover. She would mouth something to Joe, but he couldn't hear or understand what she was trying to say. He felt close to her somehow, which he needed badly.

When the *halutzot* had gone, Joe rolled over, glancing toward the girl's bed, expecting another warm welcome.

The bed was empty.

Sheets and a blanket neatly folded. Very clean and neat, and that bothered Joe more than anything. After that, Joe never looked at any other beds, or paid any attention to what was going on in the room.

Then he slept throughout the day.

The next morning Joe waited for the *halutzot* to come to his bed, and at mid-morning she walked down the aisle and stood at the foot of his bed. She pulled back a towel hanging over the window and the breeze was again warm to his face. She spoke his name. She checked his pulse, looked at his throat, and then stared into his eyes for a long moment. 'You are now doing much better', she told him.

As she walked away, she glanced back, and that made Joe happy. Maybe, he wasn't going to die in Tehran and he was going to Palestine and then America to see his father and Inez. Yes, he would see his sister again, he was certain of that now.

Several days later, Joe felt much better, quite suddenly it seemed. Later that morning, the *halutzot* even encouraged him to accompany her on a short walk through the camp. He became tired before they returned to the sick tent, but with the passing of the fever he felt stronger once he had rested. When he woke up each morning, Joe was certain the fever was going away, the mouth ulcers didn't hurt as much. But with the good feeling, came a clearness of mind. In a strange way, Joe realized that being so sick had been a blessing.

Once he was no longer under a cloud of fever, his body racked with deep aching, he had too much time to think. His thoughts pushed all the awful memories of Siberia and Tashkent into view. When Joe closed his eyes, he could see his mother growing weaker each day as she gave her food to him and Nelly. He relived watching her hands trembling when she cupped them in her lap. Then, he remembered the time when mother couldn't understand Nelly and just stared starkly at her daughter. He relived the death of his grandfather and grandmother, and the horrors of watching everyone so dear to him starve to death.

Grief, like a cold strange fear, overtook Joe. Sometimes when he thought of his mother, the last time he had hugged her, Joe swore he could smell the kitchen spices, the fruit in her kitchen. But, still he didn't cry. It was much too late for that. And, no matter how hard he fought it back, the image of little Nelly curled up on the blanket, cold and dead, rushed back at him – mostly at night when the camp was dark and silent. He began to remember all those things he had tried so hard to forget.

The thoughts tormented him. Until late one night, Joe fought back defiantly against the nightmares and swore under his breath – he would never tell anyone the terrible secret surrounding Nelly's death.

***

9. Group portrait of the members of the Tehran children's transport at a refugee camp in Tehran, 1942. Zipporah Shertok is in the centre wearing the hat. United States Holocaust Memorial Museum, courtesy of David Laor.

In honour of Zipporah Shertok's visit and the improvement of the camp, the counsellors planned a 'festive programme' and made the children shoes out of cardboard. Joe remembers that his pair of shoes lasted about two days. They dressed the children in hats and clothes, and took them to see an American movie, *Gone with the Wind*. Joe thought, 'It was in colour! I saw the film, I didn't understand it, I didn't care for the film…so, I was looking for food.'

Joe learned Hebrew songs, not so he could sing them alone but so he could sing them together with the other children. He would learn anything if it meant having food to eat. And it was here in the camp also that Joe again experienced how Jews were treated differently, in much the same manner as they had been during the entire journey.

One night, when his strength was returning, he and two other boys sneaked out of the camp and ventured into the British camp located next to the children's camp. At that time there were numerous military camps around Tehran where soldiers were being trained before being shipped to North Africa or Italy. After the boys crawled under the fence they approached the tents, and could smell the sweet aroma of food cooking.

Inside the first tent they came to, they found their treasure. On the table before them sat a big bucket of hard-boiled eggs. They started eating them as fast as they could and as many as they could. 'Since then I like to eat eggs at night', Joe remembers. 'Some nights when I can't sleep, I slip into the kitchen and eat eggs before I go to bed.' When the boys left the camp, they took a bucket of eggs with them. They saved them until the next night, and Joe got so sick that night that when the two boys went back, Joe didn't go with them.

***

Within two weeks of being relocated to the orphanage, Joe suddenly lost his sight. His eyes swelled up so that he couldn't see. Boils came back in his mouth, and so many blisters that he couldn't eat even if there had been food available. Slowly the afflictions went away, but Joe began to feel horrible again. Tehran was a miserable experience. 'So, I didn't enjoy Tehran.'

15

'The Tehran Home for Jewish Children'

Since 1933 when Szold and *Youth Aliyah* began bringing children out of Germany, they were careful to screen those brought to Palestine. But in this case, it was obvious that any child who received a certificate would be accepted – the sick, the mentally disturbed – they would all be brought to Palestine, if it was at all in their power.

Over the next several days, Henrietta Szold and her assistants continued evaluating the situation in Tehran as best they could from a distance, with only the information Zipporah Shertok forwarded to them. *Youth Aliyah* was designed to handle the rescue of older children, mainly between the ages of fifteen and seventeen, but many of the Tehran Children were much younger, presenting other problems the agency would have to address. Not only had there been physical abuse, but children at that age most certainly suffered from psychological issues, brought on by other forms of abuse and trauma. The question easily became, 'how could an 8-year-old child handle seeing their family – father, mother, and sisters – murdered, survive through such a gruelling experience, and not wonder why they remained alive when other family members had perished in such a brutal way?' Szold knew that this was something they must prepare for. She had dedicated her life to the rescue of the Jewish children, all of whom were trapped in Europe, their only sin that of being Jewish. 'Women are the natural protectors of childhood...they are the guardians of the generations', she told herself many times.[175]

***

Many children, prisoners to the horrors in Europe, were protected, but many others were not as fortunate.

One child who was protected until her arrival in Eretz Israel was Stella Knobel, born in Krakow, Poland in 1931. Deported to Siberia in freight cars, a similar fate as that suffered by Joe and his family, the Knobel family were released in 1941 as Hitler attacked the Soviet Union. Stella and her parents spent over a year in Iran before joining the refugees in March 1943, arriving in Israel in April. In the Yad Vashem Museum in Jerusalem, on display is the teddy bear of that young girl, named Mishu. When she donated the teddy bear she said:

> Because I was an only child who very much wanted a sister and brother, the teddy is like family…he was my sister and my brother and I clung to him…I didn't have any other toys…he's part of my family… the last remnant of my home in Poland…I know that in Yad Vashem he'll be taken care of…I thought of burying him in the garden, but I was afraid that someone would find him and get rid of him…the thought that he could be thrown in the garbage is terrible to me…it [the teddy] is symbolic of my life.

Carefully hidden away in a drawer are two photographs of Stella's childhood. One shows Stella in Krakow leaning against the front fender of the family's automobile. Her father's chauffeur, elbow leaning against the window, smiles into the camera, as does Stella. The second old photograph frames Stella with her cousin Elisabeta before the war. Both girls smiling, hair braided in long pigtails, arms around each other's shoulders. Elisabeta and her mother, Frederica, would be murdered in one of the death camps located in Poland.[176]

***

In Tehran, Zipporah Shertok's organizational skills produced impressive results.

Hadassah fundraising had raised over $500,000 in the United States to assist the children as Shertok continued to fight for the children's release. She met with the British consul in Tehran, and with a Polish minister residing in Persia. During each conversation she was told to be patient. But Shertok knew time was one commodity she didn't have. 'The children were freezing cold, tired and irritable.'

Joe remembered that they stayed there until the wintertime of January 1943. He could speak some Hebrew, but he didn't know the Hebrew songs at all. But everybody spoke Yiddish, so Joe could talk to everyone. Placed with a group of children between nine and twelve, Joe slept on the ground in a tent. In the early fall that arrangement had been okay, but later, in November, Joe and the others would find themselves freezing on the cold ground.

At least there was some food, not enough so one could survive. 'The food there was half and half. The supervisors, our *madrichims*, spent more time with the girls than with us. It was okay. I didn't starve there, but I didn't really gain [weight] either.'

The counsellors decided structure would give the children some meaning in the mundane camp life.

> As life in the camp settled down, we decided to habituate the children to the patterns of life in the Israeli *kibbutzim*, to which they were preparing to immigrate, one counsellor remembered. When they rose in the morning, they lined up according to age and were trained to stride in rhythm, accompanied by marching songs. An original hymn entitled 'We are Ascending and Singing' was sung every morning and on special occasions. News of the world events and camp happenings was announced at the morning lineup. The day's agenda was proclaimed.[177]

As children continued flooding into the camp, the Jewish Agency recognized that to maintain the orphanage effectively it was necessary to add to the staff (the children had been accompanied by a few guides), but regrettably the number of counsellors simply didn't grow at the required level. Both the agency and *Youth Aliyah* reached out as far as Palestine in search of additional staff. But either experienced counsellors weren't available, or if located an immigration visa couldn't be obtained for them to travel to Iran.

Joe went to school, where Hebrew, the official language of the camp, was taught along with Polish and Russian. This gave the children structure and routine in their lives. After breakfast each morning, the children marched out on the field, a parade ground, and sang songs to begin the school day, even though there were no textbooks.

Once the Polish group gave permission to the Jewish community to establish a Jewish orphanage, the camp gradually improved, and paths bordered by stones encircled the area. A flagpole was raised in the middle of the parade ground. The children put up a flag, one that they had themselves sown, in the middle of a parade ground adorned with the inscription *Beit ha-Yeled ha-Yehudi*, the 'Jewish Child's Home'.

Or – 'The Tehran Home for Jewish Children.'

Late in the year the children, tired of being harassed and sometimes beaten because they didn't know the prayer to the Holy Mother, began to question: 'In the children's home where you are taking us, are the teachers Jewish? Do they speak Yiddish? Do they hit and steal bread from the children? Will we go to Eretz Israel?'

There was the constant affirmation that the children would never be abandoned, and that there was hope and a future for them in Palestine. Soon, an event would happen that would console the children's fears. For the moment.

16

Christmas in Washington D.C.

Most days during December 1942 in Washington were cold and rainy, reflecting the mood of Americans in the nation's capital. A once sleepy town, Washington had turned into the capital of a world power fighting a global war. The war was going badly on all fronts, and there lingered the worry of further Japanese attacks on the American mainland.

Downtown Washington, cramped and crowded, was a centre of activity. Construction of temporary emergency office space for the ever-expanding federal government crowded the Mall and the surrounding area. Labourers and skilled workers toiled around the clock 'clearing away earth and pavement, removing a tree to be transplanted, mixing and pouring concrete, nailing up walls. Along the blocked streets sat pile upon pile of asbestos siding, cast-iron pipe, nails, and concrete forms, wire, cement, and brick and lumber.'

To turn their minds from the dark news of the war, the dreaded daily casualty list printed in the newspapers and now rumours of millions being murdered in Europe, the people in the nation's capital redirected their thoughts to the upcoming National Football League Championship game to be played at Griffith Stadium on 13 December. The game would pit the undefeated Chicago Bears and the Washington Redskins led by their flashy quarterback Sammy Baugh.[178]

However, the Hadassah leaders in Washington had more important issues on their minds other than football. They had to find a way to get 870 Jewish children out of Tehran.

Tourover refused to give up, aware that their efforts in Washington were the last hope for these children. She, along with de Sola Pool and Warburg, went to the British embassy and met with British Ambassador Lord Halifax.

British ambassador in Washington from 1941 to 1946, Halifax was recognized as one of the chief designers of the appeasement policies before the war. His continuing efforts in the pacification arena toward Hitler, earned him a reputation as possessing 'a sweet and Christian nature' and 'half-unworldly saint', and at the same time 'half-cunning politician'. Harold Begbie, noted English journalist, described Halifax: '[he was] the highest kind of Englishman now in politics whose life and doctrine were in complete harmony with a very lofty moral principle, but who had no harsh judgement for men who err and go astray'.

A controversial file would add a unique chapter to Halifax's life years after his death. Released in 2008, the documents revealed that Halifax, at the outbreak of the war, attempted to broker a peace deal with the Nazis. He believed that by contacting anti-Nazi Germans, like former German ambassador in Rome Ulrich von Hassell, Hitler could be stopped.[179]

Despite his reputation on appeasement, in December 1942 the ambassador appeared to represent Hadassah's last hope, and Tourover was hoping to utilize his 'half-cunning' demeanour to open a door of escape for the Tehran Children. He seemed saddened, and obviously moved, that these women could not find an ally in this gallant cause. The world had suffered through three years of destruction and war and death, and Lord Halifax understood it would be a long time before the murder and destruction would end, and the world be at peace again.

In a twist of fate, the time of the year would influence the British leader's hard work in making one last attempt to save a group of Jewish children. Halifax told the ladies, 'It's almost Christmas. How sad it would make me if nothing could be done for wandering lost children at this time of love and caring.' However, he made no promises, offering, 'but I will make one last effort'.[180]

Tourover later sent a telegram to Jerusalem detailing the failures, and of Halifax's emotional pledge. This news angered Henrietta Szold. *Didn't anyone care about these children?* Szold finally had to admit to herself the answer was clear – no one, not one official in any Allied government, wanted to advance the issue – because they were Jewish children.

17

Promises of Palestine

Zipporah Shertok continued pushing forward, attempting to take the best care of the children as possible. She consistently met with Colonel Ross, who from the British standpoint oversaw the refugees and had written the report in late August and into September on the horrible conditions of the arriving refugees. She met also again with the British Consul in Tehran, and with the Polish minister who was living in Persia, all the while encouraging her staff to show the children pictures of Palestine, to create a connection with their new homeland.

With all the apprehension and fears the children suffered, the Jewish counsellors tried their best, telling stories about Palestine which were filled with sun and fruit orchards, telling them to be patient.

The children, Joe among them, began to learn about Eretz Israel, to sing Hebrew songs even though they did not understand most of the words, and to dance the *hora*. They begin to raise questions: Do Jews really live in Eretz Israel in large numbers? Do they have enough to eat? When we will get there? Will they accept us? The older ones begin to recall the Hebrew prayers of their childhood and fragments of the Bible they had learned long ago. Little by little, a craving began to stir in their hearts to settle in Eretz Israel.

Then Zipporah Shertok learned of a group of Palestinian Jewish soldiers training in a nearby camp with British soldiers, and she requested that they visit the children's camp. The thought was that if the children saw Jewish Palestine soldiers, then that would build their confidence and perhaps calm them in some manner. Despite the counsellors telling stories of Palestine, there had been incidents of mass weeping among the children, breaking out after breakfast one morning in an open field adjacent to the camp. When the adults asked one of the young girls what they were crying about, she stared up with wet eyes, answering beyond her years, 'We are crying for our parents…our fathers and mothers.'[181]

The soldiers arrived mid-morning, dressed in uniforms with colourful 'Palestine' patches across their shoulders, with armloads of fruits and candies. As the children gathered around them, the soldiers were shocked to stare into blank, gray stoic faces.

Weeping, the soldiers knelt and hugged as many as they could gather close to them treating them with tenderness and warmth. Many of the children began telling them of the horrors they had witnessed – fathers and brothers shot in front of them, of whole families buried alive – as if to tell what they had seen would make the memories melt away.

The soldiers passionately told them about Palestine, a land of fruit trees planted in straight, long lines stretching over the next peak, of hillside vineyards, vast wide deserts and the many gardens bursting with colour. They told the children that soon Palestine would be their safe home, yes, very soon, to believe and hope and pray…and yes, it would happen.

Joe didn't remember the soldiers, but he recalled how he felt when he learned that they were close to leaving the camp and going to Palestine. He felt guilt. Why should he out of all of his family that left Germany, why should he be the one that got to go? The other children seemed so happy, and Joe couldn't understand that. Hadn't they also seen horrible things happen, a mother or father shot by the Germans? A sister buried alive? A brother starved to death?

Weren't they sad inside, didn't they feel guilt like he did?

***

Despite travel certificates having been issued, at the end of 1942 there was a growing deep concern about the 870 Jewish children's safety and survival within the Yishuv. Several roadblocks, unexpectedly, had halted the removal of the refugees from Iran, and intensified the political manoeuvering to move the rescue efforts forward. Initially, the Jewish Agency had negotiated to have the children sent south to Baghdad and then through Iraq. Even though Iraq was a Muslim nation that discouraged Jewish immigration to Palestine, at first they seemed agreeable to the children travelling through their country in either sealed train cars or through Iraq airspace. But, at the last minute, the proposal was refused. Then Turkey was approached about the refugees travelling north into their country, crossing from Damascus, but Turkey wouldn't allow that.

Arranging to transport the children to the Promised Land grew increasingly difficult. The Jewish Agency attempted to persuade the Iraqi government to permit the children to cross its borders on their way to Palestine. But Iraq was unyielding because of its anti-Zionist policy. Any plans to transport the children through Turkey also failed. The American and British governments rejected the Agency's request for air transportation on the basic that they could not spare the planes. Soon it became evident that the only route that was open to the children was the sea.

***

Finally, in Washington events abruptly shifted.[182]

Two mornings after visiting Lord Halifax at the British Embassy, and what must have seemed an eternity, Denise Tourover received a telegram from British War Ministry chief John McClay in Washington. With no other country able to do anything to move the rescue effort forward, it was the British government, who had played the role of a constant burden to the Zionist movement and a restrictor of immigration to Palestine, which was the party to change the desperate situation.

It seemed that Lord Halifax, ironically, deemed that Christmas was the appropriate time to do something for the children…a group of Jewish children. He had secured passage for the children to depart the Iranian capital in short order.

***

Henrietta Szold was elated with the news, and throughout agency offices in Palestine preparations began for the children's arrival. As much as she hated it, the children would first have to come to Athlit, the same detention camp where Dobkin had interviewed the exchangees who first told of the gassings and mass murders, a place Szold described as 'a barren, ugly government quarantine station'.[183] She would do her best to get them out of there as soon as possible, but they couldn't be sent directly to homes from Athlit. If they were to relive their horrible past, it couldn't be done in new homes. Instead, temporary centres would be designated throughout Eretz Israel for the children to be nursed back to physical and mental stability with assistance from trained doctors and counsellors. There the children would be showered with warmth, love and affection. Something a child should never pass through childhood without.

***

When the travel notification finally came, the camp had just two days to get the children ready for departure. For those in charge, there were so many pressing questions that had to be answered: surely blankets should be left behind, shouldn't they? After all, it would be hot in India, wouldn't it? Would medicines be available along the route?

The endless waiting, rumours of 'leaving tomorrow' only to be proven untrue, grew into intense frustration for the children and adults. Joe, even at such a young age, was by now a veteran of long journeys, and he wouldn't have any of it. Just like when the trains were going to take them out of Russia, and with excitement they had walked most of the night, only to see no locomotive. No, he wouldn't believe it until the trucks came and took them away.

Even most of the adults refused to believe, despite assurances from the Jewish Agency. This had gone on now for weeks, since September and October. Hadn't there been assurances before? Several times they were informed that the Iraqis agreed to let the children travel through, or that Turkey was close to granting permission, only to rescind permission the next day.

Then, when it became evident that this time leaving for Palestine may actually be true once two dates were given as departure dates. One group would leave on 2 January and the other group on 6 January 1943. And when the news swirled through the camp that, yes, they were finally leaving, the children became so excited that any resemblance of routine quickly vanished, other than the children busying themselves packing the few belongings they possessed.

This news didn't only stir excitement in the Tehran camps, but among the Jewish population of Palestine once the news reached the *Yishuv*. Up until this point, any news coming out of Europe concerning the Jews was always profoundly depressing. On 4 January 1943, just as the children departed Tehran, headlines in a Hebrew newspaper declared: 'Reality Surpasses in Horror the Darkest Prophecies', and Yishuv residents read that 75 per cent of the Jews of occupied Europe had been murdered. The number of Jews under Nazi occupation was estimated to be 8 million, fixing the number of victims at 6 million killed.

Strangely, leaving the camp turned into an unpredictable drama. During the seven months the camp had offered the children some hint of stability with routines and an ordered life. They saw the same faces every morning and looked forward to some content times during the day. They had become familiar with what they could expect of the people around them, and in turn what was expected of them. So, once they were informed that they were scheduled to leave soon, old fears and dreads flooded over them.

The counsellors watched as the children reacted in different ways, unpacking and repacking their meagre belongings, confused about what they needed and how long the journey would be to Palestine...'though their belongings were pathetic bundles of torn and tattered possessions. They held on to every foul-smelling rag, ripped pair of shoes, or frayed photograph, refusing to let go of the little that was theirs...'[184]

Those last few nights in the camp, as they anxiously awaited the trucks 'were filled with the sound of weeping, such as we had not heard for a long time.' There was nothing the adults could do to stop it.

The next morning, the first trucks pulled into the camp, and immediately the children began pushing and shoving, fearing that if they didn't find a place on the first several trucks, then they wouldn't get to go.

David Laor was there to assist in the loading. 'The children arranged themselves as they wished and not according to age groups. The infants were accompanied by their nurses and we also had a good many eighteen-year-old boys, who left with us under the pretence of being younger, to avoid conscription. They all had their bundles in their hands, containing all their possessions despite our instructions. We preferred to overlook this, also.'

There was sadness also because the children had grown over the years to mistrust anyone, even the adults taking care of them in Tehran. There was a fear of what lay ahead. With the journey taking them to Palestine, many of the children realized they were being taken even further away from families still in Russia. Joe Rosenbaum's memory faded in and out because once again he had become exhausted and sick. In the back of his mind, he thought that he had come this far…but he wasn't certain that he could make the journey much further.

Laor and the other counsellors tried their best, all the while respecting the efforts, the bravery and tenacity of the Jewish Agency. Many of them stayed until the very last, watching them load up and finally leave the camp. Among the ones who stayed was Zipporah Shertok.

'Tzippora [Zipporah] Shertok accompanied us,' Laor remembered:

> …through the whole whirlpool departure from the Tehran Jewish Children's Home, our camp. She was scared that our departure would be complicated for other reasons: the pressure from the Persians, who did not want the tens of thousands of refugees flooding into their country, had expedited our leaving. We would get to India as had other Polish refugees sent there, but there was still the possibility that we would not be able to continue to Palestine. This worry had robbed her of sleep. Only I shared her awareness of the danger, but I tried to hope for the best, and I had faith in Tzippora's dedication to our cause. And so, on that cold winter morning we left Tehran in the convoy of trucks winding away from the camp. The abandoned tents, the empty hut, lay behind us with the snowy mountains in the background. A new chapter had begun in our lives. We had left this important and decisive station on the long road that we had travelled, that still had not come to an end. Ahead of us lay yet another station on the journey to our final destination – Palestine. Eretz Israel.[185]

For the next 36 hours a column of canvas-topped trucks followed narrow, mountainous roads.

When the trucks pulled into Bender Shapur, the children saw the harbour, and anchored at the dock there was the welcome sight of the ship that would take them on the last part of their journey. On 11 January 1945, the children and adults boarded the British ship *Dunera*, bound for Karachi, India.

Shertok was deeply moved as she said goodbye and went ashore. To those on the ship looking back at the shore, she looked 'small, devoted, resourceful…she had given herself utterly to "our cause", and many wondered where she drew her physical and spiritual strength from.

Long after the ship was out of view in the horizon's haze, loaded with its precious cargo of 750 children; Zipporah Shertok stood at the pier and stared at the empty horizon.

She was content that she had done her best.

PART FOUR

January 1943 – February 1943

18

Bender Shapur: Another Journey Begins

'So then, on January 8, 1943, they took us by trucks to a ship', Joe recalls as the last part of his journey began. Though there would still be hunger and illness to deal with – Joe would almost die in a British hospital in Karachi, India – at least the children were, at long last, out of Tehran and on their way to Palestine. 'Those that escorted us from Tehran to Palestine took more care of us than the supervisors when we went from Russia to Tehran.'[186]

In Iran, the Polish officials had placed the children under the care of the Jewish Agency, with specific orders from Henrietta Szold that all precautions are taken to secure the children's safety and well-being. In the trip out of Siberia months before, any effort toward organization to achieve a semblance of order, other than that offered by the Polish army, was simply overwhelmed by the sheer numbers of children. This was also the case in the escape from Central Asia, across the Caspian Sea and into Iranian territory. But from October 1942 onwards, Jewish children were under the guarded, watchful care of the Jewish officials, fervent Zionists who understood if there was to be a future in the new land of Israel it would require children who would grow up to be that next generation.

Beneath the haze of a humid morning, Joe and the over 700 children spent their last day in Persia sitting on folded blankets on the pier, eating fruits and nuts. They heard rumours that they were going to India – and then on to Palestine. Sitting at the edge of the sea, Joe's eyes burned from the sunlight, and his stomach tossed nauseously. As much as he saw the excitement among the other children he wasn't excited about being on a ship. Joe wasn't as excited as the other children at all. 'Trucks leave, but I didn't care what was going on anymore. I was ill…they gave us food and water, and I didn't pay any attention. I was in bad shape, and even today my teeth have short roots because of my sickness. I have other illnesses, problems, today.' The lingering fever since Tashkent had come over Joe again.

At night his fragile body ached so much that he startled himself awake, and that lack of sleep had once again taken its toll on his well-being. Those few hours of sleep, were at least an escape from the nightmares that had begun when he arrived at the Tehran camp. Until Joe reached Palestine, he would relive the last time that he stared into his mother's face...of the cold touch of his sister's skin as he tried to wake her after making porridge poured into a tin can. These nightmares would stop, for a while, then begin again later in his life.

There was one question, however, that Joe asked himself that day as he saw other children, other boys with younger sisters sitting in the sand awaiting the trip to Palestine – *Why couldn't Nelly be here with me?*

The rumours were in fact true, the destination was the Arabian Sea coast of West Pakistan, specifically Karachi where a British hospital was located and from there they would be able to sail around Yemen and then towards Egypt. The Jewish authorities were aware that it would take a bit of good fortune for any ship sailing through the Indian Ocean to escape enemy submarines and minefields. These waters had been the scene of numerous sea battles and remained heavily patrolled by both sides.

Late in the afternoon, they were loaded onto the SS *Donora,* a converted cargo ship that would take them out on the Caspian Sea and to Karachi.

It was a large ship, and because it was built to haul freight there were a few cabins reserved for the crew and some passengers. The children and adults were crowded into a hall next to storage spaces. There were few toilets and no showers. Refugees were allowed to mill about in limited designated areas on the deck. There were not enough life preservers and the heat was over-bearing, and as the journey began the swaying of the ship caused many of the children to become seasick. Because there were no facilities for washing, the children soon became filthy and infested with lice. The food was inedible. And they were all told to expect enemy planes and minefields throughout the trip.

As shadows fell across the high embankment that kept high tides from flooding the buildings and the train tracks running near the port, the SS *Donora,* with her precious cargo, lifted anchor and made her way to the Caspian Sea.

The 750 children, accompanied by 116 adults, had spent 41 months escaping both the Germans and the Russians. There now remained another 40 days before they reached Palestine.

***

The transferring by General Anders of his army headquarters to Iraq had begun in September and was completed by the second week of January, just as the children sailed southwards.

Quizil Ribat was a small village of primitive huts surrounded by Polish troops bivouacked in an ocean of tents. 'The heat was terrific', Anders wrote, 'and I well remember the joy of making my first call on the hospitable manager of the oil refinery at Khanaqin, where the rooms were air-conditioned'.[187] Soon after arriving, Anders learned that there had been an outbreak of malaria, which took many months for British medical officers to get under control.

From his base in Iraq, Anders then flew to Cairo numerous times to meet British officials concerning the organizing of the Polish army. It was during these meeting that Anders was presented the initial details of an African offensive; plans that included Polish troops fighting alongside the British.

It was in these Iraqi camps, where Polish soldiers were fed and treated well, that Anders felt he now commanded a valid fighting force. Later in the year, June 1943, American General George S. Patton would review these Polish troops for the first time, and describe them as 'the best-looking troops, including the British and Americans, that I have ever seen'.

Nevertheless, as the Tehran Children departed Bender Shapur on the SS *Donora*, Anders received a telegram from General Sikorski relating disheartening news: 'The Soviet government had handed a note to the Polish government-in-exile in London informing them that all Poles remaining in the Soviet Union and originating from the provinces under Soviet occupation would be considered Soviet subjects'.[188]

Anders wanted to respond at once. But he hesitated.

Thinking back to the exodus from Russia, politicians had demanded that he leave the Jews behind to certain death, instead of evacuating with his troops to Central Asia. Anders had simply resisted such notions. He took the Jews with him.

But now this was a betrayal by the Soviets, a powerful ally of the Polish people. Would the Allied leaders stand up to Stalin at this critical moment in the war? How would this affect the morale and, most importantly, just as the momentum in the war was being regained from Germany's armies, would his men continue to fight for the Allied effort? Anders, once again, had reached a crossroads in his life that he had to manoeuvre through with great care.

The general was unaware that two months before, in October 1942, Soviet-Polish relations had begun to unravel. It was clear by then that the Soviets would be content to liberate territories from Nazi control, only to prepare such countries for 'Soviet domination'. That same month, the Soviets presented a note to Polish Foreign Minister, Count E. Raczynski, informing him that the Soviet Union would no longer permit any future enlistment in the Polish Army of Poles still in the Soviet Union.

'This cruel and illegal Soviet decision deprived hundreds of thousands of Poles of their citizenship,' Anders stated. 'It was a heavy blow to all of us, for it meant that most of us had friends and relatives doomed to remain, unheard of, in the Soviet Union for the rest of their lives.'[189]

In the end, Anders knew what action he must take if he were to handle this situation correctly. He would leave it to his troops, the ones who would spill their blood on the battlefield, to make the decision whether to continue to fight, or not.

***

Henrietta Szold had been awake long before the sun came up over the hills outside her Eden Hotel apartment window. Now, carefully as she did each morning before going to the *Youth Aliyah* office, she watered each pot of flowers, their scent filling the room. And, of course, there were the dead flowers that she couldn't stand to throw away. For all her flowers were precious to her, their colourful presence and the handsome smell that prompted her to say to a friend once, 'The air of my room is fragrant with the perfume of orange blossoms. I wonder how orange trees stand it.'[190]

She stepped to her desk and picked up a telegram that had arrived the previous day.

The children had departed Persia by ship, and were heading out into the Indian Ocean. This information lifted her spirits, and Szold was happy; at last they were heading home. But that also meant they were on the move placing them in great danger, and that deeply concerned her. She was still upset about the lack of assistance from both American and British governments. That all had to be set aside now, for with the children's arrival would arise another problem. Not a problem unknown to *Youth Aliyah*, however, because Szold and her staff faced the dilemma whenever children arrived from Europe. The *Yishuv* wasn't unified as far as types of schools, but the Jewish settlement maintained a divided system based on political parties flourishing within Zionism. The General Zionist centre and the Labour left wing focused studies on history and literature, more of a secular education. The Mizrahi, a right-wing thinking group, dictated education as the study of the *Talmud*, the central text of Rabbinic Judaism, and the details, unyielding orthodox compliance.

And therein was the problem that Szold knew she would face.

Because the system within the *Yishuv*, as Szold knew, never worked perfectly, each group wanted the new arrivals converted to their teaching. Each new immigrant would be affiliated with a Zionist group, a specific philosophy, based on the association and belief of their past. But the children coming to Palestine, some as young as three, would be influenced into believing whatever a group would taught them.

The Tehran Children were very different from the children they had managed to rescue from Europe since 1933. These children had suffered greatly. First, they would have to be restored physically and, perhaps more importantly, brought out of depression and mental maladies.

No, Szold promised herself, these children had to be handled with delicate counselling, touched with the patience and love of a mother, and not that of political ideologies.

Szold's preparations included bringing the children to Athlit, 'a barren, ugly government quarantine station she despised', but a necessary location. Aware of the conditions of the children – needing rest and food – they would stay at Athlit for as short a time as possible, Szold decided, then they would then be sent out to temporary centres located all over the country for perhaps five or six weeks. At that time, the choosing of permanent homes would depend on their past and on their religious relationships.

Organizing her counsellors in Palestine, she told them, 'It is for you to heal wounds inflicted by malign cruelty, to replace the wrenches of ties that bound a [generation] of children to father and mothers scattered to the furthest corners of the earth, to restore confidence in men and their works and to encourage aspiration and direct it into channels of action toward culture and peace.'[191]

Szold had made another decision in those weeks awaiting the children's arrival. She would meet them at Athlit, and personally talk to each child no matter how long it took. It was that important.

***

Joe didn't care any longer because on the ship sailing toward India the fever burned like a fire on his insides. 'I was ill again…in bad shape, and I didn't pay attention to what was going on.'[192] It was the third time Joe had fallen ill since Tashkent, and once again he doubted that he would ever be well again, or to look upon the land of Palestine. Joe had hidden away in a secret box inside of his mind all his hurt and fear so that no one would know.

One of the older children who was not as ill as Joe, remembered the deplorable conditions onboard the ship:

> [Due to the overflow of passengers]…for much of the day, the children were instructed to stay below deck, where the heat was oppressive. The constant swaying of the boat caused severe sea-sickness. The children vomited over themselves, and, because of the crowded

quarters, sometimes on others. Without facilities for washing and changing of clothes, the youngsters' clothes soon became filthy and beset by lice. The available food was most unappetizing, not too surprising during a brutal war.[193]

19

Karachi…

Ten days later, on 31 January, as the SS *Donora* docked in Karachi on a stormy rainy day, the officers of the Bombay Jewish Relief Association met the boat and were dismayed at the condition of the children. Immediately they dispatched a telegram to the Jewish Agency in Jerusalem:

> CHILDREN COMPLETELY DESTITUTE DESOLATE CONDITION NEEDING BADLY CLOTHES SHOES VITAMINS STOP HAVE COLLECTED STERLING ONE THOUSAND URGENTLY REQUIRE AT LEAST FURTHER THREE THOUSAND COMMUNICATE HENRIETTA SZOLD CABLE REMITTANCE URGENT.[194]

Located on the Arabian Sea coastline, Karachi was a major seaport known as Uroos ul Bilaad, 'City of Lights', or 'The Bride of the Cities' because of its liveliness. It was also known as the 'City of the Quaid', the birth and burial place of Quaid-e-Azam, the Great Leader, Mahammad Ali Jinnah, the founder of Pakistan's independence four year later.

Eliott Jaroslawicz was on the ship with Joe, and he remembers vividly the sights he witnessed in Karachi. In the marketplace, he was startled to see graceful women wrapped in captivating sarees making their way through crowds of deformed beggars:

> There was [were] a lot of very poor people. And the men with the head wrapped around (turbans). And people washing themselves in the street. Big trucks with water and they had a shower on the side…I remember I saw the first time the snake. A snake charmer whistled to a snake! And I saw somebody walking with a monkey on his shoulder. And there were monkeys holding hands of children. And when a cow goes by, everybody goes on the side to let it pass.[195]

However, this was not the Karachi most of the children saw when they arrived. For them there was only poverty, filth and a people that they had never laid eyes upon before. Starving people swam out to the ship, begging for any food that the refugees had for them to eat. But they had no food to share. 'People, half-naked with towels on, they would climb up with a rope to get whatever is left on the ship – garbage. The food was rotten, but the British soldiers would toss it to them.'[196]

Then army trucks came for the children and drove them far inland to the camps that would be their home until another ship came to take them to Egypt. The British army camp was located outside Karachi, guarded by Indian soldiers, in colourful, royal uniforms. To the children, these soldiers spoke a strange language that they couldn't understand – English.

'Our next stop on the way to Palestine was Karachi, which was in India and under British rule', Joe remembers. 'They took us to one of their camps. Here I got sick again. I had all kinds of problems, I don't know exactly. They put me in a tent hospital, not a building. I stayed there for about two weeks.'[197]

It was a recently constructed camp, surrounded by open fields, sectioned off by ropes into units that housed smaller groups of children, usually of about the same age. Each living section was connected by pathways lined with white rocks, so once the sun set the camp was in complete darkness. But the soldiers built fires around the camp to keep away hyenas, which the children heard yelping at night.

10. Group portrait of members of the Tehran children's transport during a stopover in Karachi whilst en route to Palestine. Unites States Holocaust Memorial Museum, courtesy of Aaron Rubinstein.

Soon, it was evident to the children that this camp was more orderly with four or five children assigned to each tent. The military camp was clean, organized, with a precision the children hadn't witnessed during their long journey. On the third day in the camp they had a surprise when the soldiers gave each of them pith helmets and shoes and white shorts and shirts. Within the week the military recorded photographs of the children exercising on the parade ground and playing soccer with the Indian soldiers. One photograph showed children sitting at a table, the adults standing behind, as they ate from tin cups and plates. One of the smaller children in the foreground sat with his pith helmet on this head, refusing to give up his gift even while eating.

All of them are smiling. It had been a long time.

***

Karachi's military importance in the war began eleven years before, in 1932, when a de Havilland monoplane arrived at Drigh Road airfield from Bombay with bags of mail. Within a decade, Karachi Airfield was crowded with United States Air Force personnel manning an installation built to assemble crated combat aircraft. On 12 March1942, ten crated P-40s had arrived by ship from Australia and were gathered to fight against the Japanese in the Pacific Theater. Supply flights originated out of Karachi, orchestrated by the USAAF Air Transport Command delivered badly-needed food, medicine and weapons to eastern India and China.

By late October, four months before Joe Rosenbaum lay in the British Hospital in Karachi, again near death, the Indian Air Task Force was activated, joining the 7th Bombardment Group, the 51st Fighter Group and the 341st Bombardment Group. On 11 November 1942, the IATF would bomb Shinghbwiyang, Burma with nine of the assembled P-40s causing heavy damage. The IATF 9th Photographic Reconnaissance Squadron, with F-4 aircraft, would later fly their first mission on 1 December from Karachi to Kunming, China.

***

On display at *Yad Vashem* in Jerusalem, there was a faded photograph of a small child with a large bow in her hair, just over two years old when she arrived in Karachi. Vera Brand née Lifshitz held a doll, and in the background, was a row of tents. The doll's name was Lala, Polish for doll, given to her by an Indian soldier.

Born just three weeks before her family was deported from Lvov, Poland, Vera followed the same journey as the other children. Though not Jewish –

her father was allowed to join Anders' Army – Vera would leave Karachi by ship and travel on one of the same trains as Joe out of Egypt to Palestine almost a month later.[198]

***

On the same day the Tehran Children reached India, at 7:35 a.m. Field Marshal Friedrich von Paulus surrendered over 90,000 German troops to Soviet Army Lt. Fyodor Ilchenko in Stalingrad. A month before, the Russian army had announced that 22 German divisions in Stalingrad had been surrounded by the Red Army.

The tide of war had definitively turned in the Allies' favour, for with the fall of Germany to Russian forces the *Pittsburgh Post-Gazette* announced 'British Seize Forts in Tripoli' as the British Eighth Army, commanded by General Bernard Montgomery, defeated Italian forces holding the city.[199]

The same week, on 27 January, B-17 and B-24 bombers from the American Eighth Air Force launched the historic Wilhelmshaven bombing mission, the first such operation against the Nazis' homeland. In the attack 137.5 tons of munitions were dropped on the port destroying tactical naval facilities.

Not all news was good, however. In German-occupied Poland, Jewish residents in the Czestochowa ghetto, in June 1943, launched the Czestochowa Ghetto Uprising. The *Jewish Fighting Organisation*, formed by Mordechaj Zilberberg and others, was about 300 men. In late January the resistance was crushed. Of the over 48,000 residents originally placed in the ghetto for deportation to slave labour and killing camps, perhaps 3,000 were still alive and were shipped to Treblinka concentration camp.

All perished.

Even as the war ground on and American soldiers continued to die on foreign soil both in Europe and in the Pacific theatre, some normalcy of life in the world continued. The last week of January saw the movie *Casablanca*, staring Humphrey Bogart and Ingrid Bergman, released. Unintentionally, at the same time, President Roosevelt was in Casablanca, the Moroccan capital, meeting with Winston Churchill. At New York's Carnegie Hall, Duke Ellington premiered his jazz symphony, 'Black, Brown, and Beige'.

***

Anders, as often good commanders do, sensed the attitude of his soldiers beginning to change. 'Our soldiers, who instinctively knew what the truth was and how things stood', Anders later wrote, '[they] were growing impatient, and I sympathized with them'.[200]

No longer satisfied to hold back his opinions, Anders, on 2 February had written to General Sikorski and the President of Poland, Raczkiewicz:

> Our present experience is the most difficult which can befall a soldier and a citizen. We have fought for Poland without interruption since 1939. Now, in this fourth year of hostilities, we clearly see that our eternal enemy loses strength...the whole world is aware of the fact that Germany will be defeated, but our hearts are still full of anxiety, because we feel that the victory of Soviet Russia would mean deadly danger for Poland...it is quite clear to us that the Soviets have deceived us and this must be proclaimed everywhere.[201]

Anders wrote in his letter to Raczkiewicz, after detailing the experiences of his army since leaving the Soviet Union: 'A great majority of our men have families still in Poland. We wish to go back to them, and we are perfectly aware of the fact that should the Bolsheviks enter Poland we shall never see them again. This must be understood by our great allies, and it is our task to make it clear to them.'[202]

With these actions, Anders knew he had presented the situation to the best of his ability. Now he must have patience while he waited, because the fate of himself and his army was not in the hands of a general poised to give an order, but in the hands of his soldiers. As it should be.

Anders then turned his attention towards another problem which had presented itself.

Over 4,500 Polish soldiers under his command presently stationed and training in Palestine were of Jewish descent. Anders and his officers were aware that they would be facing desertion issues, concerns brought to their attention by British officials and Polish commanders who were both aware of Zionist feelings stirring in the Jewish soldiers. All Polish soldiers, including the Jewish soldiers, had taken an oath in Persia to the Polish cause. But with these soldiers stationed in Palestine, the situation offered an opportunity for them to abandon the army.

In August 1943, when the army issued temporary passes, over 800 soldiers would fail to return to duty.[203]

Anders decided on the matter and moved quickly, issuing instructions reflective of his opinion: 'The Jews are fighting for their freedom, and I do not intend to stand in their way.' He issued undisclosed instructions to 'not pursue the deserters. I considered the Jews who saw their first duty in the struggle for Palestine's freedom, had every right to that view.'[204]

By the end of the following year, over 3,000 Jewish soldiers had left the Polish army ranks.

After two weeks in Karachi, at last a ship had been dispatched to India to take the children on the remainder of their journey to Egypt. As a parting gift, the British military arranged a concert for the children in the camp the night before their scheduled departure. Intrigued by the strange, exotic instruments playing, one small girl was noticed sketching the musicians in her diary.

20

…And then to Aden

The children were loaded on trucks at the British camp on 6 February 1943, and taken back to the harbour where they had arrived several weeks before, and put aboard the ship waiting for them.

Joe almost didn't make the trip. But at the last minute, Jewish authorities walked through the hospital and asked that even the sick children should at least be given a chance at surviving the last leg of the journey.

Then the SS *Noralea* departed for Egypt. Conditions on the *Noralea* were deplorable. Again, the children were forced to endure extreme heat and crowding below deck, living in stale air.

However, the children were once again encouraged as they arrived in Aden, a seaport city in Yemen with an eastern approach to the Gulf of Aden, a beautiful port with mountains and seagulls following the ship as it slipped into the harbour which lay in the crater of a dormant volcano that formed a peninsula, joined to the mainland by a low isthmus.

Because the ship wasn't going to remain in the Aden harbour long, the children were ordered to stay on board enduring over-crowding and the suffocating heat. Suffering even more were the women and girls who had to stay below deck because the British officials didn't want to take the chance of offending the Muslims.

The ship pulled away from the harbour late the next afternoon, creating an excitement throughout the ship. What the children didn't know, but British officials were well aware of, was that the last route of the journey would take them through waters that would be mined, and airspace frequently patrolled by Italian warplanes. The captain let the adult leaders know that he also expected to be trailed by enemy submarines.

'We were bombed by the Italians', Joe remembers of the trip. 'There was an alarm to go down [below], but I only went down one time, and after that I didn't care and stayed on deck. I didn't believe they could hit us.'[205]

Joe Rosenbaum and the Tehran Children weren't yet out of danger.

***

On 4 February 1943, two days before the *SS Noralea* sailed into the Aden harbour, the remnants of Rommel's once proud Afrika Korps withdrew into French Tunisia.

A month later, on 6 March 1943, General Erwin Rommel attacked the British Eighth Army at the Battle of Medenine, his last futile offensive in Africa which ended with the loss of 52 tanks, and he then withdrew.

On 9 March Rommel returned to Germany, still a hero in the hearts of the German people. Two months later, on 13 May 1943, the famed Afrika Korps surrendered.

21

Eretz Israel Awaits...

Until early 1943, news from Europe was bad and continued to hang like a veiled darkness over the *Yishuv* in Palestine. Several months before, in October 1942, exchangees interviewed upon their arrival at Athlit Detention Camp had finally confirmed the greatest fears of the Zionist leaders and the Jewish people.

Thousands were dying in the Nazi 'Valley of Death' as Ben-Gurion referred to the *Shoah*, the Holocaust, and it appeared that not much could be done about it. Meanwhile, the news of murders, and gassings, and crematoria continued to hang over the land like smoke from the ovens themselves, burning the flesh of the European Jews.

Kept secret as for as long as possible from the public, in January 1943 the *Yishuv* learned the news of the Tehran Children heading to Egypt. Although it was only a small group, especially considering the millions of Jews who had disappeared from the map of Europe, this rescue went to the centre of what Zionism stood for. 'Bring the children home', Ben-Gurion had urged.[206] Once the news spread that the children were at last on their way, the populace was captivated and to the *Yishuv* these children represented a rebirth of the lost European Jews.

The children were coming home.

***

A week before, on 10 February, Henrietta Szold had sent Hans Beyth, one of her associates in the *Youth Aliyah*, to Suez to prepare for the children's arrival as the ship made its way northward through mined waters, managing to survive the occasional bombing by Italian planes. Beyth's orders from Szold were to, by all means necessary, keep the arrival date secret as he passed on any information through a code which he kept hidden in his shoe.

Whenever anyone in the *Youth Aliyah* office inquired about Beyth they were told he was at home suffering from the flu. Meanwhile, socks, skullcaps and large quantities of food were collected without explanation. There was more good news, badly needed, when Szold received cables from Hadassah in America. Monies were being sent.

There was a place on the Haifa road where Henrietta Szold occasionally found the peace she desired, a brief shelter away from her responsibilities. It was a lone ancient sycamore tree, twisted and damaged with wide-reaching branches. Whenever she had a moment, no matter how brief, she would get her driver to stop the sedan and she would walk up to the tree and sit in its deep shade, feeling the nobility that it held, bent and twisted and burdened by centuries of storms – but never broken. Henrietta often thought when she was alone that 'it was rooted in the land, and so was she.'[207]

On this particular afternoon, Henrietta was weary. She had worried over the children and felt an aching sickness consuming her. Several of her aides noticing that she was weak and advised her to rest. No, she had told them, there would be time for rest later, but for now that wasn't possible.

That morning, she had received a message from Hans Beyth from the Suez, informing her that the children were scheduled to arrive by ship later that day, and then leave for Palestine the next morning by two trains, secured by the Immigration Office of Zionist Labour. If all went as planned, he had written, the children would reach Athlit camp within 24 hours.

Two days? She could hardly believe it.

It had taken seven hard months of negotiating and political manoeuvering from Ben-Gurion, Hadassah and many other Zionist officials to finally secure passage from Tehran to Egypt. Szold could only wonder why it should have ever been so difficult to save starving, frightened children.

But even with the children drawing ever closer to Palestine, still she worried. There had been times when other refugees were close to freedom and unforeseen circumstances had dictated horrible outcomes. Two incidents lingered in her mind, the first being the sinking of the ship, the *Patria,* on 25 November 1940.

The SS *Patria* was a twelve-ton, French-built ocean liner, which in the last week of November was carrying 1,800 Jewish refugees from Nazi-occupied Europe. British officials had seized the ship off the coast near Haifa, and, in an effort to present a dramatic example of the *Patria,* and to discourage the illegal immigration; the passengers were deported to Mauritius.

Zionist authorities openly opposed such British actions, and Haganah, the Jewish paramilitary organization, planted a bomb intended to disable the ship so it couldn't sail from Haifa. Haganah misjudged the explosive power of the bomb, and the *Patria* regrettably sank sixteen minutes after the explosion, killing 267 refugees.

The other incident Szold reflected upon was on 12 December 1941, when the ship *Struma* sailed from Romania with 769 refugees on board. An old cargo barge, built to haul livestock along the Danube, owned the distinction of being the last vessel to leave Europe once the war began.

Commissioned by the Irgun, a more radical underground group whose members had broken away from the Haganah, the *Struma* sailed from Constanza in Romania, a major embankment port for Jews attempting to leave Europe for Palestine. Despite poor living conditions for the passengers and faulty engines, the ship reached Istanbul on 16 December 1941, where they were greeted with disappointing news. The passengers were told they wouldn't receive visas to enter Palestine, and to make matters worse entry into Turkey wasn't going to be permitted.

After two months in quarantine in the Istanbul harbour, on February 23, Turkish officials ordered the boat to be towed out to sea. The next day the boat sank in an explosion. Only one passenger survived. Although the exact cause behind the explosion was never determined, reports passed to Szold suggested a Soviet submarine had mistakenly torpedoed the *Struma*. Szold, looking back on these two sad incidents, grew more anxious and apprehensive, and she would remain concerned until the children were truly safe.

She walked down the hill toward the sedan waiting at the road. It was time to leave her place of peace and return to Haifa. Her driver opened the door. Szold entered and sat on the back seat. He pulled out onto the highway and headed south as Szold gazed out upon the land that she grown to love since arriving over twenty years ago. If the information Hans Beyth had forwarded to her from Egypt was correct, the children would be home soon, and there were many tasks yet to be completed preparing for their arrival. Still, they had to pass through the desert to reach home, a thought that gave her pause. 'Save the children', Szold whispered.[208]

***

If ever there was a child weary of travelling it was Joe Rosenbaum. Childhood for Joe and the other children had been a long journey of camps, disease and death. During the voyage on the *Noralea* most of the children remained sick, and weak, but were continually encouraged by the idea that Egypt was not that far away, two days, three days at the most. At night, when they were put to bed, Joe would will himself to sleep, dreaming of the orchards of fruit and flowers that the Palestine soldiers told them of when they visited the Tehran camp.[209]

He wasn't sure if the other children knew, but for Joe learning to survive from camp to camp meant watching other people. The ship's crew, for example, seemed anxious, constantly watching out over the waters. Joe was right, because what the children didn't know was that since departing Yemen the *Noralea* had been sailing through heavily-mined waters. With no mine-sweepers to clear their path, the captain followed smaller boats that could more easily see the mines laid by Allies during the North Africa campaign.

The trip became even more difficult as the *Noralea* neared Egypt. Constant alarms sounded, suggesting the sighting of enemy boats, or a U-boat rumoured to have swerved into their path. The precious cargo of children was constantly herded below deck.

Then, on the afternoon of 17 February, the SS *Noralea*, with the children lined along the rail, gawking in wonder, slipped out of the Suez Canal waters and docked at Port Said, Egypt.

One of the older counsellors pulled out the flag from the Tehran camp and unfold it. 'We hoisted our flag emblazoned with the *Magen David* and the words 'Tehran Jewish Children's Home'.[210]

***

Small boats drew along the *S.S. Noralea*, as Joe and a small group of children were instructed to follow several adults down a walkway to the smaller boats. The children clutched thick, canvas bundles, their only possessions in the world. Joe watched anxiously as the infants and attendants were taken ashore and then elbowed his way to the front of the queue, waiting for the next boat.

Then another boat pulled up alongside the ship, prepared to load the next group. The children climbed down the ladder, followed by the adults. Pulling the bundle close to him, Joe stared at the shoreline. Several large ferries criss-crossed in front of their boat, and as they slipped closer he saw old houses with grand balconies, reminding him of the old section of Cologne neighbourhoods where his mother would take him on weekend walks to visit her aunt. Joe, of course, didn't know the name of the city sprawled out before him along the Mediterranean Sea coast, but they had arrived in Port Said, Egypt, just north of the Suez Canal. Joe didn't care. But as the salt air blew in his face and as the boat slipped toward shore, Joe could sense that this place was the beginning of freedom that he had so often been promised.

Several counsellors stood in front of the boat, facing the children. They yelled out that they were all going to sing a song, thankful that they had at long last arrived in Egypt. At first Joe didn't join in because he didn't know the words. But when he finally did try to sing, a knot swelled in his throat. So much…so much had happened. All the more reason to be happy as, after all, they had made it to Egypt and would be in Palestine soon.

Joe looked out on the ocean, the waters the colour of copper pennies. He looked as far out as he could where the water danced magically beneath the sunlight. He began singing, the words resonating loud and strong, until his voice broke.

'We ascend and sing, above death and ruins...'

***

For a moment fear gripped the children.

Along the pier were a line of soldiers, and from their past experiences they had learned that soldiers were mostly never good news. But these soldiers were different because they wore the same uniforms that the soldiers who had told them about Palestine had worn. And they were smiling. The soldiers began tossing the children small packages with portions of rations. Joe caught one parcel and opened it. There was a note, written in Yiddish: 'Blessed be the ones who come. You shall never be a refugee again.'

Those who first greeted them were Jewish military engineers who had received word that these children were coming. Anticipating the arrival of the transports, the solders had collected funds throughout their camp and prepared gift packages for each child. Each package contained a slip of paper:

> We, a unit of Palestinian Jewish soldiers doing its work on alien soil, have had the great good fortune to be the first to welcome you home and to give you the traditional blessing of our people: 'Peace be unto you'. Blessed be you in your coming, [young] brothers and sisters. It is you and such as you who give meaning and purpose to our participation in this war. You are the reason for which we throw ourselves into danger and hardship. Your coming is only a token of the coming of multitudes after you. It forces us and encourages us to labor beyond our strength for the salvation of the others to follow you.

In one bag a child found a paper that read: 'To You, Child That Goes Up to the Land: This is the name by which I wish to call you. I will not call you a refugee child for, from this moment on, you are a builder and a pioneer. You will work in the Land and build the Land and love it. And so, you will forget the cup of grief from which you have drunk to the full.' The note was signed – A Jewish Soldier.

The boy beside Joe started laughing out loud. He was taller than Joe, but just as skinny and very pale. His was smeared with black ointment on crusty scabs, his head shaven to rid him of lice. A worn, thin shirt hung on him as if he were a scarecrow. Ragged trousers were bunched at the waist, a belt buckled tightly. But he was laughing, chapped lips stretched over his teeth. When he noticed Joe staring at him, he stopped laughing and stared back at Joe for a long moment. Then with a weak smile spreading across his face, he handed Joe the small piece of paper from his parcel. Joe read it: 'And the children will return to their homeland. Jeremiah 31:17.'

When they reached the pier, the soldiers pressed closely around them and with tears in their eyes began handing out sacks of fruit. These were Palestinian Jewish soldiers, Haganah, who had raided the military canteens of any items they thought the children might eat.

This was at a time when news of Hitler's 'Valley of Death', as Ben-Gurion had referred to the Shoah, had begun to trickle into Palestine. The scope of the mass murders stunned the soldiers, but at the same time had reinforced their urgency to fight Hitler's armies. Throughout Eretz Israel, the news of the children coming home now held an extra meaning to the rescue. But even with the horrifying truth of the *Shoah* exposed, the soldiers weren't prepared for the sight before them that morning as the children disembarked.

Many of the children were barefoot; all of them were thin and pale. They were obviously exhausted, scruffy and neglected, despite desperate efforts by the Jewish Agency. Some of them wore oversize, flopping shoes without laces on sockless feet. They hugged ragged bundles, their only possessions in the world, close to their hearts.

Seeing this pitiful sight the soldiers wept.

They closed in even tighter around the children, speaking in Yiddish, Hebrew, and Polish. They wore uniforms labelled 'PALESTINE' with a little star, and they played harmonicas and sang songs to the children. As the soldiers hugged them, Joe felt surrounded by fathers, someone who would protect them all. For the first time, in a long while, Joe felt as though another human truly cared for him. Cared whether he had food and water to eat and drink, and cared whether he lived another day.

The children and soldiers mingled, and patiently waited on the pier until all the refugees had disembarked. Then they were led into an enormous, metal building where food was laid out on long tables.

Joe ran up to the table and couldn't believe what he saw. Food – vegetables, fruits, desserts – so much food he was overwhelmed! He didn't sit like the others but just stood at the table and ate, hesitating only to stuff an orange into his trouser pocket.

Around him, soldiers cried as the children told them of the horrors and tragedies they had witnessed. Little girls hugged the soldier's necks and told them of watching their father being shot in front of their homes. Boys sat on the floor, with three or four soldiers gathered around, as they told of mothers and sisters being buried alive.

Joe stopped eating and listened.

One girl told the story several times of when her mother and six children were forced to dig a pit and then the Nazis buried them alive. These stories were told in Polish and Yiddish, and then many of them asked whether there would be anyone in Palestine who could take them back to their homes in Poland.

His hatred for the Germans came rushing back at Joe. He was very sad that Mother and Nelly weren't there with him, but if any of the soldiers asked him his story he wasn't going to tell them one word. Not about his mother dying. Or the frigid, biting cold of Siberia. Not of poor Nelly. Not of her death. And for sure, he couldn't talk about what had happened after that.

***

The next morning, the soldiers raised a blue and white flag on a pole just outside the huge building and they sang 'Hatikvah'. That night the children camped by the Wells of Moses, on the east side of the Gulf. It was the traditional camping place of the children of Israel after the crossing of the Red Sea when they came out of Egypt.[211]

22

A Train to Palestine

18 February 1943. The next morning beneath a tea-cup-blue sky two trains, glistening in brilliant sunlight, slipped northward through an immense brown-sugar desert.

Organized by representatives of the Immigration Office of the Zionist Labour, the trains had departed the Egyptian seaport of Suez shortly after sunrise. On board were Joe Rosenbaum and 750 children, accompanied by 369 adults. Henrietta Szold had given orders that the Athlit Detention Camp in Palestine, located twenty kilometres south of Haifa on the Mediterranean coast, would be their journey's end.

Haggard and thin, the children appeared ghostly and gray-faced, described by authorities, who would later greet them in Palestine, as 'pitiful beyond description.'[212] A deep suffering was locked in their eyes after months of exhaustion, hunger and disease. Many wore British-issued pith helmets to hide recently shaven heads done to prevent lice and most were dressed in trimmed-down, worn adult trousers, shirts and dresses. In fact, the appearance of the children was so shocking that Szold feared parents and family members wouldn't recognize them once they arrived in Palestine. For that reason she insisted that each child be photographed with their names. What she wouldn't be prepared for later, as they arrived, would be their faces – reflective of the lives they had lived for four and a half years. She saw no trace of childhood in their faces – no mischief, no laughter, only cold remote suspicion.

Who were these children who had had their precious childhoods stolen from them? Who were these innocents who should never have suffered starvation and cold in Siberia? Or the heat and dysentery in a tent camp outside Tehran?[213]

They were Jews, who happened to be children from Germany and Poland who had lived contently in the 1930s in cities such as Warsaw, Hamburg and Cologne, went to school and played happily in the streets, as war clouds gathered over Europe. They had lived typical lives, prayed in the synagogues and remembered warm kitchens that smelled of fruits and cooked potatoes.

Distantly they could still remember quiet lives in a clean apartment above the bakery, and of a mother feeding them a warm breakfast before sending them off to school. One of their fathers was a rabbi in Siedlice and his daughter could still remember the sweet polished smell of the *Beys Medrash*, where there were many books to read. There were two brothers on board the train that morning whose father had been a *shoykhet*, a man who slaughtered animals for kosher meat according to Jewish ritual law. Two older girls and their younger brother sat in the back of the train surprised that they had all survived and talked of precious memories of picking vegetables with their father and mother in the Czerniakow area and selling them in the Warsaw market. There was a boy on the train whose father was a forest manager, and he would take him to work many times with a lunch bag filled with cheese and fruit. An eight-year-old girl sat in the front of the train and she remembered going to school in Kaluszyn. Her father had escaped to Brzesc, and she was sadly certain she would never see him again. Another child had a father who owned a dairy in Czarny Dunajec. Another whose father was a shoe-maker, and his customers were rich country squires and government officials. Another whose father owned a textile mill in Lodz at 220 Piotrkowska Street where there were more than a hundred workers. Another whose father was a book-keeper who knew politics and predicted there would be a war with Germany. Also among them was a brother and sister whose father owned a bus that ran between Stoczek and Lukow, and they had lived well until the Germans came.

A happy, content and cherished world that was to never return for these children.

Children on a train to Palestine. New citizens for the land. They could only wonder what lay ahead for them all.

***

Joe Rosenbaum lay on the floor as the trains departed Egypt and headed north through the Sinai Peninsula, that area the ancient Egyptians had named *Mafkat*, 'land of the green minerals'.[214]

He heard laughter all around him. All the other children were happy, and all he could feel at that moment was guilt that he had survived. Would he ever speak for everyone in his family, those who hadn't survived? Would he remain silent, the one who had watched the death and suffering, forever the witness and not the victim?

Sometime later, Joe managed to get to his feet, staggering against a seat where a girl, older than himself, stared up at him. She smiled briefly. Joe gathered himself, and then pushed and shoved against a wall of thin, bony arms and legs, forcing his way along the aisle. Past the larger children, he stood before an open window, staring for a long moment over the vast desert.

Like all of the Tehran Children, Joe was terribly thin, with hollow eyes set in a bony, lean face. He had almost died a month ago in a British military hospital in Karachi, India. Several weeks on, a photograph taken at the Athlit refugee camp would show a miraculously transformed Joe. This was after the children were rested, fed and the fears of the future mostly vanished from their thoughts. Joe would be smiling, his hair grown out and thick, his arms and legs again muscular and tanned from the desert sun. He wore a sailor cap skewed back on his head of tossed, uncombed hair.

On that morning, as the crowded train continued along the coast, many of the children held small blue and white Zionist flags in their small hands. As the children had unloaded on the pier, Palestine Jewish soldiers handed out the flags, along with sacks of candy and foods. The children had sung a Hebrew song in appreciation of such kindness... *We are all children of Mother*... But unlike the other children who delighted in the colourful flags, Joe didn't care much for decorations when there was so much food available. During his journey there never seemed to be enough food or water, or enough blankets to shield them from the bitter cold, or proper medicines to protect them from the disease raking their frail, young bodies. After the soldiers presented them with sacks filled with food, Joe was determined to never suffer hunger again. Instead of a flag in his hand the next morning, Joe boarded the train with his pockets crammed full of oranges and plums.

Although he often thought of them all – grandfather, his mother, his family members who had perished or vanished – it was Nelly he thought of the most. She should be here on the train, standing by him, holding his hand, afraid because she was different from the other children. So young, innocent and damaged. Joe imagined removing an orange from his pocket, peeling it, and handing the fruit to his sister. She would've liked that, gently smiling up at him.

Eventually Joe forced his thoughts away from Nelly and instead remembered how in Tehran, seven months ago, Jewish soldiers visited the children's camp. That was when the soldiers passionately told them about Palestine, a land of fruit trees planted in straight, long lines stretching over the next peak, of hillside vineyards, vast wide deserts and the many gardens bursting with colour.

As Joe stepped away from the window and looked for a seat, he desperately wanted the soldiers' stories to be true.

Later, the trains veered away from the coast and soon the sea was hidden behind clusters of sweeping sand dunes. There was flat desert as far as the children could see.

Weary, they silently sat in their seats with hands clasped in their laps like obedient school students. For a long time the only sounds were that of the continuous clacking of train tracks.

After another ten kilometres, out beyond the train windows, gradually the land transformed from desert sands to chocolate, rock-strewn mountains and sparse clusters of lush, green trees, yellow-gold fruit orchards and ploughed fields. Suddenly, there at the side of the track in bold black letters, a sign appeared – EGYPT-PALESTINE.

The border! They were in Palestine! The children jumped to their feet, wept, laughed and cheered.

Joe's heart swelled in anticipation. The soldiers' stories were true about fruit trees and gardens. And soon there would be all the food he could eat. Over that next hill perhaps. Joe covered his face with open hands as his thoughts turned to his mother and sister. Only a few short months ago, amidst the trials and sorrows, abuse after abuse, surviving in filthy camps, of disease and hunger, the exhausting work details – to have dreamed of ever seeing this land, Palestine, seemed impossible.

23

Home

The Egypt-Palestine border faded into the distance, ten kilometres behind the trains. Well into Palestine now, the land suddenly appeared green with ploughed fields in neat rows, flowing out over the hills. In the morning sun, off in the distance white buildings, scattered evidence of settlements, rested against the background of the sea.[215]

Once the trains had crossed over the border from Egypt, each train stop became a celebration with the yelling out of Polish cities names to the children, seeking any recognition from one of the young, searching faces, in hopes that some long-lost child might be found.

To Joe and the children, it was an amazing and unexpected sight. The throngs of people waving and yelling out to them. And the oranges! One had never seen such fruit in Europe or Russia.

The trains passed into Rehovoth, twenty kilometres from Tel Aviv.[216] This town had been established 50 years before by Polish-Jewish immigrants on land purchased from a Christian Arab. In Rehovoth, the trains were swarmed by thousands of well-wishers, school children, women's organizations, Arab school classes, all who had travelled there from throughout Eretz Israel, greeting the anticipated passengers with gifts and songs. Above the station a large banner spelled out the message: 'And the Children will return to their Homeland.' When the trains finally pulled away from the station to continue northward, a man, dressed in a Polish uniform ran onto the platform, yelling out one of the children's names. A girl on the train, certain it was her father, shouted, 'Stop the train!' Her mother, leaning out the window to get a better view of the soldier running beside the train, fainted in the aisle. The children waved and shouted at the soldier. Only after the officials reassured the woman and daughter that the soldier, who turned out to be her father, would follow their train to Athlit camp, did they calm down.

Once out of Rehovoth, the trains gained speed and struck out toward Lydda, a major railway junction just four kilometres away.

This final day of Joe's journey would soon fade into a distant memory, passing in and out in his mind because he had been very sick since leaving the British camp in Karachi. Years later, he would read books, written by the

11. Members of the *Yishuv* (Jewish community) greet the Tehran children as they arrive by train in Palestine. United States Holocaust Memorial Museum, courtesy of David Laor.

older children and adults, relying on their memories to recall exactly what he had been through.

Ten miles north of Tel Aviv, the coastal plain town of Lydda, according to the Talmud, was fortified in the days of Joshua, the son of Nun. Again, large crowds of yelling and waving well-wishers lined the tracks and crowded the station's platform. Sacks of candy and fruits, and flowers were passed through the train windows. Young boys climbed up on signs, so that when Joe stared out the window they glanced into each other's faces. The local boys gawked at the thin, sickly children staring back at them through hollow, empty eyes. The boys perched on the signpost wore thin sweaters, khaki shorts and thick socks that came almost to the knee. Strangely, the boys standing on the ground still had their caps on, but the boys who had climbed the signs had removed their caps, holding them curled in their hands. Maybe it was out of respect, or maybe they had removed the caps so that they could get a better view of the strangers, Joe thought.

These boys staring at them were healthy, and happy. Joe looked away, certain that his appearance looked odd to them, and for some odd reason the caps made him jealous. These caps had no frays along the edges; they weren't worn thin, like the sweaters his mother had worn in the Siberian camps. It was as if the caps were new, as though they had been worn new just this morning to come to the station and see Joe and the others arrive. Joe knew these boys would never know what it was like to go hungry, or to be so ill you thought you were going to die, or to watch a mother or a sister die right in front of you.

Joe stared out at three boys sitting on top of the railway sign. The one in the middle gazed in the windows until his eyes met Joe's stare. He was about the same age as Joe, and strangely, Joe remembered the young Russian soldier who stood by the trains in Nemirov. In both cases – the young Russian soldier, who had been there to force them from their homes, and this young Jewish boy, who had no idea the suffering Joe and the others had been through – just for a brief moment Joe saw in each a faint glimmer of compassion.

The next stop was Hadera, founded in 1891 as a farming colony by Jewish immigrants from Lithuania and Latvia. As the trains pulled into the station, the children leaned out of the window waving their tiny blue and white flags. Thousands of deeply-moved people again swarmed the station platform, passing out cakes, sandwiches and fruit to the children.

And then, the trains were off toward Haifa.

***

12. Eliahu Dobkin of the Jewish Agency (left) and Henrietta Szold, founder of the Hadassah Women's Zionist Organization (second from left) await the arrival of the Tehran Children. Athlit, Palestine, February 18, 1943. Copyright United States Holocaust Museum; courtesy of Israel Government Press Office.

Henrietta Szold waited at Haifa station. The train was running late, and she stood patiently under the shade of the platform roof away from the midday sun. An assistant walked up to her, informing her that the trains were, in fact, only two miles away.

It won't be long now, Szold thought. She, and the Jewish population of Eretz Israel, had been anxiously awaiting the safe arrival of these children for months. She also knew what this meant. With the rescue of these children, now there was at last hope for the Jews.

This day felt differently within the very soul of each Jew in Palestine. The children signalled that if one really considered the meaning of the small hands extended out the train windows, blue and white Israeli flag waving – it was truly a resurrection of the lost.[217]

***

At noon the train pulled into the station. Joe leaned out the window to get a better look at the scene on the platform. Though there had been so many people at the other places where the train stopped, this was by far the largest crowd, stretching out beyond the loading ramp and the road opposite the station.[218]

The sign read: HAIFA.

As the train came to a stop, the crowd sang *Hatikvah*, the Hebrew anthem.

When the train doors opened, Joe and the children poured out among the crowd, while photographers snapped pictures and school children carrying armloads of wildflowers, chocolates and, of course, oranges. Again, Joe heard the names of Polish towns called out, and occasionally a child would call back. There were people hugging all around him, laughter and crying, as weeping swept through the crowd.

Wandering to the edge of the platform, Joe looked down along the train where there stood a gathering of men dressed in suits. Among them was a woman, an old woman with gray hair and sad eyes. But as she glanced out over the joyous crowd, she was smiling.

A school teacher prompted his students to sing songs of the *chalutzim*, those who move to Israel to establish agricultural settlements. Soon the crowd, the old woman and mostly all of the children joined in. But Joe didn't sing. There was no one there to meet him like the other children, to hug him and welcome him to Palestine. And besides, he didn't know the words to the song.

The Friday, 10 February 1943, issue of *The Palestine Post* would read: 'Wandering Refugees Reach Journey's End.'[219]

Seven months later, at noon on August 28, 120 Russian-Jewish children would arrive in Eretz Israel by way of Tehran, although their route to freedom was slightly different. These children were bused through the desert and across the Yarmuk River directly to Athlit. Henrietta Szold would again stand at the Haifa train station as the last group of Tehran Children would arrive safely from Persia. She wore a wide, straw hat shielding her face from the hot sun.

And, once again, she smiled as they sang the children's songs.

***

Joe, the children and adults were loaded onto buses and driven away from the train station on the last leg of their journey to their new home, at least for the moment. The children were used to not staying in one place long. Was there any reason to expect any different now? But, as initial sorting out started taking place, Athlit Detainee Camp would be that home.

Located on the coast, twenty kilometres south of Haifa, the transit camp wasn't deemed 'Palestine proper' as far as the Jewish Agency officials were concerned but for now it would have to serve a purpose. Officially a detention camp built by the British during the Mandate in the 1930s, it was constructed to detain Jewish refugees illegally immigrating into Palestine. But what the British built for bad purposes, as far as the Jews were concerned, the camp would be utilized for good by the 1940s as holocaust survivors, released from Displacement Camps in Europe, would be briefly interned at Athlit awaiting their release into Eretz Israel.

That afternoon, beneath the evening sun dulled behind rolling, gray clouds, the buses pulled up at Athlit. When Joe looked out the window, his reaction was like that of most of the children. Their hearts sank when they saw a camp surrounded by straight, barbed-wire fences, perched guard towers and soldiers with guns.

Joe had seen this before, and he didn't like the knot swelling in his stomach.

***

That same week in February, Polish General Anders received a telegram from General Sikorski stating that a month before on 16 January 1943, the Soviet government had informed the Polish Government in London that all Poles remaining in both the Soviet Union and provinces under Soviet occupation would be considered Soviet citizens (subjects).

It was a heavy blow that stunned Anders.

13. Younger members of the Tehran Children's transport are led away from the train after their arrival at the station in Athlit. United States Holocaust Memorial Museum; courtesy of David Laor.

He considered the Soviet decision to be cruel and illegal, depriving thousands of Poles of their citizenship, many of whom had fought alongside the Allied armies. Sikorski suggested that Anders discuss the situation with his officers, but the General decided to take such a decision, of whether to continue fighting the German or not, to the men he trusted most…his soldiers.

***

On 18 February, the same day Joe arrived at Athlit Camp in Palestine, Nazi Propaganda Minister Joseph Goebbels delivered a speech at the Berlin *Sportpalast*. The message was simple and direct: *Total War*.

The underlying message was one that for the first time the Nazi leadership admitted that Germany faced dangers in the following days. Realizing the tide of the war had turned against the Fatherland, Goebbels insisted that 'the German people continue the war even though it would be long and difficult because', he emphasized, 'Germany's survival…was at stake'.[220]

Even with this awakening realization spoken from the mouth of one of Hitler's inner circle, as the war continued into 1944 and the German armies pressed on all sides, more resources were blindly committed to the purpose of killing Jews.

***

Fears among the children gradually subsided as they unloaded from the buses, entered the gates and went through the process of being registered. Later, they were then sent to their huts. The children realized that this wasn't the type of camp they had lived in for over four years.

Everyone treated them so warmly.

Women volunteers wearing aprons greeted the children with smiles and hugs. They were led into long, narrow buildings and shown the unbelievable sight of beds covered with clean sheets, thick blankets and pillows with 'welcome home' signs on top.

Dolls were handed out to the girls. Joe glanced over to his left and saw a room with shelf upon shelf filled with stacked clean clothes waiting to be distributed to them. They were given glasses of milk and then shown where to take hot showers. Joe stood under the hot water for as long as they would let him, chose new clothes from the shelves and then shyly asked if he could have another glass of milk. Sitting at the table he dozed off, until one of the kind ladies showed him to his cot. She removed the sign, and Joe collapsed on top of the covers. The pillow was so soft, and he remembered that he had not slept in a real bed with sheets and a pillow since they left the apartment in Cologne. The milk warmed his stomach and slowed his mind.

As sleep slipped over him, Joe realized just how tired he was. But he had been tired for a long time and, amazingly, this would be the first night in five years that he wouldn't go to bed hungry. He would go to sleep in a bed and his stomach would be full. There would be no fear, only apprehension of perhaps what tomorrow would bring. He would worry about family another day. So, finally, Joe slept content and safe, and as happy as he had been since leaving Cologne.

Sometime during the night, beneath the new stars of Palestine, curled beneath crisp, clean sheets, Joe dreamt of his mother and sister Nelly.

And in his dreams there was, at long last, hope.

PART FIVE

April 1943

24

Yaffa, the Oldest

In Palestine, we were put in a camp called Athlit. This was a British camp, and they de-liced us and disinfected us. We were a bunch of funny people, with all kinds of skin rashes and other sicknesses. We were stuck there for three days. A few of us had parents in Palestine and they were taken by their parents right away. After three days, they cleaned us up a little bit, gave us some clothes, and sent us to different places to recuperate.[221]

-Joe Rosenbaum, *My Saba*

Patience proved to not be a virtue for these children after all the months and years of mistreatment. Still, Joe was surprised by the abundance of food, and fresh bread piled high in the middle of the tables. Although amazed and grateful that there was food, Joe and the other children couldn't help but be suspicious of those who attended to them. These caretakers smiled and appeared to love the children, giving them anything they wanted, but the children watched cautiously for any sign that the situation would change.

On the second day the interviews began and the children were asked a lot of questions. It reminded Joe of when the Russians in Nemirov asked his grandfather and mother where they desired to live. The answers the deportees gave to the Russians really didn't matter, Joe thought looking back on that day. Their fate had already been decided as they were shipped to Siberia, where his grandfather and mother had both died of hunger.

In Palestine Joe was asked basically the same question: 'Where would you like to go – to a kibbutz, a school or to a family who might adopt you?'

'None of those', Joe had answered.

The woman stopped writing, looking up at him.

'I have relatives', he said.

'Here, in Palestine?'

'Yes, an uncle, and he will come soon.'

She smiled, turning back to the paper in front of her. 'Then we shall make a note of that.'

But so far, no one had come for him.

This caused periods of terrible loneliness that overwhelmed Joe as he watched the older children refusing to be separated, even briefly, from their younger sisters, brothers and cousins. They showed a fierce loyalty towards siblings and relatives, and the caretakers seemed to understand this show of protection and let the children be. As Joe watched all of this around him, he became anxious that no one knew he was there at the camp. Maybe his uncle would never come for him. Maybe, no one would ever come for him, and he would become a forgotten refugee all alone in this new land. What would happen to him? Would a family ever take in a total stranger into their home to live with them? The sad thing was Joe should have been happy, Palestine meant safety, bread to eat and the beginning of a new life for him.

Each morning the children were led from the huts past the barbed-wire fences, boys on the left and girls on the right. After breakfast they were allowed out into a central square, where they were encouraged to play and run and enjoy the fresh air. But instead, the children simply spent their time milling about, some standing in a group in the dark shade of a single tree. There were no emotions, no happiness, no echoing of laughter as there should have been. Joe stood away from the others, alone at the fence. Perhaps too much had happened too quickly.

Most of all, what Joe wanted more than anything else was his childhood back. The old woman he had noticed at the Haifa train station was doing all she could to help the children realize just that.

Through the assistance of Polish and Yiddish interpreters, Henrietta Szold personally interviewed the Tehran Children, uncovering their age, background information about their families and the kind of homes that they came from but most importantly, to Szold, their 'religious background'.[222] An assistant wrote down what the children told Szold, and a nurse was always present in the room. The one aspect Szold feared the most was that any of the children could become pawns within the religious factions in Eretz Israel. How the children answered the questions determined for her whether they were sent to either orthodox or liberal families or groups.

During the time of these interviews, two stories emerged that spread throughout the camp.

The first story was of Sarah, about five years old, who appeared to be the youngest of the Tehran Children, and it was believed that she was an orphan. Eventually, she was sent to a *Youth Aliyah* camp and the leader and his wife nursed her frail body back to health. They approached Szold about adopting her, and she told the couple that she thought it was a great idea. But then hesitated, thinking that there had to be someone in their chaotic world who was looking for Sarah. Concerned that the couple would one day have to give up Sarah, Szold suggested that they delay the decision for a while and advised them that 'you have your own lives to establish. Sarah will be cared for, wherever she goes.'

In Ahawah, near Haifa, Sarah began life again and was loved in the settlement. A year later, a telegram arrived at the Youth Aliyah office: 'Please wire immediately fate of my daughter six years old, born in Wilno, Poland, evacuated from Middle Asia to Haifa. Worried absence. Message.' The wire was signed 'Father of Sarah'. Szold, remembering that small voice that told her to hesitate about Sarah being adopted, sent a message to Sarah's father that his little girl was indeed alive and healthy again.

The other story involved the interview of three children who were brought to Szold, two brothers and a sister who had spent four months in a home receiving clothing and medical care. After Szold interviewed them she informed the children that because of their ages, they would be sent to three different groups, but she carefully explained they would be able to see each other. But the children refused to be separated. Szold explained again her decision, but again the children refused. Finally, the girl leaned toward Szold sitting directly across the desk: 'You must understand that such a thing is impossible', the girl said firmly pointing at the youngest boy. 'You see, my little brother has no mother any more and no father. We are his mother and father now and have to take care of him. He's only a child, do you understand?'

'I myself will look after your little brother', Szold said.

'Oh, no', the girl answered. 'You have not understood at all. I'm sure you would take care of him. But I am his sister; I must be his mother now. I must look after him. If you take us away from him, he will cry all the time. You wouldn't want that, would you? And I would cry all the time, too.'

Szold remained silent for a moment. 'Good', she agreed. 'You can all three stay together. You are a good sister.'

The little boy came to Szold. 'Give me your hand and promise', he said. 'Swear that you won't take me away and I will believe you.'

Szold took his small hand and promised.

During this interview process, Henrietta Szold talked with young Joe Rosenbaum who was feeling much better by this time and very anxious about where he would end up. He remembers very clearly the encounter with the gray-haired lady with piercing dark eyes, and her warm smile: 'I remember that she asked me how I felt, and I told her that I had been very sick on the train. Then, she asked me, "Are you being treated okay? Do you go to synagogue, do you light candles?" As hard I tried, I don't remember exactly what I told her.'[223]

The appearance of the children transformed quickly, impressing Szold. However, it wasn't their appearance that she was concerned about as the concealed hurt she knew had to be inside the heart of every child there. Several months later, she would reflect back on those hectic days in the camp when the children arrived:

> In their years of hopeless wandering as they were herded from place to place, the children had slept in [the] woods, had bordered on starvation, and were exposed to disease. Clothed in near-rags, these wild, frightened young ones needed a great deal of attention, both physical and psychological…the past week I have continued the individual examinations…If my health were up to the mark, I should doubtless find the conversations illuminating. At all events, they reveal a state of degeneration among our tortured people that cannot but arouse anxiety.

But on 18 June the children were dispersed to other locations and Szold would write an entry in her diary showing that she, at last, was optimistic about the children:

> I spent the week rushing hither and thither, and succeeded practically in completing the survey of the Tehran Children in their permanent placements. On the whole I am pleased with what I have seen of them. They are apparently making good progress toward normality. They study with vim. Most of them have already acquired enough Hebrew to carry on a conversation. They are no less ready to do the work assigned to them. What pleases me most is that they are beginning to frolic, to be children. They will snatch back a little of the heritage of youth that the Hitler war robbed them of.

On his third night in the camp Joe went to bed and listened as the smaller children cried. They cried every night since arriving at Athlit. Frightening cries, begging for a light against the surrounding darkness, cries for protection from the jackals heard roaming out beyond the fences. And they cried because their small bodies were so weary.

Joe rolled over on his back, and stared at the ceiling. He clutched the bread given to him at the last meal of the day. Like most of the others, Joe slept refusing to take off his clothes or to give up his bread. But on this night, Joe got out of bed and stood by the bed beside a wooden chair. He took off his new clothes, neatly folding the trousers and shirt and placed them on the chair back. He tucked his socks in his shoes as his father had shown him when he was a young boy in Cologne, and then got back in bed.

Joe took the bread lying beside him on the pillow, clutched it tightly to his chest just as he had done every night. Then, he stretched out across the bed, and set the bread in the chair.

After a long moment, he half-whispered, 'Yes, they will come soon.' Something told him that he hadn't lied to the woman who had asked him the question.

***

In several days Joe was sent to one of 'eleven preparation camps' in the northern part of Israel and not that far from Haifa because he was so ill. 'I was sent to a place in the northern part of Israel, it was then called *Kfar Ha'Noar Hadait*. There I got a real good bed and blankets and three meals a day. I couldn't believe it.'[224]

Life was even better there, although there were still many children who slept in their clothes and hid food beneath the beds. Late at night Joe could hear weeping as the other children thought of their fathers and mothers.

During the day cars would pull up at the gate and parents or family members would come to take away another child.

Still, no one came for Joe.

***

Over the next six weeks Joe watched families arrive at the village anxiously searching for their children. Many times when the family approached them the children wouldn't even recognize them. They tried to persuade the children that they really were an aunt or an uncle, or cousin, and that they should leave together. For that reason, Joe soon learned to stay to himself and not make friends. What good would that do to make another friend, when there was the possibility that their relatives would simply take them away, leaving Joe alone? No, Joe decided, staying to himself was the best thing to do.

What Joe wasn't of aware of was that the *Youth Aliyah* had sent out lists throughout Eretz Israel containing all the children's names. This assisted the relatives who were searching throughout the country in knowing which of the eleven camps their child might be located.

In the case of Joe's family, they had, in fact, found cousin Shlomo. And they were close to finding Joe.

***

After four weeks watching families come and take their children, the number
of children who still remained with Joe dwindled. He grew nervous, asking
himself with doubt 'How could they not find me? Mother always told him
that she a brother living in Palestine. Where was that brother?'

***

Another week passed. During those seven days, six more children left with
families.

But Joe refused to give up. He hadn't given up in Poland as the German
soldiers forced them away from home, and neither had his mother. He hadn't
given up in the horror of the Siberian camps, and neither had his mother
until the day she became so ill that she didn't care to live any longer. Or on
the march southward when he and Nelly were on their own. He hadn't
surrendered to fear in Tehran, or given in to illness when he almost died in
Karachi. Joe realized, that even at his young age there seemed to be purpose
for him surviving.

Joe waited another day. And then another.

Then one late afternoon something extraordinary happened.

Gray clouds anchored on the horizon across the sea reflecting Joe's
continual worry. He was talking to several boys as they stood in front of their
building, and didn't pay any attention to the bus pulling up outside the gate.
It was now a common sight for vehicles to pull in and out during the day. He
did notice a girl only because she was very pretty as she walked up to one of
the camp administrators. The administrator perused the area and pointed
to the group of boys, and she walked over to them. She stepped on the porch
and out of the sun, and when she was closer Joe noticed that she was tall with
dark smooth skin and wide eyes. She stared at him for a long moment. Then
she said 'Yossi?'

This shocked Joe because no one had called him by that name since since
Siberia. 'Who are you?'

'Are you Josef Rosenbaum?' she asked.

'I am, but who are you?'

'I am your cousin', she said in German, 'the daughter of Sophie'.

'And who is Sophie?'

'Your father's sister.'

Yes! He remembered and his heart lifted. She was family.

'I'm your cousin, and I told the man in charge that I came for you, to take
you to Tel Aviv for a whole week so you can have a reunion and know your
family again.'

Joe didn't know what to say – a whole week with family – he would like it to be forever, but he was so overwhelmed at that moment he didn't care.

The girl went in with him to the barracks, and waited while Joe packed some clothes and personal items. After he was ready, they walked together across the opening and toward the gate.

'I'm glad I found you, now you'll be with family during *Pesach*. You should be glad for that.'

Joe was more than just glad. He didn't know exactly how to feel right now. 'Can you do me a favour?'

'What is it, Yossi?'

'Don't talk to me in German', he said. 'I hate Germans. Do you speak Yiddish?'

This all seemed to embarrass her and she nodded.

They walked silently together, and with each step Joe's heart lifted. When they reached the gate, he stopped. 'I don't know your name...what is your name?'

She smiled. 'I am Yaffa. I am the oldest.'

25

Family in Tel Aviv

During the bus ride south on the coastal road to Tel Aviv, Yaffa asked Joe questions, but not too many because she wanted him to save his stories for when they arrived at her parents. They are anxious to hear him, she told Joe. 'Yaffa was then sixteen or seventeen, a beautiful girl, but I didn't appreciate it yet. I was too young.'[225]

Simon Rosenbaum's sister and family left Germany in 1932, and moved to Palestine. Joe didn't remember any of them because he was such a small boy when they left. The only relative he did remember from that time was his mother's brother, Anschel, and that was because he owned a chocolate store.

Sophie Rosenbaum married Shimon Balzam, who was actually a friend of Joe's father. They had three children, Yaffa, Shulamith the second daughter and Israel, the son. Joe found the Balzam family very happy, and they were glad for him to be there.

They lived in the back of the store where Mr Balzam made and sold all types of hats. *Kova tembel*, khaki hats to wear for protection against the sun. And other hats for women and children.

After they had welcomed Joe, his aunt showed him around where they lived in the back where there was a sink and a toilet just outside the building. Joe found out the first night that the two adults slept in the back but the children slept in the store front. When any of them needed to take a shower, they would go to the home of Uncle Anschel. An inconvenience maybe to the others, but considering Siberia, Joe thought of it all as a wonderful convenience.

Once Sophie had finished showing Joe around they sat on a cloth couch in the apartment, and she asked Joe to sit by her and tell her his story. It was then that Joe asked her, 'Don't speak German to me. Please don't speak German.' Sophie never asked why, as if she understood the hatred in Joe's heart towards the people who had hurt him so much.

Over the next hour Joe told her all that he could remember. He told her that her father died in Siberia, and that his mother had died there in the same camp also. He told her of how they went south with the Polish army, and that everyone thought things would get better then. But things didn't get better. Their situation only became worse in a place named Tashkent. Joe hesitated and then quietly told his aunt that Tashkent was where Nelly died, starving to death in that awful place as he hunted for food like a dog. Sophie cried. When Joe told her that her brother had died there too, she simply couldn't cry anymore. Instead, she sat quietly as Joe told her of his time in Tehran, and the last seven-month journey on the boat. Both Joe and Sophie laughed when he told her about the train to Palestine, and what a happy time it was when he learned Palestine and America weren't as close together as he had always believed.

Should a child ever go through this? Joe wished they were all with him, everyone who had died not just family. But each person who had perished on the journey numbered in the hundreds, so many people that his aunt's house wouldn't be large enough to hold everyone. Thousands of them, they would be in the house, the yard, up and down the street, stretching out so far away that he couldn't see their faces…Joe would lean out the window and yell, and let everybody who would listen know how wonderful and glad he was that it had all been a dream . . . a nightmare…and they were all alive.

He sat still for a moment and an awkward silence fell over the room.

Then, suddenly without Joe knowing he would speak, the secret gushed out, bursting his insides. And, Joe became someone else sitting on the couch, his aunt tightly hugging him, as the words spilled out so fast. The truth about Nelly's death.

That morning when Nelly died, Joe had run to another hut to let his uncle know. Joe wasn't crying, but inside the bitter pain was almost more than he could bear. Several of the adults walked back with Joe. They covered Nelly's body with a blanket, and Joe went and curled up in the corner. The men talked among themselves in a whisper, and his uncle occasionally glanced back at Joe.

And then what happened – they didn't ask Joe, they just did what they had to do to survive. In a way, Joe always understood what they did next he just could never accept it.

Instead of burying his sister, the men wrapped her in the blanket. And, when they were certain none of the Soviets were around, they carried her out to the end of the street and tossed her like garbage in the dump.

Why hadn't he said something? Joe asked. His aunt grasped him tighter.

Why hadn't he stopped them? Joe and Sophie wept together.

Later that afternoon, it was Joe's turn to ask about how they found him after all this time. Sophie related a story to Joe that amazed him.

'I didn't know this but Shlomo had been picked up a week or two weeks before me.' His cousin had ended up in a Jerusalem hospital where he was being treated by a Jewish-German doctor named Vallach. It was a twist of fate that the doctor shopped for chocolates at Uncle Anschel's store one day and Vallach told him that he was treating a kid with a funny German name – Zali Buglikter. Anschel excitedly explained that his sister had married a Buglikter, and that it was likely that his patient could be his sister's son they had been searching for.

The next day Uncle Anschel went to the Jerusalem hospital and there was Shlomo. He took him back to the Tel Aviv apartment, where Shlomo told Sophie, 'You know what? Yossi is here, too. But where, I don't know.'

So they searched through the camp list and found Joe's name. Yaffa came two days later. They talked all the afternoon, and finally Joe realized he hadn't been told how Uncle Anschel got to Palestine. Like most of the stories told that day, it involved a degree of good fortune.

Anschel was a big, strong man and one night in Cologne a Nazi picked on the wrong guy. Anschel beat him almost to death and had to flee, so he struck out to Belgium. He had enough money to pay his way into Palestine, about 1,000 pounds sterling, so he bought his way in. Later, he brought his wife and three children over, just before the opening days of the war.

The next day, the two families met, and many of the stories were told over again.

Joe stayed in Tel Aviv through Pesach, ten days. Then it was time to say goodbye. As he rode on the bus that headed north out of Tel Aviv, warm sunlight shone through the window onto his face. Shortly thereafter he dozed off to sleep, and dreamt of the family – those at Sophie's home and those who had died. Suddenly awakening, he realized for the first time truly that another season in his life was about to begin.

When he closed his eyes again, he didn't dream, but remembered…

…on the last day in Tel Aviv before he left, they had all gone into the city. They took him to Dizengof Plaza, an iconic public square in the heart of the city. Uncle Anschel insisted on taking a photograph of Shlomo and Joe, two surviving Tehran Children, who stood close and smiled at the camera.

In the background was the garden and fountain, and in the sitting area, three strangers sat on a park bench, locked in conversation, captured in the image's background.

Joe was squinting into the sun.

***

The bus delivered Joe back to *Kfar Ha'Noar Hadait*. After several days Joe was called into the administrative office, and told he would be sent to *Kfar Ha'Roeh*, and that a foster family would soon come for him.

***

The defeat of Hitler in Europe had uncovered the darkest side of Germany when the concentration camps where the Jews had been murdered were discovered.

Even as reports filtered out of Europe over the last fourteen months, what Allied soldiers walked upon in the Polish and German forests was unimaginable. Soviet troops liberating the concentration camps in Poland had fought back German Panzer divisions once poised for conquest at the gates of Stalingrad and Leningrad. Then a winter offensive had broken the German lines and they had chased Hitler's once invincible divisions back across the Russian plains to the outskirts of Berlin.

Majdanek, the first major concentration camp liberated, was discovered by advancing Soviet troops on 24 July 1944. Auschwitz was liberated on 27 January by the 322nd Rifle Division of the Red Army. Buchenwald would be liberated on 4 April 1945, the first camp liberated by US troops. These were hardened, seasoned soldiers who had survived much for their victory but when they witnessed the horrors within the camp fences, many broke down and cried.

***

Stories began to circulate among the soldiers and beyond the barbed-wire fences and SS watch towers. Thousands of tales of horror and murder. Survivors told what happened each day when trains arrived, like a story from Treblinka death camp, located in a forest northeast of Warsaw, four kilometres south of Treblinka train station. Upon their arrival, the refugees were forced off the train in short order, and then lined up on the platform and sorted into groups – men, children and women, all separate. They were all forced to undress; workers immediately picked up all the clothes and carted them away. Then the people were forced to walk naked through the street towards the gas chambers.

The inmates told them in trembling, hushed voices of how the Germans had called the ramp leading down into the gas chambers 'the street to heaven', *Himmelfahrstrasse*. Jews called it the *Ascension* and *The Last Road*. The operation was completed in maybe ten minutes, of undressing and walking down to their deaths. The women took longer because they had to first have their heads shaved.

The stories of such brutalities shook the soldiers. One witness, a Polish railwayman, told of a policeman after he had caught two Jewish boys who had attempted to escape.

> ... He [the policeman] did not shut them in a wagon, since he was afraid to open the door in case others would escape. I asked him to

let them go. The assassin did not even budge. He ordered the bigger boy to sit down on the ground and take the smaller one on his knee, and then he shot them both with one bullet. Turning to me, he said: 'You're lucky, that was the last bullet.' Round the huge stomach of the murderer there was a belt with a clasp, on which I could see the inscription 'Gott mit uns','God is with us.'[226]

All the extermination camps were located in Poland; the camps positioned in Germany were utilized to house prisoners and slave labourers. It was from these camps that Himmler's SS farmed out slave labourers who were sent to places like Peenemunde, the centre of the Nazi rocket project production of the V1 and V2 rockets that fell on London producing such deadly results. The prisoners were ill-fed and forced to work in horrible conditions until they died at their work stations. Then the German camps simply shipped more labourers to the sites. The extermination camps served one purpose with staggering precision – to murder as many Jews as they could, a purpose the Nazi hierarchy remained steadfastly focused on even as Soviet troops poured into the Berlin suburbs.

Geoffrey Megargee and Martin Dean, lead editors of the *Encyclopedia of Camps and Ghettos, 1933-1945* of the United States Holocaust Memorial Museum, identified 42,500 Nazi ghettos and camps throughout Europe, and that between 1933 and 1945 estimates were as high as 15 to 20 million people died and were imprisoned in these places.

On 15 April British Forces liberated Bergen-Belsen, a complex of camps located eleven miles north of Celle, Germany, a small town on the Aller River. It is estimated that over 50,000 prisoners died in Bergen-Belsen. Most were Jews.

Originally built as a prisoner-of-war camp, thousands of Jewish prisoners evacuated from outlying camps flooded into the camp as Allied armies continued their advance. In July 1944 there were around 7,300 prisoners. The number quickly swelled to over 60,000 in a camp designed for a much smaller prisoner population. Food, fresh water supplies and sanitation facilities rapidly diminished and deteriorated. Outbreaks of typhus, dysentery, and typhoid fever killed thousands of prisoners in January and February 1945 as they waited for the Allies to free them.

When Montgomery's forces entered the camp, they found over 60,000 prisoners seriously ill. The dead lay scattered throughout the camp, conditions had deteriorated so badly that German officers approached the British under a white flag requesting assistance so that the outbreak of typhus wouldn't spread from the prisoners to the guards.

British Intelligence Officer Derrick Sington witnessed the haunting scene as he entered Bergen-Belsen:

It reminded me of the entrance to a zoo. We came into a smell of ordure – like a monkey camp. A sad, blue smoke floated like ground mist between low buildings. I had tried to imagine the interior of the concentration camp, but I had not imagined it like this. Nor had I imagined the strange, simian throng, who crowded the barbed wire fence surrounding their compounds, with their shaven heads and the obscene striped penitentiary suits…We had been welcomed before, but the half-credulous cheers of these almost lost men, of these clowns in their terrible motley, who had once been Polish officers, land workers in the Ukraine, Budapest doctors and students in France, impelled a stronger emotion, and I had to fight back my tears.[227]

Over half of the prisoners were women, most of whom were Czech, Hungarian, German or Polish Jews who had watched their families being murdered in the extermination camps. During the war and for months after the liberation many were too ill to recover and over 50,000 died in Bergen-Belsen camp.

Among those thousands was Anne Frank, whose diary was found by Otto Frank, a surviving family member when he returned to Amsterdam after the war. It was first published in 1947, and then published in English in 1952 as *The Diary of a Young Girl*. Her tragic story was one of thousands repeated by innocent Jewish children who had no way of escaping once Europe fell under the shadow of Nazism.

The Frank family had moved from Frankfurt to Amsterdam in the early 1930s. When Hitler's army invaded the Netherlands and the persecution of Jews began, the family hid for two years within several concealed rooms within a house. Eventually they were betrayed to the Gestapo and sent to concentration camps. Anne and her sister Margot ended up in Bergen-Belsen as the Soviet army advanced into Germany. In March 1945, less than a month before British soldiers would liberate the camp, Anne Frank and her sister died of typhus.

The tragic ending of Anne's story sadly had the same ending as thousands of other children in wartime Europe. They would never escape 'the valley of death' created by Hitler's hate. They would instead die in filthy ditches of disease, or in the gas chambers of Dachau, Auschwitz or Treblinka. Or be murdered and buried in mass graves in the Russian forest. Anne and countless other children would die there smothered in evil – never to see the valleys of Palestine, the trees and vineyards.

Ohrdruf concentration camp, located south of Gotha, Germany was liberated on 4 April 1945, by the 4th Armored Division accompanied by the

89th Infantry Division. It would be the first camp liberated by United States troops.

General Dwight D. Eisenhower, Supreme Allied Commander, on April 12 visited the camp joined by Generals George Patton and Omar Bradley, as they reviewed the horrible carnage. Shortly after his visit, Eisenhower sent a wire to General George C. Marshall, head of the Joint Chiefs of Staff in Washington:

> The most interesting – although horrible – sight that I encountered during the trip was a visit to a German internment camp near Gotha… the visual evidence and the verbal testimony of starvation, cruelty and bestiality were so overpowering as to leave me a bit sick. In one room, where they were piled up twenty or thirty naked men, killed by starvation, George Patton would not even enter. He said that he would get sick if he did so.[228]

Eisenhower didn't make such a visit out of curiosity, instead he explained his purpose of walking the campgrounds, 'I made the visit deliberately, in order to be in a position to give first-hand evidence of these things if ever, in the future, there develops a tendency to charge these allegations merely to "propaganda".'[229]

Several weeks later, Eisenhower related over the telephone details of what had been found to Winston Churchill. On 24 April the Prime Minister had arranged for the photographs of the victims to be circulated to the Cabinet. 'Here we are all shocked by the most horrible revelations of German cruelty in the concentration camps', he wrote to his wife.[230]

26

'For your Freedom and Ours'

14. Eva Litman, a Jewish child, greeting General Wladyslaw Anders with flowers. United States Holocaust Museum, courtesy of Halina Peabody.

There is no record in General Anders's writings after the war as to whether he received word that the Tehran Children had finally reached their destination in Palestine. Perhaps, in the obscure fog of war and the preparing his troops for battle in North Africa, Anders felt he had done all that he could to save the Jewish refugees by evacuating them out of Siberia.

However, the week the Tehran Children arrived in Palestine in February 1943, Anders received a disheartening telegram from General Sikorski stating that Poland wouldn't be free after the war, but would remain under Soviet rule. 'This cruel and illegal Soviet decision deprived hundreds of thousands of Poles of their citizenship', Anders would later write in his autobiography.[231]

Then, several months after Joe and the children reached Palestine, Anders finally received appalling news concerning the fate of his missing Polish officers. In late 1942 Polish railroad workers started hearing rumours from local citizens in Smolensk, a city on the Dnieper River 360 kilometres southwest of Moscow, about mass graves of Polish soldiers near Katyn. After several graves were uncovered, the information was turned over to the Polish Secret State, who in turn reported it to the German army. In early 1943 Rudolf von Gersdorff, an intelligence liaison officer with the Wehrmacht's Army Group Center, acted upon this information, and troops were sent into the Katyn Forest, near an area named Goat Hill. Even for the German troops, what they uncovered was shocking.

'On April 13, 1943, the Germans broadcast a report that the corpses of thousands of Polish officers had been found buried at Katyn…the German radio was naturally suspect', Anders wrote, 'but nevertheless we were already well aware that something dreadful had happened to the missing officers'.[232] Naturally, the Polish government mistrusted Stalin as much as the Germans, as the Soviet leader dismissed any involvement in the murders, suggesting that it was simply Nazi propaganda. Eventually, the truth was exposed and painfully clear.

In May 1940 Stalin had ordered the massacre of the 15,000 Polish officers. Many officers were killed at the NKVD prison at Kalinin, the process described by a soldier who was there: 'They thought they were going home and so a band played as they marched out of the camps.' Instead each officer was led into an isolated cell and 'two men held [the prisoner's] arms and a third shot him in the base of the skull'.[233] Those prisoners who weren't executed at Kalinin were transported first by train and then loaded on buses and driven into the Katyn Forest, a wooded area at Gnyozdovo, outside Smolensk in Russia. There, they were executed with pistol shots to the back of the head, piled in stacks and then buried.

With the Soviet denial, the Polish government-in-exile asked the International Committee of the Red Cross to visit the massacre site, and at the same time requested official reports on the missing Polish officers imprisoned at Smolensk from the Soviet officials. On 25 April 1943 Stalin broke off diplomatic relations with London and established a Soviet operated Polish government-in-exile.

Eugenia Huntingdon, the wife of a missing Polish officer, had witnessed the shameful conditions of the Polish troops after their amnesty a year before. She stood in the midst of a train station and saw troops sprawled out in the street, dying while waiting on the trains. Now, twelve months later, much had changed. The Polish troops were well fed, clothed in thick British uniforms and being trained on vast parade grounds outside the camp. Eugenia met with Anders at his headquarters in Buzuluk, searching for any information on her husband. He could offer her none at that time. She arrived in Tehran in April 1942. As Joe and the Jewish children departed by ship for Palestine in January, Eugenia had stayed in Iran working at the Polish headquarters as an editor of the Polish weekly *Zew*. Several months later, she secured a new position as a secretary and Russian translator at the British military headquarters.

It was during that time that she received the horrible news about the massacre. Heartbroken even years later, her memoirs published in 1986 conclude with this simple, emotional line: 'My husband's body was found in a mass grave among thousands of other Katyn victims.'[234]

***

Anders received more disheartening news on 4 July 1943, after a Liberator bomber took off from the Allied airstrip in Gibraltar. The airplane banked and circled out over the harbour, climbed up into a brilliant afternoon sky, levelled off normally and seemed to be heading to London. Then suddenly the aircraft lost speed, trembled in mid-air and then crashed into the blue-green waters below.

On board was the Prime Minister of Poland's London-based government in exile, and Commander-in-Chief of Armed Forces, General Wladyslaw Sikorski. Accompanying Sikorski on the plane flight was his daughter, his chief of staff Klimecki, his British liaison officer Victor Cazalet and several other personnel.

Concerned that the news of the Katyn murders would have a demoralizing effect on the Polish troops in the Middle East, Sikorski had departed London on 25 May 1943 to meet personally with the troops and with General Anders.

Anders was in bed ill with malaria when he was informed of his superior's death: '...on July 1943 news reached us from Gibraltar that General Sikorski had been killed in an air crash. Anders had flown to meet with Sikorski in Cairo only the month before. It was a profound shock to the whole army. To me it brought great grief, for we had respected each other, and his death had come at a time when the differences in our points of view – which had arisen over our attitude to Russia – had been resolved.'

Sikorski's body reached Plymouth by boat and his funeral was conducted at Westminster Cathedral on 15 July. Anders was depressed that he could not attend the funeral but he was simply too ill. The British CiGS, Field Marshal Lord Alanbrooke, wrote:

> The service was too theatrical and fussy to stir up my feelings till the very end. But when I saw the empty stand where the coffin had been with 6 'sierges' burning around it, and on either flank representative 'colours' of regiments borne by officer parties it struck me as a sad picture of Poland's plight: both its state and its army left without a leader when a change of tide seems in sight. I was very fond of Sikorski personally and shall miss him badly.[235]

Alanbrooke's image of Poland's plight reflected what Anders thought of Sikorski's untimely death. Within weeks broadcast news reported that a new government had been appointed, and with that Anders recognized that Sikorski's death was being exploited by a number of politicians, saying 'in whom we had no confidence at all'. Anders strongly felt that Poland's future would have been in more capable hands if Sikorski hadn't died, because he was greatly respected by the Allied leaders. 'There is every reason to believe', Anders later admitted, 'that if it had not been for his death the Polish cause would have been much better defended later'.[236]

Anders turned his attention to regaining his health because there was much still to accomplish in the war. The doctor ordered complete rest to overcome the malaria bout and the general spent several weeks in the Lebanon Mountains until he was fully recovered.

***

In August 1943, Anders and the Polish II Corp arrived in Palestine for the last phase of their training. Then, joining in the fight in North Africa against General Rommel and his famed Afrika Corp, the Poles quickly established themselves as effective fighters. Once Rommel was defeated at El Alamein in October 1942, the Polish forces were transferred to the Italian Campaign.

The last straw for Anders was the Yalta Conference.

During the discussions many leaders throughout the world thought that Roosevelt and Churchill had given Poland as a gift to Stalin. The decision whether to continue to fight, or refuse to any longer spill Polish blood for the Allied cause, was left to Anders and his officers. Anders, in turn, deferred the decision to his soldiers, the ones who would pay the ultimate sacrifice if they continued to battle.

During the battle at Monte Cassino, Anders had threatened to withdraw his troops and radioed Wladyslaw Raczkiewicz, President of the Republic, that he, Anders, could not accept 'the unilateral decision by which Poland and the Polish nation are surrendered to be the spoil of the Bolsheviks...I cannot, on good conscience, demand at present any sacrifice of the soldiers' blood...'[237]

However, once it was considered that the British had no reserves to call up and fill the gap if the Polish army left, the Poles decided to stay and fight on, ignoring the betrayal of their country by Allied leaders. From January to May 1944, Allied forces launched numerous attacks on a German fortified abbey located on a high mountain top. The Polish II Corp took the heavily-armed citadel after a furious assault, opening the road to Rome for the advancing Allied forces. After the battle, American General Mark W. Clark stated: 'The Polish II Corp fought so splendidly under General Anders that it accomplished the nearly impossible – it took Cassino which had been extremely difficult.'[238]

***

Late in the afternoon the day after the German-fortified abbey had been taken, the sun descended the ancient Roman hills and the light turned a dull gray. Anders walked up the steep, rocky slope toward what remained of the abbey, only desolate broken columns, enormous heaps of ruins and rubble. Earlier that morning at 9:50am, a regimental flag was raised over the abbey ruins as a Lancer bugler played 'Kraknow Hejnal,' the medieval Polish song. At the command post, soldiers wept openly.

Even for a battle-hardened general such as Anders, the scene before him gave him dreadful pause. He later wrote:

> The battlefield presented a dreary sight. Corpses of Polish and German soldiers, sometimes tangled in a deadly embrace, lay everywhere, and the air was filled with the stench of rotting bodies. There were overturned tanks with broken caterpillars. Crater after crater pitted the sides of hills and scattered over them were fragments of uniforms, helmets, tommy guns, Spandaus, Schmeissers and hand grenades. The slopes of hills where fighting had been less intense were covered with poppies in incredible number, their red flowers weirdly appropriate to the scene.

After the war, on the western side of the hill in the Commonwealth War Graves Cemetery, British, New Zealand, Canadian and other Allied soldiers were laid to rest. The Polish government-in-exile had built the memorial on the site of the *Dolina Smierci* (Valley of Death) between Monastery Hill and

Hill 593, where thousands had perished. The American dead were buried at Anzio. The German dead were buried 3.2 kilometers north of Cassino.

At the entrance to the Polish military cemetery, an inscription reads:

> We Polish soldiers
> For your Freedom and Ours
> Have given our Souls to God
> Our bodies to the soil of Italy
> And our Hearts to Poland.

Towards the end of the war the Polish army would fight for the liberation of Bologna, Italy, from Nazi forces. After Germany's surrender, Polish soldiers remained camped near Ancona to guard and support swelling numbers of refugees flowing into newly-formed displacement camps.[239]

Anders departed Italy five months later still bitter about the betrayal by the Allies towards Soviet control of his homeland. He knew the Russians; he had fought two wars against them. He knew Stalin, and was well aware of the dictator's ambitions towards the whole of Europe. The treachery was still heavily on his mind as he left behind his soldiers, writing:

> I left Italy on October 31, 1946, travelling by way of Verona, through lovely mountain scenery marred by never-absent signs of war-bombed towns and villages, wrecked railway coaches and vast dumps of unused ammunition. My long war service in Italy had ended and I was going, not home, but to exile. Somewhere in the east there was a red glow in the sky as from a distant fire.[240]

27

A New Life

Six weeks later, Joe was sent to a village settlement near Hadera in central Israel. *Kfar Ha'Roeh* was occupied by families who possessed simple but private homes. Each owned a small parcel of land on which they farmed, raised chickens and built barns for cows.[241]

Before finally departing *Kfar Ha'Noar Hadait*, the officials told Joe that a foster family would be waiting for him to arrive at the settlement and they would take him with them. But when he arrived, Joe found that he had arrived too late to meet with the family.

From what Joe was told it was a great opportunity for a child if a family chose you. But it also took a bit of luck. A family, who received funds from the *Youth Aliyah* to foster a child might come to the village looking for a boy, but maybe just one of a certain age. Or they might desire a girl, with a certain colour of eyes or hair, or maybe a bigger or smaller child. So, to be chosen by a family a child had to fit into what the family was looking for in a son or daughter. Joe also understood that besides being a commitment by the family, it was also a commitment by the child, because you had to work a half day for your new family, and then go to school for the remainder of the day.

No one at the settlement could explain to Joe why he was too late that day, but the administrators told him not to worry, that other families were coming to the farm village to look for children.

One day a family arrived for Joe. It was a time when Joe could have been content and happy. Instead, the experience sent him on a dark spiral that took him months to recover from and, so deep that to this day, he doesn't remember what happened to him with that family. Over 60 years later, on a trip to Israel, Joe asked Tsvi Weinberg, the head *madrich* (teacher), 'What happened there? Why did I leave so quickly?'

The *madrich* couldn't give Joe an answer. All either he or Joe could remember was that after a week Joe ran away from the family, and returned to *Kfar Ha'Roeh*, shaken and frightened. Trembling, he told Weinberg that he wasn't ever going back to that house. Weinberg quietly listened and then reassured his student, 'Go back tonight, and I'll figure something out tomorrow.'

Joe refused.

***

The Jewish Agency eventually found another family for Joe, a young couple with two sons aged five and three. Then there began a part of his life filled with peace and happiness that he hadn't experienced since he was a child in Cologne.

The mother's name was Leah and she was a wonderful presence in Joe's life from the first day, treating him as though he was her true son. Her kindness would affect and guide his life from that time forwards.

However, Leah's husband was a different kind of person, the opposite of the gentle, kind woman. Joe would always consider him 'a grown up, stupid guy', who always teased Joe 'in a wrong way'. What did this grown man expect Joe to know at thirteen? It was true that Joe couldn't read or write, but was that his fault with all that he had been through? When would he have had time to be educated moving from camp to camp, and hunting for food like a wild animal? If Joe didn't know something, he would make fun of him in front of everyone,and Joe would never understand what Leah saw in her husband.

This was an important time in Joe's life, and for all the Tehran Children, in that now that they had survived a horrible experience they needed love and nurturing and guidance – exactly what Leah provided for Joe.

For many years later in life, Joe would stay in touch with Leah, and he brought his sons Amir and Ori to meet her.

It was a pleasant time for Joe because Shlomo was sometimes next door, visiting with Leah's step-sister. This idyllic life would last until August when Joe went to school, learned Hebrew and mathematics, although he didn't like either of those subjects. He started out in the third grade, but he was soon promoted to fourth grade, and it was then that classes changed to include more Hebrew and mathematics and reading and writing. Also, it was here that Joe, for the first time, studied geography and he was surprised to learn that Palestine wasn't anywhere close to America!

***

Joe was very content living with Leah. He once again felt truly loved by someone, he had playmates in her sons and he just did his best to avoid her husband. And Joe discovered that he was good at learning and loved school now that he had that opportunity.

But unbeknownst to Joe, events were unfolding that would drastically change his life again, and there would be little he could do to stop them.

Aunt Sophie, shortly after Joe spent Passover week with them in Tel Aviv, had written to Simon Rosenbaum, Joe's father in New York, relating the stories Joe had told them. The news of the death of his wife, daughter and parents shocked Simon and Inez. Simon, learning that Joe had survived, insisted that his son travel to America and once again be a part of his true family.

Simon and Inez wrote to Joe about coming to New York. The letters from his father were written in Hebrew, so Leah translated and Joe would write back in Hebrew. It was from those letters that Joe understood that his father insisted that he come to him, and that he would never give up until his son came to him. The problem for Joe was that he had mixed emotions about leaving a place where he was finally safe and happy living with Leah, and he had worked his way up to the eighth grade.

Joe was torn on what was the right thing to do, but eventually he felt as though this decision was no longer his to make, that it was being decided for him. This letter-writing back and forth had started in 1944 when the war was still in its full fury. But by May 1945 the war in Europe ended. Then both Aunt Sophie and Leah told Joe, 'Josef, you are young, and your father is married now. He has a wife and a daughter, and you'll be a whole family. It's time to go.'

Two things bothered Joe. First, he had known his father when he was six, now he was fifteen. During that time Joe was aware that he had changed a lot. How much had his father changed? He had, after all, remarried a younger woman. How would she accept a stranger coming into her family, even though he was a son?

The other thing that bothered Joe was America was such a different place, a new language, and he would have to adjust to each new aspect of life there. Trying her best to persuade her brother, Inez sent photographs. It was obvious that he was being convinced to leave Palestine, the place he loved. He had started a good life there, 'eating, working and enjoying dancing, and the other children'. Joe seemed to get along with everyone. Each day was a gift. When he turned fourteen, Joe had his *Bar Mitzvah*, not that big of a deal really for him, 'but Leah tried to make a big deal of it, and held a party in the store'. Inwardly he had told no one, Joe had made his decision not to go to America in spite of the insistence from Leah and Aunt Sophie. And it was a secret as to why Joe had made that decision.

Maybe it was the burden of deciding whether to go to America, or not. Or having the *Bar Mitzvah*, that time when a boy passes into another season of life, that of manhood. Or maybe it was all brought back by the parties, the dancing and the friends who often brought along younger brothers or sisters. Perhaps the darkness that gradually crept into Joe's mind would have happened anyway.

But then began the awful nightmares, nightmares about Nelly that stole his new-found peace. In these haunting dreams the room was always still, no air, no movement, as if the very world had died. Joe went to Nelly who was lying in the sun-drenched tossed blankets like a frail bird. When he dared to reach out and touch her hand, the coldness shocked Joe into the realization that Nelly would never wake up again. Ever. Still, he risked touching her pale, gray cheeks as if perhaps he was wrong. Maybe his sister was just asleep. Her cheeks were cold, a dull chill he would never forget as long as he lived. He fell back on the floor, pulled his knees under his chin, his arms circling over his head…thinking of the food he searched for so that he and Nelly could survive, every morsel of food found in the alleyways…pieces of cake, perhaps a slice of bread, a half-eaten vegetable…it was only rubbish to those who casually tossed them into the bins. But for Joe those scraps represented life, it was food to keep him going, to look after Nelly. In the end he realized it was this food that was the reason why she had died because he had been selfish with it. Why hadn't he let her eat when she was so hungry that morning? They had saved two pieces of bread, after all. But Joe had said, 'No', thinking he was doing the right thing. Instead, Nelly had died in her sleep. She had so deserved to live.

As the nightmares worsened and became more vivid and frightful, Joe started to wet the bed at night.

Leah set up appointments with several psychiatrists, who after interviewing Joe diagnosed that the boy was insecure about the situation and not able to talk about his guilt over Nelly's death. They explained that keeping it trapped within made the guilt more powerful.

Joe stayed at home constantly, refusing to go out and play with the other children. He was embarrassed. And he was aware that if he went out to a dance or a place where his friends met, that they would have their younger sisters with them, and Nelly should have been with him. Leah never gave up, taking him to doctor after doctor, because watching Joe go through so much pain caused her to suffer also.

One night, Joe began talking about Nelly's death to Leah, and once the words began, it flowed like hot tears from him. They cried together, and then Joe told her something – it would sound horrible, inhuman and brutally cold to anyone who wasn't there at Tashkent and just trying to live – when he told her how Nelly hadn't received a proper burial as any human deserved, Leah wept as hard as he ever had.

Leah still wouldn't give up and made an appointment with a woman doctor.

This doctor treated Joe in a very different way. She was kinder, more direct with Joe and gradually through her treatments turned on a light in the darkness haunting his life.

On one visit she asked, 'What's very dear to you, Joe?'

The answer was easy for Joe because each day he took with him a large, thick notebook in which he placed his homework and notes. It rarely left his sight. For a boy who loved school, it was a valuable possession.

He told the doctor about his notebook.

'Okay', the doctor said, 'take the notebook…and put it right under the sheet where you wet the bed.'

Joe looked at her. 'I don't want to do this, I need my notebook.'

But the doctor insisted.

When Joe went home and told Leah what the doctor had suggested, she agreed. She told Joe not to worry, to put the notebook beneath the covers as the doctor told him and everything would be fine. 'It was a big notebook where you wrote your homework, or your notes that you took in class', Joe fondly remembers. 'A thick notebook that was very important to me because if I didn't have this I didn't know what was going on.'

But, as Joe trusted Leah, did as he was told. He didn't sleep that night. Or the next night.

Several nights later, Joe slept all night without any problems. Within a week, Leah told him to go to bed without the notebook under the covers. The doctor's treatment had worked. Joe slept throughout the night and didn't wet the bed. What a relief it was for Joe when he realized the problem was gone.

With that out of the way, the family once again insisted that Joe should go to America and visit his father and Inez. He loved Israel, which by now was a nation of Jews, and he was afraid that if he went to America his father would keep him there, even if he wasn't happy. But what bothered him most of all was that someone other than himself was trying to make the decision for him.

Leah sat Joe down one day and told him, 'You have to go.' It was that simple. She explained that it was his father and sister and that he had to go to his family. If Leah, who Joe loved dearly and he knew how much she loved him, thought it best, then Joe knew, 'that's how it's supposed to be.'

Once the decision was made, Uncle Anschel wrote to Simon Rosenbaum that this son was coming and that he had taken care of the details. He would be travelling fourth class and Anschel gave him the name of the ship.

***

The day that Joe was to finally leave Israel for America was naturally a sad one for him and Leah, but it was also chaotic.[242]

Uncle Anschel had organized each step of Joe's departure and trip. Rosie, his oldest daughter, drove Joe to a hotel in Haifa and had arranged for a couple to come for Joe and take him to his ship. But the next morning Joe's problems began because nobody came for him. So he decided to go himself and hired a cab to take him to the harbour. When Joe arrived at the pier, he discovered that he had brought along his small suitcase with him, but he had left behind a briefcase with all his travel papers. He made a quick trip in a cab back to the hotel, retrieved the briefcase from his room and hurried back to the harbour. Joe made his way onto the ship moments before departure.

Joe never saw or heard from the couple his uncle had arranged to help him. But it didn't matter anymore. Joe was on the ship and it would take him to America, and to his father and sister.

***

As the ship slipped through the metal-gray waters of the Bay of Haifa, soon to be in the open waters of the Mediterranean, Joe stood at the railing staring at Mount Carmel in the background. Looking at the mountain, a thought struck Joe. Haifa was Palestine, now Israel – and he was leaving home.

Was this something he really wanted to do?

This was where he had found his freedom, even as that hungry, ill and scared young boy on the train to Palestine. This Israel, and wonderful, sweet Leah, his friends, all the family he really knew, it was all here and he was leaving them all behind. He really didn't know his father at all. And America? Inez's photographs had showed him that it was such a strange place.

All these doubts swirled strongly in his mind.

The strange thing was how could he have forgotten such a valuable briefcase filled with his papers? How had he been so careless, a mistake that could have cost him from being reunited with his father? That act of leaving behind the briefcase at the hotel, an ominous beginning to his trip, the possibility of why he had let such a stupid thing happen, bothered Joe and haunted him during the trip.

Maybe, Joe had left behind the briefcase at the Haifa hotel because deep inside, he was angry about leaving Leah and Israel. Maybe he didn't want to go to America.

28

America and Reunion, 1946

The America Joe travelled to was a nation that had undergone a sweeping transition since 1939. That year before the war, the country had struggled through the Recession of 1937-1938 as unemployment sky-rocketed to more than 25 per cent, industrial production was down 30 per cent, both statics at almost the same levels as 1929 and the beginning of the Great Depression. Economic historians noted that private sector employment didn't exceed those levels in 1929 and 1937 until the start of the Second World War.

The post-war economic boom, beginning in 1939, unfolded in Europe and lasted until the late 1970s as, worldwide, countries enjoyed economic growth. Even countries devastated by the war began to grow economically with such high levels that Italy would be known as the 'Italian Economic Miracle'. In America, housing growth (15,000,000) provided homes for veterans and their new families. This was the era of new and better, as new products came on the market for consumers to buy and air conditioning and television sets began to fit into every living room. Good days had indeed returned, and America was ready to revel in the prosperity.

Joseph C. Goulden, in *The Best Years: 1945-1950*, explained the elation spreading over America just after the war:

> August 1945 found America victorious in places other than the battlefield. The Great Depression fell along with the Axis powers, and the word 'want' took on a new and not entirely negative meaning: when citizens wished to buy something, there was not a shortage of dollars, but of the articles they wanted to carry home from the stores. When the war ended, Americans had jobs (53,000,000 of them, with unemployment less than two per cent) and Americans had money ($140 billion in liquid savings, in war bonds and in banks and in their wallets, about three times the national income in 1932). Although most people expected some inevitable painful bumps as the economy shifted from war to peace, Americans nonetheless entered the post-war era confident that the bread lines were gone forever.[243]

Americans wanted to forget about the war and turned to entertainment for their escape. Robert Penn Warren's novel portraying Louisiana governor

Huey P. Long, *All the King's Men*, was released in 1946, along with Albert Camus's dark novel *The Stranger*. Frank Sinatra hit the billboard charts that year singing new songs like 'There's No Business, like Show Business'.

America seemed to be gradually becoming comfortable with no more war, but there was one social problem that remained to be dealt with in the months after the war – The returning soldier – and it was a movie that brought this reality to the attention of the American public.

Director William Wyler filmed a movie based on the novel *Glory for Me* by MacKinlay Kantor. The movie was centred on three Second World War soldiers returning home to small-town America. *The Best Years of Our Lives* chronicled the veterans as they returned from war, struggling with the changes in themselves, and the families they had left behind.[244] The American public was hungry for such a movie describing the transitions many veterans faced once they returned home.

In Europe once great cities lay in ruins, flattened by British and American bombing. Now it was time to restore the war's wastelands and America joined in with a programme named after Secretary of State George Marshall, to provide food, clothing and economic assistance. Just a year previously, Marshall had been Chief of Staff commanding the largest army in history during the war. With the purpose of rebuilding those European countries, America would invest over $13 billion to the Marshall Plan ($130 billion in today's economy) in aid over the next four years beginning in April 1948.

America had turned to its bitter enemy with a helping hand. America had welcomed its soldiers back with open arms, offering them a future. And now America would be the new home for Joe Rosenbaum.

***

Joe's trip took three weeks.[245]

The ship he travelled across the Atlantic on was a 'troop haul', a ship built to transfer soldiers. It was three storeys high and throughout the ship, to manage such a large number of people, over 300 hammocks were tied up along walkways and halls.

Alexandria, Egypt, was the first destination after departing Haifa. As the troop ship entered the harbour there were many small boats surrounding the ship and children swimming in the water, waiting for gifts to be tossed down to them. By then, the loneliness of not knowing anyone on board began to bother Joe. But watching the children laughing and swimming in the water below reminded him of when they had sailed into Suez after a seven-month journey. The difference was that on that day he had been very happy. Now – well, now, he wasn't so sure.

After picking up passengers in Alexandria, the ship sailed that night to Piraeus, Greece, near Athens. There a large number of passengers boarded, one was a boy about Joe's age. In a short time they became friends despite a language problem. Joe only spoke Hebrew and the new boy spoke Greek. However the boys soon learned to communicate, which was fortunate for Joe. After a brief stop in Gibraltar the ship headed out to sea, where the waters were rough and tossed the ship. Joe became violently ill so his new friend took him up to the top level, where the fresh air made Joe feel better.

Then the day came when the ship sailed into New York Harbour, and everyone on the boat was excited and crowded along the deck railing. Such tall, grand gray buildings to stare at, and there off to their right was the Statue of Library that Joe had heard so much about on his journey. The 6 July 1946 cover of *The Saturday Evening Post,* painted by Norman Rockwell, displayed the Statue of Liberty as workmen painted and restored the torch that she held high.

Later, there was a long line on the walkway as they unloaded onto a large, crowded pier.

The passengers then formed into another long line to present their papers, finally exiting through a series of doors. Outside, Joe looked for his father, or Inez, who were supposed to meet him there. Inez had sent Joe a photograph, so that he could recognize them. He recognized no one.

Against the wall was a line of benches.

Joe walked over and sat down, his two travel bags at his feet. All around people waved and hugged, greeting their families, laughing and crying. Through the doors the Greek boy, Joe's friend, emerged. He was quickly surrounded by people hugging him and patting his head. The boy never saw Joe, but Joe saw him and watched the happiness on his face. Then suddenly they were gone, disappearing into the thick crowd.

Joe looked around.

He didn't see Inez or his father.

He would wait.

***

The shadows had grown long along the pier by late afternoon and the air was crisp. Joe felt lonelier now than he had at any time during the trip. 'The day went by and soon most people went home, and I was left alone', Joe says.

In a while, several women approached Joe. They were surprised when he answered their question which they asked in Yiddish, 'Who is supposed to come and pick you up?' Joe answered that either his father or sister were coming. They identified themselves as members of the *Hias*, the Hebrew

Sheltering Aid Society, an American charitable organization that assisted Jewish immigrants.

'Do you have his address?'

'No', Joe answered. 'I know he lives in New York, and he is supposed to pick me up. Or my sister.'

'Okay', they said, 'why don't you wait here, we will put you up for the night, and tomorrow we can figure out what to do with you'.

At least there was someone who cared what happened to him, Joe thought. But he was also afraid that if he left the pier he would miss his father or sister, and then would they ever find him? New York looked like such a big place. In a few short minutes Joe didn't have to make that decision.

Suddenly he recognized Inez as she walked up because she had sent photographs. And, she had recognized him, because she ran up to him and hugged and kissed him for a long time.

They sat together on the bench. Joe finally asked, 'Where's Papa?'

'He came already', Inez said. 'Twice, Josef, and it's not his fault because we were told you were on a different ship. Papa had already come twice, so I came. This is my second time.'

'I'm glad you're here', Joe said.

'And I came later, because I didn't want to miss work.'

'It's okay, I'm glad anyway.'

Joe stared into her face. Inez was now nineteen, and he tried to remember how old she was when he last saw her. Memories came to him from a time when they were playing in the side yard beneath the trees, images of himself, Inez and Nelly standing beneath the warm sun posing for photographs. It seemed like the family was always taking photographs. All of it came rushing back to him and in his mind it was again 1938 when he and his sister last saw each other, a week or so after *Pesach*, when father travelled to America and Inez was sent to Belgium and they were all at the Cologne train station. Joe as seven or eight then, Inez was twelve. Another lifetime. Now she sat beside him a grown woman, all of nineteen, staring at him as she placed her hand on his.

What kind of life had she had? Was she happy in America with Papa? Did she have a boyfriend? Had she ever been hungry and frightened and afraid to die like he had? Joe was certain she would tell him everything soon enough. Joe would tell her about his journey. He was also glad for his sister – at least she had never seen the horrors of Siberia or Tashkent or Tehran. At least Inez didn't have to watch mother or Nelly die.

Inez took her hand off of his hand, she stared searchingly into his eyes as if she saw the pain he had suffered, and she brushed his cheek with her fingertips. 'Come, Josef. I'll take you to Papa's house.'

***

It was a reunion that Joe had tossed about in his memory constantly on the three-week trip across the ocean to America. The first time that he would see his father. From his childhood in Cologne, he had only vague memories of Simon, a man who stood tall and always had a sharp sense of humour. But how much had the war and the time away from family, other than Inez, changed him? And would his new wife accept him as part of the family, or would she consider Joe an intruder? Joe was happy that he had come to America, but still there was anxiety gripping his stomach.

It all started well enough when Joe and Inez arrived at his father's house, and there he met his step-mother and his step-sister Evelyn. As they sat and talked, Joe realized that Inez didn't live with their father because she had her own place, but she said she was going to spend some time there with them because it was *Shabbat*. It wasn't long into the discussion that Joe began to learn about several hurdles that he was going to have to overcome. First was his appearance. When he got off the ship he was wearing shorts, very short like children wore in Israel, sandals and a shirt. His father said that tomorrow he would give Inez money and she would take him to the store and buy him long pants and shoes like children wore in America. Joe learned quickly that he didn't like the fabric rubbing against his legs simply because he had never worn long pants before. Secondly, he was pleasantly surprised that he could easily communicate with his step-mother because she spoke Yiddish. But his step-sister spoke only English, which meant it was harder to communicate with her.

That night his father did *Kiddush* and Joe helped because he knew some of the songs, but some of the songs he didn't know. It was obvious to Joe that his father was very religious, and he spoke the old Hebrew, the language of religious Jews. At dinner that night they didn't ask Joe many questions. He thought maybe they wanted to give him time before he had to remember and tell them about the terrible events he had experienced. But it was a good dinner, and Joe felt comfortable eating and discussing what he considered small talk with his new family.

After dinner Inez stood and said, 'I'm going to take Yossi downstairs and we're going to talk.' They communicated well because his sister spoke Yiddish and German. Joe had asked Inez at the pier when she picked him up not to ever speak German, he never wanted to speak German again. When Joe asked this, his sister stared at him. Joe told her that he hadn't spoken German since the day their mother died. He and Nelly spoke Yiddish, and to Joe the whole world spoke Yiddish.

But as Inez and Joe rose from the table, his step-mother asked, 'Why don't you take also Evelyn?'

Inez picked up several plates and glasses, clearing the table. 'I want to talk to Yossi now, I haven't seen him for a long time. I want to talk to him alone and besides I can talk to Evelyn tomorrow or the next day.'

His step-mother's face darkened. 'I would like it better if you took Evelyn with you to talk to Josef.'

Then an argument built up between them, words spoken low but very sharply back and forth between them, and then it became loud and angry. They yelled at each other in English, so Joe didn't understand what was going on. When he asked his father, he told Joe, 'Oh', they had a fight'. All because this woman wanted Evelyn to go with us, Joe thought. Why was that so important? Joe couldn't understand. Inez and Joe were siblings, and until today they hadn't seen each other in over seven years. What could be the problem? That night upset Joe greatly. He would learn that his father and she had been married a year, and to a fifteen-year-old boy that didn't make her and Evelyn family yet. Maybe later, maybe twenty years later she would be part of the family.

That night Joe was disappointed with his father because none of that scenario made any sense. But at that time Joe didn't talk about it with his father. Only several months later would he discuss it with him. Was his wife more important than anyone else? He also reminded his father that he had disrupted his new life in Israel to come to America. That had to mean something.

That night though, Inez forcibly got her way.

She took Joe for a walk on that July night. It was about seven o'clock and it was a nice evening and they walked and discussed what had happened since they were separated so many years ago. And soon all the walls of time broke down and they became brother and sister again. But also during that walk Inez let Joe know of possible problems that might be coming their way.

***

So another life began for Joe, this one in America with his new family. Although it had started ominously, Joe was in many ways happy that he had travelled to America to be with his true family. Then something happened that made him a little concerned.

His father decided to send Joe to a *Yeshiva*, an orthodox Jewish institution that focused on the study of traditional religious texts. Each day Joe went to school with boys wearing *peyotes*, the long locks on each side of their faces. They studied in Old Hebrew, which Joe didn't speak, and even after they translated it into English that didn't help him either because he didn't know English. The only aspect enjoyable about going each day was that his father gave him a quarter every morning, and Joe would use the money to buy *knishes*, a snack food with several kinds of fillings, covered with dough either baked, grilled or fried. When Joe asked his father for two quarters each morning, he gave them to him so Joe had 10 o'clock *knishes* and 1 o'clock *knishes*. But even with wonderful *knishes*, Joe thought, they certainly weren't a good enough reason to go to *Yeshiva*. He was miserable.

Joe did go to the *Yeshiva* for six weeks, and then came home one day and told his father that he wasn't going back. His father became upset, wanting to know why he would come to America and then rebel against him like that. Then Joe understood. His father wanted him to wear *peyotes* like the other boys, so that he would look like his father had when he was fifteen.

Joe had had enough. 'I said that's it, I don't want to go to the school anymore, and I don't want the *knishes* anymore. My father was very upset that I was rebelling', he remembers when he realized that his father wanted to live his life through his son. But Joe's feelings ran much deeper than that. 'At the time I had my doubts about religion, together with losing Nelly, for which I blamed myself a lot.' He told his father that he wouldn't go to this *Yeshiva*, but he would go to another one. For Joe, religion wasn't that easy.

Joe would go and live with Aunt Betty, the younger sister of Joe's mother. She had come to America with her son, Simon, who was two years younger than Joe, and they could go to school together. Joe enjoyed going to the new school with his cousin because he studied the New Hebrew, which he knew well. English was taught also, but Joe didn't pay much attention to learning English although the other children picked it up listening to the radio and reading newspapers.

Two events in 1947 deeply influenced his remaining days in America. First, Joe changed physically. With all the food to eat, meat which they didn't get in Palestine and glasses of milk, he grew from just over five feet tall, to over 5'9' in a short time. But there was a problem with him growing so quickly and he became ill. The doctors diagnosed Joe as having developed rheumatic fever because his heart couldn't keep up with the growth of his body.

Joe moved back in with his father and was confined to bed. Inez brought him several books in English and she encouraged him to read them. For several days the books sat on the table beside the bed. Joe remembered how hard English was for him in the school, and he didn't want to deal with all that, especially when he was ill. Then, he became bored and lonely, and to offset this one day he picked up one of the English books and began to read it. At first it took Joe two hours to read just one page because he didn't understand it or know how to pronounce the words. But he stayed with it until he could read English.

Little did he know how that one act of reading English would shift his thoughts and change his life.

***

Towards the end of the year Joe was well enough to get out of bed. His father put Joe in another school, a high school, which would one day become Yeshiva University in New York. His age placed him as a junior. Joe immediately realized that he was overwhelmed in his studies, unable to keep up with the other students.

It was also at that time that Joe's Jewish beliefs began to change and diminish because he really didn't know what to believe any more. He supposed that he still believed in religion, but the question he continued to ask himself was how much did he believe?

When Joe turned seventeen he went to his father and told him he was going to stop school because he hated it, and he couldn't keep up with the studies. To Joe's surprise, his father agreed with his decision.

Joe told him that he would go to study groups in the evenings in Borough Park, a neighbourhood in the southwest part of Brooklyn and a religious place, and he could study Judaism there.

With all of these changes in his life and the setbacks, Joe still had a plan. He would study what he wanted to study, find a job and work, and when he turned eighteen, when his father couldn't stop him because he wouldn't be a minor any longer, he would return to Israel.

***

Joe continued to live with his father, began to work and to learn English. At first he worked at unskilled tasks, taking the subway to Manhattan from Brooklyn, and working at it for several weeks until he had enough money to support himself. In those days he paid Aunt Betty ten dollars a week to live with her, leaving him with about ten dollars a week. Inez brought him more books and encouraged him to read them, but he simply set them aside.

He spent the evenings working at odd jobs, and the mornings searching for the next job. To pass the time Joe went to the 42nd Street Theater where he stumbled up something he loved. He watched movies sometimes three times because he loved watching them, but also because he was picking up English from the dialogue. Joe thought Edward G. Robinson was a wonderful actor. One day he watched *Casablanca* six times until he got a headache. Eventually he understood enough English, although he couldn't speak it, when people spoke to him.

In the evenings, Joe went to a synagogue and attended Jewish lessons for several hours, and there he met some guys who spoke to him in English, which he now understood. They became friends.

From endlessly watching movies, and having conversations with his new friends at the synagogue, Joe found that he could go home at night and read the books Inez had brought him.

Joe began to make friends, and during that time he learned that he had another love. Music. So, he bought records and a phonograph, and went to parties when his friends invited him so that he could listen to records. Joe made more friends, who eventually introduced him to the opportunity to join the Israeli 'illegal' underground that was fighting the British. In America, Joe joined the Stern Gang, named for their leader, Yair Stern, a philosopher and poet. By now Stern had been killed by the British, but the surviving group developed into a deeper and more sinister underground. In Hebrew the Stern Gang was called *Lechi*. And the group Joe belonged to was called *modaon*, a club, busy in taking up money to support the underground in Palestine so that they could fight and kill British soldiers. In America the *Lechi* wasn't illegal, so this fundraising was upfront.

But in September 1947 the Stern Gang assassinated Count Bernadotte, a United Nations official, who was attempting to arrange peace between the *Yishuv* and the Arabs. This drove Joe's organization underground, and they obviously had to be more careful with their activities.

Joe's life in America – although it had started badly with his relationship with his step-mother and then becoming ill – gradually improved and Joe was content. Movies. Music. A purpose with the *Lechi*. Then Joe read of a world event that would shift his life.

The State of Israel was declared.

He had been considering going back to Israel for a long time, and this historic event convinced Joe that he could go back. He was eighteen now and he could make up his own mind about such matters.

In March 1949 he sat down with his father and Inez and told them of his decision. His father was firmly against him going back. But Inez, as Joe thought she would, took his side and told him that he should do what he thought was right. Give it some more time, his father said. Give it a week and think hard about it. But for Joe, the hard journey he had travelled as a child, trying to survive in first Siberia, then Russia, had taught him to follow his instincts and not to allow anyone else's opinion sway him. No. He would go back to Israel.

29

Israel. March 1949

Joe Rosenbaum returned to Israel on board the same ship on which he had travelled to America three years before. 'Inez's boyfriend, Herbie, drove me to pier and I paid 45 dollars for the voyage', Joe recalls. No one else was there to see him off, and the knot of restlessness that Joe was so familiar with burned in his stomach. He felt as though he was 'going home', but there were many things he'd miss about America.[246]

***

During the years when Joe Rosenbaum lived in America, reuniting with his father and sister, the land of Palestine had gone through many changes. It was now the nation of Israel.

Journalist Naomi Shepherd explains in her book, *Ploughing Sand: British Rule in Palestine 1917-1848*: 'British Rule [the mandate] protected the Zionist beachhead in Palestine during its most vulnerable, insecure period during the 1920s and 1930s.' But for whatever purpose one could find something good of British rule in Palestine, at the end of the Second World War. The *Yishuv*, the Jewish community in Palestine, however, began pressuring the British government even more during the months after the war concerning her immigration regulations. Jewish holocaust survivors, once again detained in displaced person camps much like the camp Ben-Gurion had visited in late 1945, didn't want to return to Europe and their homes where neighbours had turned against them. Instead, these refugees who wanted to start life over again in Palestine, were turned away by the boatloads or detained in Athlit, or sent to Cyprus.

Drained of blood and money, Britain announced in 1947, that it would withdraw from mandatory Palestine. The United Nations General Assembly then proposed a plan to replace British rule with an independent Arab State, an independent Jewish State, and the City of Jerusalem to exist under an International Trusteeship System.'

The Jewish agency accepted the plan. But the Arab League and Arab Higher Committee of Palestine rejected the resolution, and suggested that they would reject any plan of partition. On the following day, 1 December

1947, Arab violence against the Jews broke out across Palestine. The Jewish Agency, which was by now the shadow government of the Jewish community, now had no other option.

On 4pm on Friday 14 May 1948, in the Tel Aviv Municipal Museum, members of the *Yishuv's* shadow government gathered at a hastily-prepared meeting to declare independence for the small nation. The Israel Philharmonic Orchestra began the meeting playing the Zionist song 'Hatikvah', which would become the Israeli national anthem. The document was just 979 words, and it took only seventeen minutes for David Ben-Gurion to read the document out over a radio broadcast. The last words he spoke over the microphone to the infant nation were that the proceedings declared, 'The establishment of a Jewish state in Eretz Israel, to be known as the State of Israel.'

The last British soldiers left at midnight, and the next morning at 5:30 air raid sirens sounded for the first time over Tel Aviv as Arab war planes appeared over Israeli skies.

During the 1948 Arab-Israeli War the Arab countries (Egypt, Syria, Transjordan, and Iraq) largely outnumbered the Jewish state. The *Haganah*, the Israeli army, besides being outnumbered in troop figures, possessed few weapons, planes or tanks. Despite the overwhelming odds (one *Haganah* commander when asked by Ben-Gurion the night before the declaration of their chances of victory, answered '50-50'), Israel won her independence. On 20 July 1949 a final armistice agreement would be signed. It was a total Israeli victory as Israel kept all the land designated to them by the Partition Plan, and captured 50 per cent of the area intended for the Arabs.

The conflict would be known in Hebrew as the *Milkhemet Ha'Atzma'ut*, The War of Independence, or *Milkhemet Ha Shikhrur*, the War of Liberation. The Arabs, dazed by their devastating and unexpected defeat, would call it the *Nakba*, the 'Catastrophe of Palestine'.

***

The return trip took three weeks and once Joe arrived back in Israel he went to see Yaffa, the beautiful cousin who had come for him at the camp in Galilee. After all, Joe reasoned, she was the one who had started him on his new life after the journey. She now lived in Haifa and was married to a captain in the Israeli navy. After staying with Yaffa for a day, he travelled to Tel Aviv and stayed with Sophie.

They no longer lived in the shop but had moved to an apartment upstairs in the same building. He told Sophie that he only needed to stay for several days until he could join the Israeli army, so she let him stay in the back of the shop, which he had to himself. The next day Joe went to the military office and told them that he wanted to join. The officer informed Joe that he was too late and that the war would be over in several months. It was now April and the war would end in May, and that they weren't recruiting any more soldiers. Before sending him away, the officer assured Joe that they would contact him when he was needed, possibly in about a year.

Once again Joe was at a crossroads in his life. His plans once he was back in Israel were detoured. He needed something to do for a year until the military needed him, and he didn't want to 'live in a store full of hats', so he found a kibbutz that needed workers and he stayed there for six weeks working in the fields. He travelled to Tel Aviv to see Sophie during *Yom Ha'Atzma'ut,* the national day of Israel celebrating independence. It was during this holiday when Sophie asked Joe if he liked what he was doing, did he like the kibbutz? He told her, 'no'.

'Why do you stay there?' Sophie asked.

'Because, I have no other place to go.'

She smiled. 'Why don't you stay here? You can get a job. If you need to kill a year, get a job and do something.'

Joe went back to the kibbutz, gathered his few belongings and came back and stayed with Sophie in the back of the shop full of hats and started looking for a job. One of his uncle's friends was a barber, and it was suggested that he might like that. But after several days he decided he didn't want to be a barber. One day, when he was eighteen, he began missing his parents. At this age father and mother should be here to guide, and offer advice. The only advice Joe received was from his aunts and uncles in Tel Aviv telling him to find a job, make a living, after all he had to eat, and then go from there.

Eventually, Joe found a job – or the job found him.

One of his cousins, Alex Feldman, came to Joe one day and told him that he had a bicycle that he didn't use any longer, and that Joe should take the bicycle and go and look for a job in the city. Finally Joe found a job. A large department store named *Madim* sold men's clothes, slacks, suits and shirts and was owned by a German who came to Palestine years before and had the money to start such a business. Joe's work was to be at the store by 7:00am and clean the top two floors where the selling took place. The third floor was where women sewed the clothes. His work day was from 7:00am until 1:00pm, a break until 4:00pm, and then work until 7:00pm. The three hours in the middle of the day quickly became boring for Joe because he didn't have a home to go to during that time. But the pay was about four times what boys his age were making, about forty *lirot* a month. 'It killed my day', Joe recalls, 'because I didn't know what to do with the three hours in the middle of the day. I took the bike and biked around…there was no reason for me to hang around'.

After several months Joe started going out after work, usually around 8:00pm, into the city. This would begin Joe's lifelong love of music. One friend he met, nicknamed Tino Rossi, invited Joe over to listen to records, the first time he had ever heard classical music. That night it was Beethoven's Nineteenth Symphony, which strangely Joe found boring in the beginning, but finally he fell under Beethoven's spell. He told all of his new friends that he had, at last, 'found something that he wanted to hear more of'. Then, one of cousin Shlomo's friends who owned a large apartment gave Joe the keys so that he could go over and listen to all the music he wanted. That experience ignited in Joe a desire to study classical music. He bought a harmonica, taught himself to play, but soon that didn't satisfy his desire to learn. Tino, his friend, introduced him to a student of a composer. Joe started taking lessons, but soon realized that to really be good at classical music one must start around five or six years old. He was nineteen now. But he had found something in life that he really loved, and that meant he had to make another decision in life without anyone to guide him.

Joe had to find a new job that would allow him time to play his music.

***

Joe knew that taking a job working in the garage of the Tel Aviv Police Headquarters that paid half of the department store job wouldn't go down very well with his uncle.

'How much are you making now?'

'Twenty', Joe told him.

'You're making twenty lirot? Half what you made before? Are you crazy? Are you out of your mind?'

Joe said, 'I am paying here only ten. Ten is enough for me to spend, I don't need that much and I don't care for money.'

His aunt finally calmed her husband down, and she told him that at least Joe was working and paying for living with them. For Joe, it was another example of a young person not having someone to guide him concerning money. But Joe did realize that he didn't have a profession.

After he had been working at the station for several weeks, Joe became friends with Sergeant Bass, a man about ten years older than Joe and from Czechoslovakia. One day Joe told him that he was going to join the military as soon as they needed him. Bass gave him the name of a cousin named Polifka already in the military working in the armoured division. He assured Joe his cousin would help him out if he'd contact him once he joined.

For a time Joe was happy. He worked making ten *lirot* which Joe thought was a lot of money in Israel in those days, and he listened to music. After all, Joe didn't care about money; he was trying to make up for lost time.

In February 1950, about a year after Joe returned to Israel, the military called him up. When he took his initial physical examination, they immediately identified that Joe showed evidence that at one time he had suffered from rheumatic fever. But the military still wanted him, and Joe was assigned to a medical office job. It took him several months to contact Polifka, who was now an officer, and he told Joe that he would transfer him to his division. Joe began writing to Inez in America, and mentioned in one of his letters that he was selling cigarettes for 2 *lirot* so that he could take music lessons. She wrote back, unaware that he was so interested in playing music, suggesting that he return to America and enrol in Julliard, a good school to study music located in Manhattan. Realizing that might be a possibility, Joe decided to give the situation some time. He wasn't learning music as quickly as he wanted to because he could only afford to take lessons every two weeks. But Joe still believed in what he was doing.

He was in his second year in the military, assigned to Polifka's division now. Once again, Joe was at a crossroads in life, looking for answers.

***

Polifka liked Joe. One day he took Joe aside and they had a very important talk.

He said, 'Listen, you came here as an ordinary soldier, and I gave you your first stripe. I gave you the second stripe, and I'm going to give you a third stripe. What I want you to do is to sign up for five years in the army, go to an officer seminar and I'll make you my assistant. In another year, you'll make lieutenant.'

Over the last months Polifka had represented something that had always been missing in Joe's life – true friendship and a genuine love for someone. They were the best of buddies, and Joe liked that. So, for the time being, Joe left things alone knowing that in another year he would be up for discharge and then he could make a decision. It was a decision, Joe realized, that Polifka probably wouldn't like.

****

At the end of 1952 Joe was scheduled to be discharged, so he went to see Polifka and told him he wanted to have a serious talk. 'I hate to hurt you, I hate to go against you, but there is something in me that I cannot change.'

Joe told his friend about his love of music and that his deepest desire was to study it and play at a professional level. He told Polifka about the letters he and Inez had written each other, and that she had told him that he could stay with her and enrol in one of the best music schools in America.

Polifka looked at Joe. 'What's going to happen to my plan? You have a future working here with me. You could make a career out of it.'

'I don't like this, having somebody above me.'

'What do you mean? You can become a major.'

'But, there's always somebody above you', Joe said. 'I want to be free, to write music the way I want to write it.'

Joe told Polifka that he needed to be discharged early so he could return to America before he was 21, which was in March. That way Joe would still be considered a child of his father meaning that Joe would automatically be considered a citizen of America.

As much a Polifka tried to talk him out of it, he agreed to discharge Joe earlier than scheduled.

***

February came and time was running out for Joe. He went to the American Embassy and began processing papers to travel. Because he wasn't a citizen of Palestine, the authorities told Joe to fill out some forms, go to a doctor and get an examination, and bring them back. An inconvenience, Joe thought, but no problem. So, Joe went to the military doctor, who gave him a physical and an X-ray.

The next week he went back to the doctor's office and the doctor told Joe that he wasn't going to allow him to travel. Joe was stunned when the doctor told him 'You have TB.'

'What's TB?' Joe asked.

What the doctor described to Joe that morning both scared and depressed him. America, music, and everything that Joe had longed for was suddenly a distant dream. 'Your lungs are infected. And you have a high fever, which you've probably had for several months, which makes you very contagious. You should be in a special hospital today.'

Joe still couldn't believe it. He didn't cough, and for sure he hadn't coughed up blood. But when doctors ran a saliva test it confirmed Joe's greatest fear. Then the news turned worse when they told him that he would be in the special hospital that treated this disease for at least two years. Antibiotics in 1953 were largely unknown in Israel and there was no cure for TB. All doctors could do was to attempt to slow it down, or in some cases perform surgeries and cut out parts of the lung. Lastly, they were honest with

Joe and told him that, in most cases, people with TB lived no more than to the age of forty, or maybe forty-two.

Much later, while undergoing treatment at the hospital, Joe found out how he had contacted the disease. He played the harmonica in the army and there were two other guys who played with Joe. Because each of their harmonicas with different, often they would switch and play each other's instruments. One of those soldiers had come to Palestine as a refugee from Romania. He had TB and Joe and the other soldier had contracted the disease from him.

The news broke Joe.

All that had happened to him over the last several weeks crushed his life dreams just when he was sure his life had finally turned around. 'My dream of music went down the drain. I was depressed', Joe admits. 'Emotionally and physically I should have had a breakdown. I should have committed suicide. I was fighting. I didn't want to give up. I still believed.'

At that time he had a girlfriend, Soshana, and over the last months they had many discussions about what they wanted in life. She was only seventeen and had to finish school. Joe had told Soshana his plans of going to America and studying music, and being honest with his feelings he told her that he wasn't taking her with him. They discussed that when she graduated from school maybe she could come to America and visit. It was what Joe remembered as a 'far dream'.

When Joe told Soshana that he was ill she was shocked. Joe's fears came to be. She came to visit him twice in the hospital, wrote Joe several letters, and then drifted out of Joe's life. In a way he didn't blame her at all, as he was contagious and that frightened her and she heard people talk when they told Joe 'You're going to be here a few weeks and then you're going to die.' She wasn't naïve like Joe and knew that TB was common all over Europe, and it was a sickness for which there was no cure.

When Soshana left, Joe was all alone just as when he was that small boy on the journey when Nelly died, and that was the very thing he dreaded.

Arriving at the hospital, there wasn't a patient room available for Joe so they placed him in a room next to the showers and bathrooms. Joe stayed in the room for a few days, then the nurses placed him in a room of eight to twelve people, a narrow room with rows of beds close to each other. Over the next month, two nurses contracted TB along with several of the girls who cleaned the room. Joe finally realized, and admitted, just how ill he was.

Depression fell heavily on him. His dream of music was gone, returning to America was impossible, and if what the doctors were telling him was true he didn't have that much time to live. It seemed crushing that he had survived all that he had endured as a Tehran child, only to die in a TB ward in Israel.

Lying in the bed at night, Joe's mind began to take him back to the camps where as a child he and others had been forced to survive in row upon row of beds in the Siberian cold or the desert heat. On those nights long ago, he would lay there and listen to the cries of other children, from hunger or weeping for a mother or father they had seen murdered by the Nazis. Instead of depressing him even more, those thoughts strengthened his will to survive. When thoughts of committing suicide came to him, Joe pushed them away. He had survived the war, against all odds, now he was going to fight this disease.

It was harder than he imagined.

Every time Joe tried to pick himself up, the disease seemed to push back harder. His life since Cologne and during his plagued journey had been a series of physical tests and illnesses trying his strength and resolution. Now he was painfully aware that this disease threatened him more than any other test he had survived thus far.

One day the doctor walked through the double door and sat on the edge of Joe's bed. He told Joe everything he knew after thoroughly checking him out. The news wasn't good. Joe's lung problems were on the left upper side. If the disease were on the right side with three lobes, then they would have performed surgery to remove the diseased area. But the left side had only two lobes, each depending on the other to work, so surgery wasn't possible. The doctor went on to describe a technique designed in the late 1920s where the lung is deflated by pushing air into it with a large needle. Then penicillin and other drugs were injected into the lungs. The theory behind this procedure was to assist the lung in resting and, with the administering of antibiotics, promoted the healing of the diseased area.

Although initial results didn't show much improvement, Joe remained unwavering when every two weeks he underwent X-rays so the doctors could monitor how the treatments were working. Joe was told that there was some progress, but that it was moving slowly. To lift his spirits Joe was placed in charge of entertainment. He enjoyed that. Once, when his aunt came to visit, she asked if he needed anything. Joe told her to ask his cousin, Alex, if he would bring him a radio that would give him news and more importantly music. With his new radio and being in charge of entertainment, Joe didn't have as much time to lie around. Now he had something to occupy his mind.

The other patients loved gathering around the radio listening to music. They loved it when Joe made *Purim* a special holiday, because he made every holiday a big event, lifting the spirits of the ward. But the radiation treatments gradually took their toll on Joe's immune system weakening him more and more, until soon he became tired of being in charge of entertainment.

One day a phone call from a good friend gave Joe a lift – and almost killed him.

Tommy, who owned a Harley-Davidson motorcycle, asked Joe if he wanted to get out of the hospital for a while and go for a ride. Joe quickly took him up on it, and slipped out of the hospital ward unnoticed. They rode around the countryside for hours. Joe held on tightly riding behind his friend. The sun and wind felt pleasing on his face, and at least for a while being ill seemed only a bad dream as they travelled mile after mile. Suddenly Joe became severely ill. Joe returned to the hospital with a high fever and his lungs full of water. After pulling two litres of water from his left lung with a needle, the doctor angrily asked Joe why he did something so stupid. Then he firmly told Joe that he was to be restricted to bed until he was better.

The doctor's insistence probably saved Joe's life.

Joe turned back to his radio to pass the days, until one morning, the doctor, with a nurse accompanying him, approached Joe's bed. He informed Joe that there was a new drug that would be tested on TB patients named Nicotibine, and that they needed four patients to be guinea pigs, take the drug and see what would happen. Would Joe consent to be a part of the experiment?

It wasn't a hard decision for Joe, 'because for two years now he was healing, but he wasn't healing.' The doctors and treatments had only stopped the disease from progressing, but it hadn't weakened it. Joe agreed to be a guinea pig.

The treatments helped Joe regain his strength and he even felt like going on short walks.

Six weeks later, a series of tests showed that the Nicotibine was doing what Joe had hoped for. He was no longer contagious and the fever was gone. He thought he was ready to leave the hospital immediately, but the doctor, after saying the treatments had cured Joe, insisted that Joe stay for another two months so they could watch and evaluate him.

It was a long two months.

But after that time in 1955, Joe was finally released from the hospital after twenty-two lengthy, worry-filled months. He found out that he was classified as a disabled veteran, meaning he would draw a pension for life, although they knew he would never have TB again.

That afternoon Joe walked out of the hospital which many times he had thought he would never be able to leave. 'I went into the city to check out where I'm going to live', Joe tells. 'I had no parents. I had no family; I mean I had family – cousins, uncles, and aunts – but they didn't want to take care of me because they didn't understand yet that I was cured by the new medication.'

Clouds rolled over the city and it looked like a rainstorm was approaching. Joe didn't care if it rained or stormed. Wonderfully, a whole new life was beginning for Joe, as it had so many times before in his life.

It was 1955 and Joe was 23 years old.

***

The world Joe walked out into that day had drastically changed during the last two years. It was as if Joe had walked onto another planet. Looking at all the different buildings, houses and new-style automobiles, Joe felt as though he had been in jail. The country had transformed into a place Joe hardly recognized.

After the flush of excitement of being free at last wore off, Joe analyzed his situation. He visited his family to let them know he was out of the hospital, living in the outskirts of Tel Aviv, and had accepted a job at the Ministry of Defence, the group for disabled veterans who supplied Joe with work and housing. He was to live in *B'nei Brak* a collection of ten buildings of shabby structures each two or three storeys high which would cost him ten *lirot* a month. Assigned half an apartment, it meant Joe would have a roommate, with one bath, one kitchen and one entrance. Joe took the bus over the next morning, and unloaded a few personal items and some clothes, which wasn't much.

The job was with a company that David Ben-Gurion had created, within the Ministry of Finance, and Joe's responsibility was mainly pushing papers from one department to another. There were offices filled with row after row of engineers sitting at cheap metal desks assisting businesses who wanted equipment such as printing machines and presses. It turned out to be boring work. But gradually Joe came to appreciate the pay, and his dream of music re-awakened in him. It was in this office that Joe would eventually meet a girl named Rina.

After a week of living alone, his roommate showed up. Joe thought the guy was a nut because he never showered and never cleaned up the kitchen or any place in the apartment. Joe was very unhappy, but was determined to stay there because it costs so little to live there. However, the final straw was one night at about 2am when his roommate opened a window out onto the street and started screaming as loud as he could.

The next morning Joe went to talk to a lady at the Ministry of Defence and told her that he had to move out. She said there was no place for him to move to just then, but if he could secure a loan maybe he could get an apartment. He got a loan, and moved into an apartment in Tel Aviv at the corner of Ben-Yehuda Street. It was an old building with some advantages and some disadvantages. There was water, so Joe had a shower and a small kitchen with a refrigerator. But to get to his apartment he had to go through the fire escape, because the apartment wasn't on the top floor but located on the roof, a converted laundry room. To go to the toilet Joe had to go out on the roof, by the fire escape, and exit on to the balcony.

Still, Joe was excited and when one of the tenants decided to sell a piano because they didn't have room for it, Joe bought it.

Not knowing how to play the piano wasn't a problem for Joe at all. He started taking lessons and because he had a piano soon had made many friends. 'Somebody knew how to play very good and they used to come over', he remembers. 'Every Friday or Saturday night I had a dozen people in my house.' The problem was that because Joe's apartment was located on the roof one could easily hear the piano from outside. 'We would have big parties and people would scream at us to quieten down. They wanted to sleep.'

Joe was lonely despite all his friends coming over, and because there had been setbacks. His music career was going nowhere. To get to work Joe had to take several buses, connecting one to the other. He soon became tired of that so he tried walking, which took about 45 minutes. Joe decided that wasn't for him so he bought a motorcycle. Gas was cheap and he arrived at work in just five minutes.

Besides solving his transportation problem, the motorcycle gave him more freedom to move about in the evening. He could go out to visit his friends and didn't have to rely on them coming to his apartment all the time. At last life was good – he had the apartment with the piano, a job, sang in the choir and a motorcycle that gave him freedom.

By now it was 1956, and Joe took a vacation, and when he came back a girl, a very good-looking one, had come to work in his office. Of course the other guys thought she was good-looking too, and they learned her name was Rina Makover. When Joe tried to talk to her she wasn't friendly at all. So Joe started communicating to her with notes passed between them. Several weeks later, Joe and Rina went out to lunch together. Joe told her he had decided to date her. Rina had different ideas, refusing to give Joe her address when he asked for it.

Joe had an answer to this problem. One day as Rina was talking to a friend in the office where her father worked Joe made a note of it. The following week he went to her father's workplace and asked for him. The man told him his father had gone home, and that's when Joe asked for their address.

'So, I came and knocked at the door', Joe says, 'at about 10:30 at night. It was July or August, very hot, very humid. I found there *Savta* (Rina) cleaning the floor dressed in shorts.' It struck him odd that she would have shorts on, even at home, because her family was religious. Rina was impressed with Joe's efforts to find out where she lived.

They went to a show that afternoon. As Joe took Rina home he told her that on *Rosh Ha' Shaneah* he would come and see her. She told him that she would be in Tel Aviv 'with my aunt and don't try to come because the first night I'm going out with my boyfriend'.

Joe knew that this guy was a fighter pilot and that presented a problem for him. 'I'll come the second night.' When he showed up, he made a big impression because he brought a large, beautiful bouquet of flowers. They went for a walk that night, and Joe knew exactly what he was going to do when the time was right. He was 25 and she was 20.

'I think we should get married', he said suddenly.

'No', she said, 'I like you a lot – like a brother.'

Joe told her if that was the way she felt about it all, then he was going to go out with other girls. He wanted to find a wife. Rina let Joe know that she understood and to go ahead and date. She thought it was a good idea.

Disappointed, Joe dated other girls and Rina dated other guys. But the more they dated others, the more they saw of each other. Things changed, a little, but not enough for an impatient Joe.

Joe joined a choir that worked with the philharmonic of Tel Aviv, met people and met a girl named Gila Dobkin. Later in life, Joe would learn that Gila became a music teacher and that she never married. Through Gila Joe found that he didn't have the one thing that successful musicians need – a melodic quality called 'absolute hearing'. Gila had it though, making Joe jealous of her in a way because when she heard a song she could write out the exact notes. Gila tried to explain to Joe that when Beethoven wrote music he knew the notes right away. Joe fully understood what that meant, and his dream of playing music professionally ended.

1958. For Joe, there was nothing left to do but return to America and go to work, start a career and enjoy being with Inez, who by now was married and had a daughter. He wrote to her and she wrote back saying that she wanted him to come. That was all Joe needed to hear. He went to the American consulate and they gave him clearance to travel to America because he had been treated for TB.

He and Rina still had a good relationship, and when she came over to his apartment he was filling out his travel papers. That was when he told her that he was going to America.

'You go, and when you're done, come back. I'll be here.'

'I'm not going to go if we're serious', Joe confronted her. 'If I go…I'm not coming back.'

He knew that this was another big decision in life, because if he went to America without Rina he knew they would live the remainder of their lives without each other. The next weekend he and Rina went to Tiberius with two other couples. On this trip their relationship deepened. Back in Tel Aviv, Joe continued to play music, sing, and slip Rina into the concerts as if she was a singer. They spent more and more time together.

Joe felt their relationship changing.

In April 1959 Rina became ill and Joe went to her house to visit her. During their time together she suddenly turned to him and said 'Okay, we'll get married.'

Joe was taken aback. 'I felt it was coming, but I didn't expect to hear it from her mouth.' He told Rina 'Okay, we start working tomorrow morning to organize it.'

The next day Joe met his best friend, Stanley, at a coffee shop and told him the news. At first his friend questioned whether Rina was serious as after all yesterday was April Fool's Day.

'Yes, I'm going to marry her', Joe told him, 'I'm not going to America. I'm going to get married.' When Joe walked out of the coffee shop he was aware of the decisions that had to be made. Decisions about their jobs and finding a place to live. There was so much to do and Joe's life was turning again. This time for the better. Joe cancelled his plans to go to America, left his work and he and Rina began searching for an apartment, which they didn't find until September.

Joe and Rina were married on 13 September 1959.

30

Stones of Memory:
23 Alexander Strasse. Cologne

*I am proud of him for surviving. He is proud of himself. He is proud that
he made it, and of the family he was able to create because of it. I am
proud of those same things.*

    *And, I am ashamed that I can share in this pride without having to
do anything myself to earn it, without having to sacrifice for it.*

Simon Rosenbaum, My Saba.

Life, despite all he had suffered, had turned out well for Joe Rosenbaum.[247]

    Joe and Rina married and remained in Israel. In the 1960s Rina had taken
a position with El-Al Israel Airlines so that she and Joe could travel without
much cost. Joe's father and sister were in America so they began to visit them,
and in 1969 Joe's sister Inez suggested that they live in America so that they
would all be closer. So Joe and Rina moved. Joe used his previous social
security number obtained while living in America in the 1940s and started
to work with his brother-in-law, and soon they became partners. After
several weeks it became evident that, although Joe and his brother-in-law
were good friends, they shouldn't be business partners. Joe got his money
out of the business venture, they bought a house and Joe went to work selling
electronic wiring for a businessman to whom Inez had introduced Joe.

    Being in sales wasn't new for Joe because he had been very successful at
it in Israel, and he loved this new business selling wiring to technology
businesses. But one of the problems Joe had to overcome was the vernacular
in America because it was so very different than everyday slang in Israel.
One day, as Joe arrived at a business office where he had an appointment,
the manager told Joe he was sorry, 'but could he take a rain check?' Joe
looked outside. It was a beautiful day, what did rain have to do with anything
about their appointment?

    Joe kept working on understanding Americans and soon his territory
had doubled in sales. The next business quarter Joe's sales numbers tripled.
Everything was going great, but then an unfortunate incident took place. The
guy in charge of sales confronted Joe about being late. He said something

about Joe's wife and that set him off. 'He opened his mouth in a very dirty way…so I opened my mouth too.' Joe was fired on the spot.

But with such a great reputation, Joe soon had a job with the competition. After a disagreement concerning commissions, Joe had enough of that situation. With all his knowledge and connections with his customer base in the wiring industry, Joe decided to start his own company. Calling up old customers, soon his new business was flourishing and by the early 1970s Joe thought it was time to expand the company and buy equipment so that they could manufacture their own electronic wiring. Joe changed from salesman to business owner, expanding and buying equipment, while taking out loans against his home.

1979. The dream took a hit, not only for Joe but for the entire nation, especially small business owners, as the prime rate rose to 18 per cent. The second largest bank in California, Crocker Bank, went under. Creditors wanted their money in 90 days from those businesses the bank had loaned money to, and Joe was one of those businesses confronted. Despite the financial setbacks Joe held on for three years, selling off parts and watching the business he had worked so hard to develop slowly go under. Privately, Joe was devastated. The pain drove him to try even harder to save his company.

Eventually, the strain caught up with him.

At 55 Joe suffered a severe heart attack. Just when the doctors were going to perform major heart surgery, he was told that a new treatment, angioplasty, had been developed to unblock damaged arteries. It could save his life. It was another fortunate turn of events for Joe.

He stopped working, sold some properties, and spent his time watching his two sons, Ori and Amir, grow up.

In 1995 Joe and Rina went to Israel for six weeks. They found they liked being back there. With the boys now fully grown, Joe and Rina decided to downsize in America and buy a condo in Israel. Life had taken another turn for Joe, as they lived six months in America and six months in Israel. Then there were grandchildren. And eventually it was in America, and not Israel, where family drew Joe and Rina back.

Life had turned into another season for one of the Tehran Children.

***

October 2007. Joe had vowed that he would never return to Germany, ever. In his mind there wasn't any reason to do so. Germany had simply been a horrible nightmare for that small boy, and to return there would have been to relive that nightmare. What purpose would it serve after all? Would seeing

Cologne again after all these years help him understand why his childhood was taken away so brutally, or why Nelly and his mother had to die?

However, events were unfolding in Germany that would eventually draw Joe back to his homeland.[248] In the 1980s the people of Germany had started constructing markers in front of the homes of the Jews who were swept up in the Holocaust. It was a gesture that hardly, in the hearts and minds of many survivors, could possibly make up for what for what the European Jews had suffered. But that act of kindness and recognition by present-day Germans of the atrocities committed by the previous generation, created an opportunity for forgiveness in many Jewish hearts.

The monuments were created by artist Gunter Demning to remember the Holocaust victims and were named *stolperstein* in German, meaning 'stumbling stone', because before the war when non-Jews stumbled over a protruding stone they would say 'There must be a Jew buried here.' 16 December 1942 had been a shameful day in German history. It was on that day that Heinrich Himmler issued the *Auschwitz-Erlass*, the Auschwitz Decree, deporting refugees to the extermination camp. It was fitting that it was the fiftieth anniversary of that infamous act when Demning began his memorial campaign. The first *stolperstein* was laid at Cologne's historical city hall; the movement caught on and by January 2015 there were over 50,000 *stolpersteins* in place in over eighteen countries in Europe.

15. Nelly and Mina's 'Stone of Memory' in Cologne, 23 Alexander Strasse, 2007. Courtesy of Rina Rosenbaum.

In the spring of 2007 Joe was invited to Cologne to participate in a memorial service dedicating the Stones of Memory for his sister, Nelly. Joe resisted. His wife and sons urged and encouraged him to go. For many years Joe had refused to consider any such thing. Nightmares and waves of guilt remained deep inside, regrets questioning why he lived when others died haunted him late at night when everyone else was asleep; forcing him to take a special sleeping pill that he could only receive from Israel.

But events continued to unfold in Germany that forced Joe to reconsider.

He was contacted by Stephan Vogel, a filmmaker who was to make a movie called *The Children's Odyssey*, based on the experiences of many Tehran Children. Vogel asked Joe if he would travel to Germany to tell his story. Ruti Marshansky, a friend living in Jerusalem, had given Vogel Joe's name when the filmmaker had inquired about needing Tehran Children to interview to get their personal story. As Joe and Vogel talked, there was one last subject they discussed that night and that was a *stolperstein* for Nelly. It seemed, Vogel explained, that a young German couple, who had sadly lost a child at birth, had bought the Stone of Memory for Joe's sister.

This act of kindness struck deep into Joe's heart. That someone really cared, that thousands of deaths of innocent people like Nelly still mattered, this impressed Joe and convinced him that maybe it was time to return home. As he prepared to travel one thought remained still and hard inside: no matter how much modern Germany and its people had changed, to Joe he was still returning to the Germany of the 1930s.

Joe, accompanied by his family, travelled to Germany and there he met with Vogel. Over lunch they discussed how the movie was going to be structured and Joe learned that he would be one of four Tehran Children telling their stories. Joe began to appreciate the project envisioned by this man sitting across the table from him. Later in the conversation Joe realized what was happening – that for them to tell their story, to expose the horror and suffering, that maybe the world could learn something about itself.

Joe agreed to everything Vogel presented that day, and several days later the filming of the movie began.

Within a week, they filmed the first scenes of the movie on the streets of Cologne. There was Joe along with the other 'children', the film crews and Joe's family as they discussed how the story should develop over the next several scenes. The first days of filming had been awkward and stiff as those horrible recollections came back to each Tehran Child as their memories were filmed. But gradually they grew to know each other and finally, one day, there was laughter. Over the next few days trust and understanding would develop among them, as they realized the power of what they were doing.

Towards the end of the week, as the day's filming ended, Joe wandered across the street, as the film crew loaded the equipment into vans. He no longer searched for childhood memories in the surrounding Cologne buildings. In fact, very few things came back to him at all.

At first Joe thought maybe it was because he had been so young, after all he was only eight years old when he, his mother and Nelly were suddenly forced from their apartment. Then someone suggested that Joe didn't recognize the city because it had been destroyed during the war by the heavy Allied bombings.

Yes, that was it, Joe thought. The Allied bombers had done their job, and now he couldn't remember. He pondered all of this as he crossed the street and walked for several blocks finally finding himself alone. He stopped at the corner.

Joe finally admitted to himself that he had been wrong. It was good that he had come back to Germany, he decided. So many thoughts had resurfaced since he arrived, memories that had been washed away through the years of the busy daily routines of running a business, selling his products and raising a good family. During all that time, Rina had been his biggest supporter.

Standing there, alone on the street corner, a question entered his mind.

When did life really begin again for him after being one of the Tehran Children? Was it when he returned to Israel? Or when he returned to America, later in life and reunited with his father and Inez? Those had all been choices. But when did fate, or blessing, or fortune, make something else out of his life? There were so many times and places to remember on his long journey.

He kept walking aware there was little sunlight remaining, but he had somewhere to go. Joe walked several blocks until he stopped at a wide boulevard, lined with modern, gray-stone buildings. Cars and an occasional bus flowed down the street. It all looked so different now to Joe, this place locked in his mind, this street where his father brought him, at barely six years old, to see Adolf Hitler.

Echoing in his mind were the thunderous yells of joy and admiration, the shrill 'Seig Heil' chants he remembered as a young boy leaning forwards on his father's shoulder, attempting not to miss anything. Joe closed his eyes. He could still see the masses lining the boulevard, arms angled out in perfect salute, the dazzling flutter of a thousand blood-red and black swastika flags in the clear afternoon breeze.

As that young boy, how was he to know of the evil present that day? The destruction and sadness that this man – Hitler – would bring on his family, killing his mother and sister, their only crimes that of being Jews? As that wild-eyed, fascinated child, how was he to know?

Deciding it was time to rejoin the others, Joe reversed his steps and headed back to the apartment. Rina would be waiting. But he still hadn't answered the question that had haunted him since arriving in Cologne, revisiting the old home. When had his life begun again?

Joe paused and suddenly he knew. On that late afternoon, Joe knew when life truly began again for him. It was here in Cologne.

It was in Germany, where the new generation, like the tender young couple Christoph and Verna Weise, who had bought Nelly's *stolperstein*, was trying hard to overcome all the darkness that had covered their nation all those years ago. He couldn't forgive the old generation, at least not now, maybe that would come later. But it was there after he had walked through unforgiveness to absolve the new generation, to forgive, where life had truly begun again for Joe.

31

The Key

As Joe walked back towards the apartment, the dying sunlight slipped behind the gray silhouettes of the Cologne buildings. In another moment Joe stood at the corner, the apartment – 23 Alexander Strasse – directly across the street. Just further down, the film crew finished loading their camera equipment, got in the vans and waved at his family standing on the pavement.

For the longest time there were no thoughts. Then, Joe stared at the apartment door, realizing that it was about this time of the evening in October 1938 when the policeman arrived, threatening his mother. She had moved quickly about the apartment gathering their things. How did she know how many items to pack? How long were they going to be gone, Mother must have asked herself. She pulled money out of the cabinet shelf, wrapped it in a scarf and placed it in her purse. It must have been so hard on her, Joe thought.[249]

She took the apartment key from the kitchen shelf and placed it in her dress pocket, a hopeful gesture from a loving mother that there had to be still a future for her children. Disappearing briefly, she came out of the side room retrieving one last, almost-forgotten item. She stood very still in the middle of the living room as shadows danced across her worried face, then turned to her son and told him to take Nelly, and that she would carry the suitcase. 'Where are we going, Mama?' She managed a smile at the question from such a small boy. 'The train station, just as the policeman told us to, Yossi. But don't worry, everything will be okay.'

The clock on the mantel chimed the late hour.

That memory rushed back at Joe like a brilliant, hot light. He would never forget that haunting moment as the three of them stood in the darkened hallway, Nelly in Josef's arms, the suitcase resting at his mother's ankles…as she took the key from her pocket and locked the apartment door.

Epilogue

When all else is lost, the future still remains.
Christian Nestell Bovee

Joe and Rina Rosenbaum live in Reseda, California, surrounded by their loving family of two sons, daughter-in-law and grandchildren who have quickly grown up and are starting their own lives. Joe's life is full – joyous holiday gatherings, friends in America and Israel. And there are the memories. Time, he says, heals many wounds, but it is family that holds the greatest healing power. Still, Joe admits, those horrifying times he suffered through during those long years occasionally haunt him, and some remembrances dwell much deeper, more painfully, than others. 'I can never

16. Rosenbaum family portrait, today. Courtesy of Rina Rosenbaum.

forget Nelly...I will never forget Nelly as long as I live', Joe admits. 'It should never have happened – to me or anyone what happened to Nelly. Never.'[250]

The story of the Tehran Children is one of those remarkable tales of the human struggle to survive. It's also one of the tireless dedications of those Zionist leaders and Hadassah to see through the rescue of the Tehran Children. Sadly, like Joe, many of the children after their long journey continue to suffer through nightmares and depression, although many were able to overcome those obstacles, leading productive lives filled with jobs and children and loving wives and husbands. The foundation for the recovery of the children was the love of the Jewish authorities in Eretz Israel when the children arrived in 1943, and the loving care of family members already in Israel, and the tremendous outpouring of adoration to them by the country. Slowly, their faith in the human spirit flourished, and the memories of hatred, hunger and hardship, that stole precious years of their childhoods, would dissipate.

However, not all of the Tehran Children lived the long lives they deserved. Thirty-five of the children lost their lives during the war that erupted in the land they had longed for when Israel declared independence on 14 May 1948.

One of the children who sacrificed her life was nineteen-year-old Hadassah (Halinka) Lampel.[251]

Born in the Polish town of Nowy Sacz, in the foothills of the Beskid Mountains in 1929, her father was a government official. The family enjoyed a peaceful life. The other girls in town would remember Halinka as a girl who loved to read, especially fairy tales. The German invasion of Poland in September 1939, as it did for thousands, disrupted the idyllic life of the Lampel home. They fled to Lvov, occupied by the Russians, and on 29 June 1940 they were loaded onto freight trains, suffering bone-chilling cold and hunger on the trip, and ended up in a Siberian camp. In this camp the slave labour was forced to live on the barest of foods while cutting trees near the Czulim River, and floating them downriver to be processed in sawmills.

When Hitler invaded Russia, Halinka and her family were swept up in the mass movement southward into Asia. In Samarkand her father died, exhausted and ill, but not before securing his beloved daughter a place with the Tehran Children.

Soon she would follow the same path as Joe and over 800 other children to Palestine. She was fourteen. Four years later, in 1947, during the initial fighting for independence, Halinka joined the Palmach, the commando unit of the *Haganah*, and trained as a radio operator at Yagur and Maoz Haim. It was quickly noted by commanders that she would eagerly volunteer for any assignment, no matter the degree of danger.

On 30 May 1948 Halinka disobeyed orders and joined an armoured vehicle force, and rode in the first vehicle to enter Latrun, occupied by the Arabs, right into a scene of intense fighting. Israeli operations began receiving radio reports from Latrun, from a woman's calm voice, detailing Arab artillery positions. Halinka told the officers that the vehicle had come under heavy fire and the commander was mortally wounded. Then the radio went dead.

Her story was one that expressed the bravery of hundreds of young people who would commit their blood to the independence of Israel. Long ago when Halinka was nine and a quiet little girl who loved school, she wrote a poem that proved to be prophetic and read it to the class, 'Halinka was a Brave Girl'.

***

Henrietta Szold lived another two years after witnessing the Tehran Children arriving amongst so much love and celebration in their new home, Eretz Israel. When asked to look back on her two greatest achievements, she answered the founding of Hadassah, the Jewish women's organization that grew from a Bible study of a few women in New York to over 350,000 members, the largest Jewish organization in the United States. Her second great achievement, she would say, was that in the 1930s she created the *Youth Aliyah* within the Jewish Agency, for one purpose: to rescue Jewish children from the fire of the holocaust. It is estimated that over 22,000 children were saved, including the Tehran Children.

At age 84, on 13 February 1945, Henrietta Szold died in Jerusalem in the Hadassah-Hebrew hospital she helped establish. She was buried on the Mount of Olives in the Jewish Cemetery on a snowy day filled with gloomy skies. Fifteen-year-old Simon Kresz, one of the Tehran Children, stood beside her grave and recited the mourner's Kaddish.

A poignant entry in her diary, found after her death and hidden away in a desk drawer, details the hurt this woman had in her life, despite her great achievements: 'I would exchange everything for one child of my own.'

***

Shamefully, once the war was won in 1945, Poland, the fourth largest army fighting in the war that suffered over 48,000 casualties, was not allowed to march in the Grand Victory Parade, a massive event held in London on 8 June 1946. It was the final chapter in a disgraceful episode of betrayal towards a gallant ally. Polish soldiers were not even allowed to return to Poland.

Anders, after the war, was stripped of his Polish citizenship and military rank by the Communist government. He remained in England where he was prominent in his government-in-exile, and held the position of inspector general of military forces in exile near Chalfont St. Giles. In 1948 he married Iryna Yarosevych, a Polish stage actress and singer, and the following year wrote of his wartime experiences in an autobiography, *An Army in Exile.*

He died in London on 12 May 1970.

With respect to his last wishes, General Anders was buried in the Polish War Cemetery on the hillside of Monte Cassino, with his beloved soldiers.

***

David Ben-Gurion was the first Zionist leader to visit a concentration camp when he stepped inside the Bergen-Belsen camp gate in October 1945. It was a sombre, still and gray morning when, as he concluded his visit, he spoke at a cemetery outside the camp, staring across the dirt-crown of a mass grave where murdered Jews were buried. 'I will not try to express the feelings within me. Such a thing is impossible.'[252]

Two weeks later, on the morning of 19 October 1945, Ben-Gurion visited Zeilsheim, a detention camp outside Frankfurt where thousands of displaced persons were being fed and receiving medical assistance. Invited to speak, he was led to a stage in the auditorium by a detention camp rabbi. The crowd burst into jubilant singing of the Zionist hymn *Hatikvah* (The Hope) and there was much crying and weeping. As the stoic leader spoke, his voice cracked as he told them that he brought them 'the message of good tidings from Palestine, who anxiously awaited their coming'. The crowd broke into cheers.[253]

It was then that Ben-Gurion knew what he had suspected. Hitler and his Nazis had, instead of extinguishing the fire of Zionism, stirred the embers smouldering in the hearts of these weary people. Hitler was dead along with his thousand-year Reich, Ben-Gurion thought, and still Zionism lived in the hearts of European Jews who had survived the Shoah.

During the 1948 Israel War for Independence, Ben-Gurion became the nation's first prime minister. In that position he witnessed vast numbers of Jews from all over the world immersed into the newly-formed country. He also worked with German leaders in forming the Reparations Agreement providing compensation to Israel for the Nazi's persecution of the Jews. He served as Minister of Defence in 1954, forging hard-line defences against Arab attacks.

Ben-Gurion, lover of political battles, resigned several times, first in 1963 and then in 1970, before finally retiring to his modest home on a kibbutz in the Negev desert. There he spent much of his time working on an eleven-volume record of Israel's early history.

He wrote of the desert and the yearning of his people to return to the land:

> When I looked out my window today and saw a tree standing before me, the sight awoke in me a greater sense of beauty and personal satisfaction than all the forests that I have crossed in Switzerland and Scandinavia. For we planted each tree in this place and watered them with the water we provided at the cost of numerous efforts…Why does a mother love her children so? Because they are her creation. Why does the Jew feel an affinity with Israel? Because everything here must still be accomplished. It depends only on him to participate in this privileged act of creation. Why does the Jew feel an affinity with Israel? Because everything here must still be accomplished. [254]

After suffering a cerebral hemorrhage on 18 November 1973, Ben-Gurion was taken to Sheba Medical Center in Tel Ha Shomer, Rama Gan. The visionary of the resettlement of the land of Israel died on 1 December, the same day as his grandson Alon, a paratrooper, was hospitalized in the same hospital with battle wounds.

Ben-Gurion was buried at Sde Boker, a kibbutz in southern Israel beside his wife, Paula. His grave looks out over the Negev desert and the Zin wilderness, a rolling landscape of etched, strange sandstone and shale formations. It is the same ground over which Ben-Gurion's ancestors walked out of Egypt, leaving behind slavery and bondage over 3,000 years ago. And it is the same desert through which Joe Rosenbaum and the Tehran Children travelled during their final day of a long journey out from the brutal fog of Hitler's Europe – on a train to Palestine – to freedom.

Notes

1. I. Fineman, *Woman of Valor: The Life of Henrietta Szold, 1960-1945* (New York: Simon & Schuster, 1961), p. 420.

Chapter 1

2   I. Kershaw, 'The Writing Life', Washington Post interview, 19 October 2008.
3   Joe Rosenbaum, telephone interview, 25 August 2015; telephone interview, 1 February 2015; *The Children's Odyssey*, film.
4   Joe Rosenbaum, telephone interview, 14 October 2014; Simon Rosenbaum, *My Saba*.
5   *Ibid.*
6   Joe Rosenbaum, telephone interview, 31 May 2016.
7   *Ibid.*
8   *Ibid.*
9   J. Toland, *Adolf Hitler* (New York: Doubleday & Co., 1976), pp. 425-426. Gauverlag Bayerische Ostmark, 1935.
10 *Ibid.*, p. 426.
11 Joe Rosenbaum, telephone interview, 14 October 2014.
12 M. Gilbert, *The Holocaust*, p. 66; Letter of 25 October 1938, from Sir George Ogilvie-Forbes to Oliver Harvey, Foreign Office papers 371/22536.
13 Joe Rosenbaum, telephone interview, 6 April 2015.
14 M. Gilbert, *The Holocaust: A History of the Jews in Europe During World War Two.* (New York: Holt, Rinehart, and Winston, 1985), pp. 67-68. Testimony of Zindel Grynszpan; Eichmann Trial, 26 April 1961, session 14.
15 *Ibid.*, p. 67.
16 *Ibid.*, p. 68.
17 Joe Rosenbaum, telephone interview, 6 April 2015.
18 M. Gilbert, *The Holocaust*, p. 68. Recollections of Rosalind Herzfeld: *Jewish Chronicle*, 28 September 1979, p. 80
19 Joe Rosenbaum, telephone interview, 30 April 2016.
20 D. Bader Whiteman, *Escape Via Siberia: A Jewish Child's Odyssey of Survival* (New York: Holmes & Meier, 1999), p. 48. I. and J. Gross, *War Through Children's Eyes* (Stanford, CA: Hoover Institution Press, 1981), p. 22
21 T. Snyder, *The Bloodlands: Europe Between Hitler and Stalin.* (New York: Basic Books, 2012).

Chapter 2

22 *Los Angeles Times*, 1 September 1939.

23   'Blitzkreig', *Time-Life Books*, p. 32

24   W. L. Shirer, *The Rise and Fall of the Third Reich: A History of Nazi Germany*, (New York: Simon & Schuster, 1960.), p. 597.

25   *The Star*, London. Friday 1 September 1939 edition.

26   M. Gilbert, *Churchill: A Life* (New York: Henry Holt & Co., 1991), p. 619.

27   N. Miller, *FDR: An Intimate Life* (Garden City, New York: Doubleday & Company, 1983), p. 438.

28   FDR Library. 'FDR's Bedside Note', 1 September 1939.

29   Joe Rosenbaum, telephone interview, 14 October 2014; S. Rosenbaum, *My Saba*.

30   Joe Rosenbaum, telephone interview, 8 February 2016.

31   Joe Rosenbaum, telephone interviews, 6, 20 April 2015.

32   Joe Rosenbaum, telephone interview, 14 October 2014.

33   *Ibid.*

34   D. Omer, *The Tehran Operation: The Rescue of Jewish Children from the Nazis* (Washington D.C.: B'Nai B'rith Book, 1991), p. 36.

35   Joe Rosenbaum, telephone interviews, 6,20 April 2015.

36   W. Anders, *An Army in Exile* (Nashville, TN: The Battery Press, 1949), p. 4-6

37   *Ibid.*

38   S. Rosenbaum, *My Saba*.

39   *Ibid.*

40   D. Whiteman, *Escape Via Siberia*, p. 7

41   Joe Rosenbaum interview, *The Children's Odyssey*.

42   Joe Rosenbaum interview, 20 April 2015.

43   Description of atrocities: H. Grynberg, *Children of Zion* (Evanston, IL.: Northwestern University Press, 1994), Chapter 'Germans, Germans, Everywhere', pp. 17-50.

44   W. Shirer, *The Rise and Fall of the Third Reich*, p. 625

45   W. Szpilman, *The Pianist*, pp. 22, 23

46   Klara Glowczewska, *Town & Country Magazine*, October 2014, p. 71.

Chapter 3

47   For notes concerning Anders' activity refer to sources: 'The Conflict Begins', *An Army in Exile*, Chapter 1, pp. 1-12.

48   W. Shirer, *The Rise and Fall of the Third Reich*, p. 903; D. Irving, *Hitler's War* (New York: Viking Press, 1977), vol.1, p. 264.

49   Source for Anders' background information: J. L. Marino, 'Polish Power in Italy', *WWII History*, October 2014.

50   Anders, 'The Conflict Begins', *An Army in Exile*, pp. 1-12.

51   *Ibid.*

52   *Ibid.*

Chapter 4

53   Trip to Nemirov: information taken from telephone interviews with Joe Rosenbaum, conducted 20 April 2015; 1 February 2016; 31 May 2016; S. Rosenbaum, *My Saba*.

54   Nemirov background: 'Massacre in the Polish Uprising', *Jewish Encyclopedia*, 1906.

55   W. Anders, *An Army in Exile*, p. 7.

56   W. Szpilman, *The Pianist*, pp. 38-39.
57   I. and J. Gross, *War Through Children's Eyes* (Stanford: Hoover Institute Press, 1981), p. 205
58   *Ibid.*, p. 109.
59   J. Gross, *Revolution from Abroad: The Soviet Conquest of Poland's Western Ukraine and Western Belorussia.* (Princeton: Princeton University Press, 1988).
60   I. and J. Gross, *War Through Children's Eyes*, p. 99.
61   Z. Zajdlerowa, *The Dark Side of the Moon* (New York: Charles Scribner, 1947).

Chapter 5

62   P. Johnson, *A History of the Jews* (New York: Harper & Row, 1987), p. 490.
63   *Ibid.*
64   C. Lanzmann, *Shoah* (New York: Pantheon Books, 1985), pp. 107-8.
65   P. Johnson, *A History of the Jews*, p. 498; L. Krugman Gurdus, *The Death Train* (New York: 1979); M. Gilbert, *Final Journey* (London: 1979) p. 70.
66   Z. Zajdlerowa, *The Dark Side of the Moon.*
67   *Ibid.*
68   Joe Rosenbaum, telephone interview, 20 April 2015.
69   Anonymous source.
70   N. and J. Smenda (eds), *Unforgettable Memories: Memoirs of Polish Exiles in the Soviet Union, 1940-1942* (Perth, Western Australia, 1985). pp. 10-13.
71   Joe Rosenbaum, telephone interview, 20 April 2015; S. Rosenbaum, *My Saba*.
72   S. Kessel, *Hanged at Auschwitz* (New York: Stein & Day, 1972), pp. 50-51.
73   *San Francisco Chronicle*, 19 May 1940.

Chapter 6

74   Commissar S. Kozhevnikov, 'The Historic Advance,' *Red Star*, 17 September 1940.
75   The source of Anders' experiences taken from W. Anders, 'In the Lubianka', *An Army in Exile*, pp. 25-37.
76   *Ibid.*
77   *Ibid.*
78   *Ibid.*
79   *Ibid.*
80   *Ibid.*
81   *Ibid.*
82   A. Applebaum, *Gulag: A History of the Soviet Camps* (London: Allen Lane, 2003).
83   W. Anders, 'Kolyma Means Death', *An Army in Exile*, pp. 74-5.
84   *Ibid.*, p. 72.
85   W. Anders, *An Army in Exile*, p. 26.

Chapter 7

86   Joe Rosenbaum, telephone interviews, 20 April 2015; S. Rosenbaum, *My Saba*.
87   I., R. Gross, *War Through Children's Eyes*, p. 159
88   H. Kochanski, *The Eagle Unbowed: Poland and the Poles in the Second World War* (UK: Penguin, 2013), p. 140.

89   Joe Rosenbaum, telephone interview, 20 April 2015.

90   *Ibid.*

91   *Ibid.*

92   N. Davies, *Trail of Hope: The Anders Army, An Odyssey Across Three Continents. (Oxford, UK: Osprey Publishing, 2001)*, p. 37.

93   D. Omer, *The Teheran Operation*, p. 69.

94   J. Gliksman, *Tell the West*, p. 266.

95   D. Omer, *The Teheran Operation*, Laor quote, p. 65.

96   D. Bader Whiteman, *Escape Via Siberia*, Lonek quote, pp. 51-2.

97   I., J. Gross, *War Through Children's Eyes*, pg. XV.

98   Joe Rosenbaum, telephone interview, 4 May 2015.

99   *Ibid.*

100 *Ibid.*

Chapter 8

101 This chapter is based on telephone interview with Joe Rosenbaum on 4 May 2015 and 1 February 2016. By now Joe is a nine-year-old boy trapped in Siberia, he is ill and hungry as he witnesses the death around him, including family members. In discussions, Joe believes that he feared getting lost, and was never certain, looking back, how lost he ever became in the forest and alone. Making use of this research, I've attempted to close the gaps on the dramatic part of Joe's story, drawing on '*a priori imagination*', basing the scene on theoretical deduction rather than empirical observation. It is a method utilized effectively by Dan Porat in his book *The Boy: A Holocaust Story.*

Chapter 9

102 Simon in New York and Inez in Belgium: Joe Rosenbaum, telephone interview, 1 February 2016.

103 Situation in Belgium: B. Wasserstein, *On the Eve: The Jews of Europe Before the Second World War.* (New York: Simon & Schuster, 2012), pp. 60, 400.

104 First attacks: *Time Magazine*, 29 July 1940.

105 *The Palestine Post*, 9 September 1940.

106 *Ibid.*, 10 September 1940.

107 *Palestine Review*, 10 September 1940.

Chapter 10

108 K. Koskodan, *No Greater Ally*, p. 109.

109 W. L. Shirer, *The Rise and Fall of the Third Reich*, p. 810.

110 *San Luis Obispo Telegram-Tribune*, 22 June 1941.

111 D. K. Goodwin, *No Ordinary Time, Franklin Roosevelt and Eleanor Roosevelt: The Home Front in World War Two* (New York: Touchstone Book, Simon & Schuster, Inc., 1995), p. 253; J. Goebbels, *The Goebbels Diaries, 1939-1941* (1983) p. 424.

112 Joe Rosenbaum, telephone interview, 4 May 2015.

113 W. Anders, *An Army in Exile*, p. 41.

114   *Ibid.* p. 44.
115   *Polish Daily*, 31 July 1941.
116   W. Anders, *An Army in Exile*, p. 83.
117   *Ibid.* p. 63.
118   *Ibid.* pp. 63, 92.
119   Rymasjewski.iinet.net: 'General Anders' Army Leaves the USSR'.
120   W. Anders, 'Those We Left Behind', *An Army in Exile*; H. Kochanski, 'Escape from the Soviet Union', *The Eagle Unbowed*.
121   Joe Rosenbaum, telephone interviews, 14 October 2014; 4 May 2015; 6 May 2015.

Chapter 11

122   Joe Rosenbaum, telephone interview, 4 May 2015.
123   D. Whiteman, *Escape via Siberia*, p. 87.
124   Anders' personal decision to evacuate Jewish deportees along with his army is documented in *An Army in Exile*, pp. 77-79, 101-102, 112-113*; N. Davies, *Trail of Hope* p. 86-87; D. Whiteman, *Escape via Siberia*, p. 89-90.
125   W. Anders, *An Army in Exile, p. 106.*
126   *Ibid.* p. 'Exodus from Russia'.
127   *Ibid.* p. 119.
128   *Ibid.* pp. 120-121.
129   E. Huntingdon, *The Unsettled Account* (London: Severn House Publishers, 1986), p. 198.
130   Joe Rosenbaum, telephone interview, 4 May 2015.
131   K. Rudnicki, *The Last of the War Horses* (London: Bachman and Turner, 1974), pp. 218-219. Sourced from N. Davies, *Trail of Hope*, p. 121.
132   S. Turner, *Hoover Institution on War, Revolution, and Peace.* Sourced from D. Bader Whitman, *Escape from Siberia*, p. 70.
133   Joe Rosenbaum, telephone interview, 4 May 2015.
134   *Ibid.*
135   D. Omer, *The Teheran Operation*, p. 84.
136   Nelly's death in Tashkent: Joe Rosenbaum, 4 May 2015; 5 May 2015; 10 August 2015.

Chapter 12

137   S. Garret, *Ethics and Air Power in World War II: The British Bombing of German Cities* (London: Palgrave MacMillan, 1993).
138   H. Probert, *Bomber Harris: His Life and Times* (London: Greenhill Books, 2006), p. 52.
139   L. Feigel, *The Bitter Taste of Victory: Life, Love, and Art in the Ruins of the Reich* (London: Bloomsbury Press, 2016), quoting Martha Gellhorn.
140   Joe's experiences in Tashkent: Joe Rosenbaum, telephone interviews, 4 May 2015; 6 May 2015; 10 August 2016.
141   T. Piotrowski, *Polish Refugees*, p. 85
142   Rymaszewski.iinet.net, 'General Anders' Army leaves the USSR.'
143   D. Omer, *The Teheran Operation*, p. 144.
144   W. Anders, *An Army in Exile*, p. 127.
145   *Ibid.*
146   E. Huntingdon, *The Unsettled Account*, pp. 213-214.

147   Joe Rosenbaum, telephone interview, 4 May 2015.

148   T. Piotrowski, *The Polish Deportees of World War II: Recollections of Removal to the Soviet Union and Dispersal Throughout the World* (London: McFarland & Company, 2004), p. 102.

149   H. Edwards, *Day of Aloes* (Halwell: Sandpiper Press, 1992); Sources from N. Davies, *Trail of Hope*, p. 182.

150   W. Rubinstein, *The Myth of Rescue* (London: Routledge, 1997); *The Nation*, 9 January 1943.

151   Circumstances surrounding 69 Palestinian Jews arriving at Athlit: T. Shabtai, *Ben-Gurion: The Burning Ground 1886-1948* (Boston: Houghton Mifflin, 1987), p. 845.

152   *The Jewish Standard*, 27 November 1942.

153   T. Shabtai, *Ben-Gurion: The Burning Ground 1886-1948*, p. 846.

154   Dobkin quotes from meeting with Ben-Gurion.

Chapter 13

155   D. MacArdle, *Children of Europe* (Boston: Beacon Press, 1951).

156   D. Wyman, *The Abandonment of the Jews: American and the Holocaust 1941-1945* (New York: Pantheon Books, 1984).

157   L. Havas, *Hitler's Plot to Kill the Big Three* (New York: Cowles Book Company, 1967), p. 70; S. Morrell, *Spheres of Influence* (New York: 1946), p. 29.

158   Joe Rosenbaum, telephone interviews, 10 August 2015; 1 February 2016.

159   H. Edwards, *Day of Aloes*.

160   I. Grudzinska-Gross, J. Gross, *War Through Children's Eyes*, p. xxiii.

161   *Ibid.*, p. xxiv

162   H. Edwards, *Days of Aloes*.

163   S. Teveth, *Ben-Gurion and the Holocaust*, p. 37.

164   Scene of Szold in her Jerusalem office and internal thoughts: J. Dash, *Summoned to Jerusalem: The Life of Henrietta Szold* (New York: Harper & Row, 1979), pp. 298-299.; R. Zeitlin, *Henrietta Szold: Record of Life* (New York: The Dial Press, 1952), pp. 183-184.

165   A. Levin (ed.), *Henrietta Szold and Youth Aliyah: Family Letters 1934-1944* (New York: Herzl Press, 1986), p. 66.

166   J. Dash, *Summoned to Jerusalem*.

167   Research on Zipporah Shertok in Tehran, October 1942: A. Eisenberg, *The Lost Generation: Children of the Holocaust* (New York: The Pilgrim Press, 1985), p. 270; D. Omer, *The Teheran Operation*, p. 183; D. Bader Whitman, *Escape Via Siberia*.

168   D. Bader Whitman, *Escape Via Siberia*.

169   N. T. Gidal, *Henrietta Szold: Saga of an American Woman* (New York: Gefen Publishing House, 1996).

170   Shertok's report to Jerusalem: Central Zionist Archives, Archive of the Youth Aliyah Department, Jerusalem: File No. S75/4852. Sourced from D. Bader Whitman, *Escape Via Siberia*, pp. 103-104.

171   D. Goodwin, *No Ordinary Time*, p. 432.

172   Account of Hadassah's efforts in Washington D.C., Chapter fifteen, sixteen: D. Bader Whitman, *Escape Via Siberia*, chapters 15-18, 19; M. Levin, *It Takes a Dream: The Story of Hadassah* (New York: Gefen Publishing House, 2002), p. 195-217; A. Levin, *Henrietta Szold and Youth Aliyah*, p. 66; M. Levin, *Balm in Gilead: The Story of Hadassah* (New York: Schocken Books, 1973), pp. 169-170, 179-181.

173   Communications between Warburg and Tourover: *Ibid.*

Chapter 14
174   The account in this chapter: Joe Rosenbaum, 10 August 2015; 1 February 2016.

Chapter 15
175   I. Fineman, *Woman of Valor*, p. 419.
176   Account of Stella Knobel: 'The Teddy Bear "Mishu", Stella Knobel's Best Friend', Yad Vashem.org.
177   A. Eisenberg, *The Lost Generation*, p. 271.

Chapter 16
178   Description of Washington D.C. in 1943: D. Goodwin, *No Ordinary Time*, p. 432; D. Bercuson, H. Herwig, *A Christmas in December* (New York: The Overlook Press, 2005), prologue.
179   H. Begbie, *A Gentleman with a Duster* (London: Mills & Boon, 1924) pp. 47, 48.
180   H. Krantz, *Daughter of my People: Henrietta Szold and Hadassah* (New York: Lodestar Books, E.P. Dutton, 1987), pp. 128-129.

Chapter 17
181   Story of Palestinian Jewish soldiers: D. Omer, *The Teheran Operation*, p. 196.
182   Lord Halifax's response: M. Levin, Balm in Gilead, p. 180.
183   J. Dash, *Summoned to Jerusalem*, p. 301.
184   D. Bader Whiteman, *Escape Via Siberia*, p. 135
185   D. Omer, *The Teheran Operation*, p. 212.

Chapter 18
186   Account of Joe leaving Iran: Joe Rosenbaum, telephone interviews, 10 August 2015; 6 May 2015; 10 August 2015.
187   W. Anders, *An Army in Exile*, pp. 131, 133, 152.
188   *Ibid.*
189   *Ibid*, p. 135
190   N. Gidal, *Henrietta Szold*, p. 35.
191   J. Dash, *Summoned to Jerusalem*.
192   Joe Rosenbaum, telephone interview, 10 August 2015.
193   D. Omer, *The Teheran Operation*, pp. 219-224; sourced from D. Whiteman, *Escape from Siberia*, pg. 138.

Chapter 19
194   D. Bader Whiteman, *Escape Via Siberia*, p. 138.
195   *Ibid.*, p. 139.
196   *Ibid.*, p. 139.

197 Joe Rosenbaum, telephone interview, 10 August 2015.
198 Account of Vera Brand née Lifshitz: 'A Doll from a Distant Land', exhibit at Yad Vashem, Jerusalem.
199 *Pittsburgh Post-Gazette*, 23 January 1943.
200 W. Anders, *An Army in Exile*, p. 135.
201 *Ibid.*, pg 136.
202 *Ibid.*, p. 137.
203 N. Davies, *Trail of Hope*, pp. 381-389.
204 S. Strzyzewski, *Dezercje Zydow z Armii Andersa w swietle dokumentow Instytutu Polskiego* (London, 2012), pp. 232, 233; Polish record sourced in N. Davies, *Trial of Hope*, pp. 391-392.

Chapter 20

205 Joe Rosenbaum, telephone interview, 10 August 2015.

Chapter 21

206 S. Teveith, *Ben-Gurion and the Holocaust*.
207 Account of Szold visiting the tree: I. Fineman, *Woman of Valor*, p. 400.
208 *Ibid.*, p. 418.
209 Account of Joe arriving in Port Said: Joe Rosenbaum, telephone interview, 10 August 2015.
210 D. Omer, *The Teheran Operation*, p. 246.
211 Camping at the Wells of Moses: N. Bentwich, *Jewish Youth Come Home: The Story of Youth Aliyah, 1933-1943* (London: The Camelot Press Limited, 1944), p. 107.

Chapter 22

212 I. Fineman, *Woman of Valor*, p. 420.
213 Description of children's background: H. Grynberg, *Children of Zion* (Evanston, IL.: Northwestern University Press, 1997), pp. 3-7.
214 Personal reflections on the train: Joe Rosenbaum, telephone interviews, 10 August 2015; 3 May 2016.

Chapter 23

215 Arrival in Palestine sources: D. Bader Whiteman, 'Welcome Home', *Escape Via Siberia*; D. Omer, 'Homecoming', *The Teheran Operation*.
216 Accounts of celebrations along the train route: A. Eisenberg, *The Lost Generation*, pp. 273-4.
217 Arrival: J. Dash, *Summoned to Jerusalem*, prologue; A. Levin, *Henrietta Szold and Youth Aliyah*, Chapter Ten: 'The Teheran Children Arrive'.
218 Joe's reflection of that first day: Joe Rosenbaum, telephone interviews, 10 August 2015; 3 May 2016.
219 *The Palestine Post*, Friday 19 February 1943.

220   Goebbels's Total War: Randall Bytwerk, 'Goebbels's speech on Total War', German propaganda archive.

Chapter 24

221   'In Palestine…': Joe Rosenbaum, telephone interview, 10 August 2015.
222   Account of Szold interviewing the three children, and the story of Sarah: Nachum T. Gidal, *Henrietta Szold: The Saga of an American Woman* (New York: Gefen Publishing, 1996), pp. 68-9.
223   Joe's brief reflections on being interviewed by Szold: Joe Rosenbaum, telephone interview, 3 May 2016.
224   Account of *Kfar Ha'Noar Hadait*: S. Rosenbaum, *My Saba*, pp. 41-8.

Chapter 25

225   Account of days in Tel Aviv: Joe Rosenbaum, telephone interview, 10 August 2015; 3 May 2016; S. Rosenbaum, *My Saba*, pp. 41-3.
226   M. Gilbert, *The Holocaust*, pp. 398-9; Zabecki, *op. cit.*, pp. 58-9.
227   D. Stafford, *Endgame 1945: The Missing Final Chapter of World War II* (New York: Little, Brown, and Company, 2007), p. 83.
228   'Ohrdruf', United States Holocaust Memorial Museum Holocaust Encyclopedia.
229   *Ibid.*
230   M. Gilbert, *Churchill: A Life*, p. 836.

Chapter 26

231   W. Anders, *An Army in Exile*, p. 135.
232   *Ibid.*, p. 140.
233   J. Zawooney, *Death in the Forest: The Story of the Katyn Forest Massacre* (Literary Licensing LLC., 2011).
234   E. Huntingdon in Tehran: *The Unsettled Account*, pp. 213-14.
235   H. Kochanski, *The Eagle Unbowed*, p. 345; Danchev & Todman, *War Diaries*, pp. 429-30.
236   W. Anders, 'The Katyn Murders', *An Army in Exile*, pp. 140-49.
237   *Ibid.*
238   J. Marino, 'Polish Power in Italy', *WWII History*, October 2014.
239   W. Anders, *An Army in Exile*, pp. 179-80; 'Polish Power in Italy', *WW II History*, October 2014, p. 57.
240   W. Anders, *An Army in Exile*, p. 304.

Chapter 27

241   Joe Rosenbaum, telephone interviews, 10 August, 2015; 18 August 2015; S. Rosenbaum, *My Saba*.
242   Joe Rosenbaum, telephone interview, 1 February 2016; S. Rosenbaum, *My Saba*.

Chapter 28

243 J. Goulden, *The Best Years, 1945-1950* (New York: Atheneum, 1976).

244 *Ibid.*, pp. 3-5.

245 Joe's life in America: Joe Rosenbaum, telephone interview 25 August 2015; S. Rosenbaum, *My Saba*.

Chapter 29

246 Return to Israel: Joe Rosenbaum, telephone interviews, 1 February 2016; 30 April 2016; 31 May 2016; S. Rosenbaum, *My Saba*.

Chapter 30

247 Joe Rosenbaum, telephone interviews, 6 May 2015; 8 February 2016; 30 April 2016; 31 May 2016.

248 Cologne, 2007: Joe Rosenbaum, telephone interviews, 1 February 2016; 30 April 2016; 31 May 2016; *To Be a Tehran Child*; S. Vogel, *The Children's Odyssey* (film, 2007).

Chapter 31

249 S. Rosenbaum, *My Saba*, pg. 11; Joe Rosenbaum, telephone interviews, 14 October 2014; 6 April, 2015; 4 May 2015.

Epilogue

250 Joe Rosenbaum, telephone interviews, 31 May 2016.

251 The story of Halinka Lampel: H. Grynberg, *The Children of Zion*.

252 S. Teveth, Ben-Gurion: *Burning Ground*, pp. 870-71.

253 Incident at Zeilsheim: S. Teveth, *Ben-Gurion: Burning Ground*, pp 770-872; S. Teveth, *Ben-Gurion and the Holocaust*, pp. 65-6; D. Kurzman, *Ben-Gurion: Prophet of Fire*, pp. 262-64.

254 From the official writings of David Ben-Gurion; *David Ben-Gurion*, Jewish Agency.

Sources

ARCHIVAL SOURCES AND PERIODICALS:

FDR Library. WordPress.com, *FDR's Bedside Note*, 1 September 1939.

Franklin D. Roosevelt. *Radio Address*, 3 September 1939.

Jewish Agency Executive, Records of. *Central Zionist Archives*, Jerusalem, 20 December 1941, 6 December, 13, 1942.

Glowczewska, Klara, *Town and CountryMagazine*, 'Sweeping Statement.' October 2014, p. 71.

Grunberg, Slawomir, *Saved by Deportation – An Unknown Odyssey of Polish Jews*: film, 2006.

Marino, James I., *Polish Power in Italy*, WWII History, October 2014, pp. 52-59,80.

Rymaszweski.iinet.net.

Rosenbaum, Joe. *To Be a Tehran Child*. Jerusalem: August 2013.

Rosenbaum, Simon (grandson). *My Saba*, Essay, 2013.

Rosenbaum, Joe telephone interviews conducted June 2014- September 2016.

Time Magazine, Books, *Tell the West*, 19 April 1948.

United States Holocaust Memorial Museum, Holocaust Encyclopedia.

Whiteman, Dorit B., 'Survivors and Escapees: Their Strengths,' *Psychotherapy*, Vol 30, Fall 1993, Number 3.

Vogel, Stephan, *The Children's Odyssey*: film, November 2008.

Washington Post. 19 October 2008, 'The Writing Life': Ian Kershaw.

The Telegraph, 3 October 2004, 'Inside Winston's Lair', Ross Clark.

Yad Vashem exhibits. Jerusalem.

Bibliography

Adamczyk, Wesley, *When God Looked the Other Way: An Odyssey of War, Exil, and Redemption*(Chicago, IL: University of Chicago Press, 2006).

Anders, Lt. General Wladyslaw, *An Army in Exile* (Nashville TN: The Battery Press, 1949).

Applebaum, Anne, *Gulag: A History of the Soviet Camps* (London: Allen Lane, 2003).

Begbie, Harold, *A Gentleman with a Duster* (London: Mills & Boon, 1924).

Bentwich, Norman, *Jewish Youth Comes Home: The Story of the Youth Aliyah, 1933-1943* (London: The Camelot Press Limited, 1944), pp. 105-111.

Bishop, Jim, *FDR's Last Year: April 1944-April 1945* (New York: William Morrow & Company, 1974).

Breitman, Richard and Lichtman, Allan J., *FDR and the Jews* (Cambridge, MA: Belknap Press, 2013).

Brown, Anthony Cave, *Bodyguard of Lies* (New York: Bantam Books, 1975), pp. 384-85.

Bulmahn, Jane Zebrowski, *Long Journey Home* (New York: Writer's Showcase, 2000).

Churchill, Winston S, *The Second World War: Closing the Ring* (Boston, MA: Houghton Mifflin Company, 1951), pp. 342-407.

Churchill, Winston S, *The Second World War: Triumph and Tragedy* (Boston, MA: Houghton Mifflin Company, 1953), pp. 346-394.

Dash, Joan, *Summoned to Jerusalem: The Life of Henrietta Szold* (New York: Harper & Row, Publishers, 1979).

Davies, Norman, *Trail of Hope: The Anders Army, An Odyssey Across Three Continents* (Oxford, UK: Osprey Publishing, 2016).

Des Pres, Terrence, *The Survivor: An Anatomy of Life in the Death Camps* (New York: Oxford University Press, 1976).

Dwork, Deborah, *Children with a Star: Jewish Youth in Nazi Europe* (New Haven, CT. Yale: University Press, 1991).

Dwork, Deborah & Van Pelt, Robert Jan, *Flight from the Reich: Refugee Jews, 1933-1946* (New York: W.W. Norton, 2009).

Edwards, Helena, *Days of Aloes* (Devon, U.K: Sandpiper Press, 1992).

Eisenberg, Azriel, *The Lost Generation: Children of the Holocaust* (New York: The Pilgrim Press, 1985), pp. 267-277.

Eisenhower, John S.D, *Allies: Pearl Harbor to D-Day* (New York: Doubleday & Co, 1982).

Epstein, Helen, *Children of the Holocaust: Conversations with Sons and Daughters of Survivors* (New York: G.P. Putnam's Sons, 1979).

Feigel, Lara, *The Bitter Taste of Victory: Life, Love, and Art in the Ruins of the Reich* (London: Bloomsbury Press, 2016).

Fineman, Irving, *Woman of Valor: The Life of Henrietta Szold, 1860-1945* (New York: Simon & Schuster, 1961).

Friedlander, Saul, *Nazi Germany and the Jews: The Years of Persecution, 1933-1939* (New York: Harper Collins, 1997).

Friedlander, Saul, *Years of Extermination: Nazi Germany and the Jews 1939-1945* (New York: Harper, 2007).

Garret, Stephen A., *Ethics and Air Power in World War II: The British Bombing of German Cities* (London: Palgrave Macmillan, 1993).

Gidal, Nachum T, *Henrietta Szold: The Saga of an American Woman* (New York (Jerusalem): Gefen Publishing House, 1996).

Gilbert, Martin, *The Holocaust: A History of the Jews in Europe during World War Two* (New York: Holt, Rinehart, and Winston, 1985).

Gilbert, Martin, *Churchill: A Life* (New York: Henry Holt and Company, 1991).

Gilbert, Martin, *The Boys: The story of 732 Young Concentration Camp Survivors* (New York: Henry Holt & Co, 1996).

Gliksman, Jerzy, *Tell the West* (New York: Gresham, 1948).

Goebbels, Joseph, *The Goebbels Diaries, 1939-1941*(Fred Taylor, editor) (New York: G.P. Putnam's Sons, 1983).

Goodwin, Doris Kearns, *No Ordinary Time Franklin Roosevelt & Eleanor Roosevelt: The Home Front in World War Two* (New York: Touchstone Book, Simon & Shuster, Inc., 1995).

Goulden, Joseph C., *The Best Years 1945-1950* (New York: Atheneum, 1976).

Gross, Irena Grudzinska and Jan Tomasz, *War Through Children's Eyes: The Soviet Occupation of Poland and the Deportations, 1939-1941* (Stanford, CA: Hoover Institution Press, 1981).

Gross, Jan T., *Revolution from Abroad: The Soviet Conquest of Poland's Western Ukraine and Western Belorussia* (Princeton, NJ: Princeton University Press, 1988).

Grossmann, Atina, *Shelter from the Holocaust: Rethinking Jewish Survival in the Soviet Union* (Detroit: Wayne State University Press, 2017).

Grynberg, Henryk, *Children of Zion* (Evanston, IL: Northwestern University Press, 1994).

Harris, Sir Arthur, *Bomber Offensive* (London: Greenhill Book, 2005).

Havas, Laslo, *Hitler's Plot to Kill the Big Three* (New York: Cowles Book Co., Inc., 1967).

Hergt, Klaus, *Exiled to Siberia: A Polish Child's World War Two Journey* (Michigan: Crescent Lake Publishing, 2000).

Herwig, Holger and Bercuson. David, *One Christmas in Washington, The Secret Meeting between Roosevelt and Churchill that Changed the World* (New York: The Overlook Press, 2005).

Huntingdon, Eugenia, *The Unsettled Account: An Autobiography* (New York: Severn House Publishers, 1988).

Irving, David, *Hitler's War* (New York: Viking Press, 1977).

Johnson, Paul, *A History of the Jews* (New York: Harper & Row, Publishers, 1987).

Kershaw, Ian, *Hitler: 1889-1936 Hubris* (New York: W.W. Norton, 2000).

Kessel, Sim, *Hanged at Auschwitz* (New York: Stein & Day, 1972).

Kochanski, Halik, *The Eagle Unbowed: Poland and the Poles in the Second World War* (UK: Penguin, 2013).

Koskodan, Kenneth K.., *No Greater Ally: The Untold Story of Poland's Forces in World War II* (Oxford UK: Osprey Publishing, 2009).

Krantz, Hazel, *Daughter of My People: Henrietta Szold and Hadassah* (New York: Lodestar Books, E.P. Dutton, 1987), pp.128-32.

Kurzman, Dan, *Ben-Gurion: Prophet of Fire* (New York: Simon & Schuster, 1983).

Lane, Thomas, *Victims of Stalin and Hitler: The Exodus of Poles and Balts to Britain* (New York: Palgrave MacMillan, 2004).

Lanzmann, Claude, *Shoah: An Oral History of the Holocaust* (The Complete Text of the Film) (New York: Pantheon Books, 1985).

Levin, Alexandra (ed.), *Henrietta Szold and Youth Aliyah: Family Letters 1934-1944* (New York: Herzl Press, 1986).

Levin, Marlin, *Balm in Gilead: The Story of Hadassah* (New York: Schocken Books, 1973).

Levin, Marlin, *It Takes A Dream: The Story of Hadassah* (New York (Jerusalem): Gefen Publishing House, 2002).

Lewis, C.S., *A Grief Observed* (New York: HarperCollins, 1961).

Lucas, Richard C., *Did the Children Cry? Hitler's War Against Jewish and Polish Children, 1939-1945* (New York: Hippocrene Books, 1994).

Lustiger, Arno, *Stalin & the Jews* (New York: Enigma Books, 2002).

Mazzeo, Tilar J., *Irena's Children* (New York: Gallery Books, 2016).

Megargee, Geoffrey and Dean, Martin, *Encyclopedia of Camps and Ghettos 1933-1945.* (Bloomington, IN: Indiana Press, 2009).

MacArdle, Dorothy, *Children of Europe* (Boston, MA: The Beacon Press, 1951), p. 13.

MacRae, Sigrid, *A World Elsewhere: An American Woman in Wartime Germany* (New York: Viking Press, 2014).

Miller, Nathan, *FDR: An Intimate History* (Garden City, New York: Doubleday & Company, 1983), pp. 438-39

Nadish, Judah, *Eisenhower and the Jews* (Woodbridge, CT: Twayne Publishers, 1953).

Omer, Devora, *The Tehran Operation: The Rescue of Jewish Children from the Nazis.* (Washington D.C.: B'Nai B'rith Book, 1991).

Persico, Joseph E., *Roosevelt's Secret War: FDR and World War Two Espionage* (New York: Random House, 2001).

Piotrowski, Tadeusz (ed.), *The Polish Deportees of World War II: Recollections of Removal to the Soviet Union and Dispersal Throughout the World* (London: McFarland & Company, Inc., 2004).

Probert, Henry, *Bomber Harris: His Life and Times* (London: Greenhill Books, 2006).

Redlich, Shimon, *Together and Apart in Brezezany: Poles, Jews, and Ukrainians, 1919-1945* (Bloomington, IN: Indiana University Press, 2002).

Redlich, Shimon, *Life in Transit: Jews in Postwar Lodz, 1945-1950* (Boston: Academic Studies Press, 2011).

Redlich, Shimon, *A New Life in Israel: 1950-1954* (Boston: Academic Studies Press, 2018).

Roseman, Mark, *The Villa, The Lake, The Meeting: Wannsee and the Final Solution* (London, New York: Allen Lane, 2002).

Rubinstein, William D, *The Myth of Rescue: Why the Democracies could not Have Saved more Jews from the Nazis*, (London: Routledge, 1997), p. 118.

Rudnicki, K.J., *The Last of the War Horses* (London: Bachman and Turner, 1974).

Schonfeld, Rabbi Moshe, *Genocide in the Holy Land* (Brooklyn, NY: BneiYeshivos, 1980).

Segev, Tom, *The Seventh Million: The Israelis and the Holocaust* (New York: Henry Holt & Company, 1991).

Shepherd, Naomi, *Ploughing Sand: British Rule in Palestine 1917-1948* (New Brunswick, NJ: Rutgers University Press, 2000).

Shirer, William L., *The Rise and Fall of the Third Reich: A History of Nazi Germany* (New York: Simon & Shuster, 1960).

Simons, Erica B, *Hadassah and the Zionist Project* (New York: Rowman & Littlefield Publishers, Inc. 2006).

Smenda, Janusz and Nina, *Unforgettable Memories: Memoirs of Polish Exiles in the Soviet Union, 1940-1942* (Perth, Western Australia: Polish Siberian Group (WA), 1985).

Snyder, Timothy, *Bloodlands: Europe Between Hitler and Stalin* (New York: Basic Books, 2012).

Spector, Ronald H., *Eagle Against the Sun: The American War with Japan* (New York: Viking Press, 1984).

St. John, Robert, *Ben-Gurion: The Biography of an Extraordinary Man* (New York: Doubleday & Company, 1959). pp. 120-21.

Stafford, David, *Endgame 1945: The Missing Final Chapter of World War II* (New York: Little, Brown, and Company, 2007).

Strzyzewski, Sylwester,*Dezercje Zydow z Armii Andersa w swietle dokumentow Instytutu Polskiego* (London: 2012).

Szpilman, Wladyslaw, *The Pianist* (New York: Picador, USA, 1999). pp. 7, 33-41.

Teveth, Shabtai, *Ben-Gurion: The Burning Ground 1886-1948* (Boston, MA: Houghton Mifflin, 1987).

Teveth, Shabtai, *Ben-Gurion and the Holocaust* (New York: Harcourt Brace & Company, 1996).

Toland, John, *The Last 100 Days* (New York. Bantam Books, 1966), pp. 130-31.

Toland, John, *The Rising Sun: The Decline and Fall of the Japanese Empire 1936-1945, Volume One* (New York: Random House, 1970).

Toland, John, *Adolf Hitler, Volume Two* (New York: Doubleday & Co., 1976), pp. 640-43.

Tomaszewski, Jerzy; Mazur, Tadeusz, *1939-1945 We Have Not Forgotten* (Warsaw: Polonia Publishing House, 1961).

Yahil, Leni, *The Holocaust: Fate of European Jewry* (New York: Oxford University Press, 1990).

Wasserstein, Bernard, *On the Eve: The Jews of Europe before the Second World War* (New York: Simon & Schuster, 2012).

Whiteman, Dorit Bader, *Escape via Siberia: A Jewish Child's Odyssey of Survival* (New York: Holmes & Meier, 1999).

Wyman, David S., *The Abandonment of the Jews: America and the Holocaust 1941-1945* (New York: Pantheon Books, 1984).

Zajdlerowa, Zoe, *The Dark Side of the Moon* (New York: Charles Scribner, 1947).

Zawooney, J. K., *Death in the Forest: The Story of the Katyn Forest Massacre.* (Literary Licensing LLC., 2011).

Zeitlin, Rose, *Henrietta Szold: Record of Life* (New York: The Dial Press, 1952).

Index